Minnows United

Adventures at the Fringes of the Beautiful Game

MAT GUY

Luath Press Limited

EDINBURGH

www.luath.co.uk

First published 2017

ISBN: 978-1-912147-06-9

The paper used in this book is recyclable. It is made from low chlorine pulps produced in a low energy, low emission manner from renewable forests.

Printed and bound by Ashford Colour Press, Gosport

Typeset in 11 point Sabon by Lapiz

This book is dedicated to my grandfather, who showed me that life can be joyous – as long as you remain faithful to your hopes and dreams.

Contents

Acknowledgements

I WILL BE forever grateful to Alice Latchford, this book's editor, for all her hard work, insight, and suggestions. So too Gavin MacDougall and Luath Press for their faith in the people and stories within these pages.

Indeed, without the stories this book would be nothing. I owe a debt of thanks to those who shared their experiences with me: Jamal Zaqout, Motaz Albuhaisi, and Moahmoud Sarsak from Gaza, Cassie Childers, Sonam Dolma, Sonam Sangmo, and Tenzin Dekyong from Tibet Women's Soccer, Keil Clitheroe, Adam and Julie Houlden, Nick Westwell, Adam Scarborough from Accrington Stanley, Dan Hatfield from Selfoss, Anton Jonas Illugason from Olafsvik, Sarah Wiltshire from Yeovil Town Ladies, Iggy from Darfur United, Mick Ellard from Southampton and Rob Heys from Macclesfield Town – thank you, from the bottom of my heart for opening up a wonderful world to me.

Introduction

A LIFE AT the fringes of football, far from the media spotlight afforded the world's biggest leagues and the most successful national teams, can be a largely anonymous one.

Supporters, players, clubs, and nations that find themselves existing right at the very edge of the game, be it geographically, politically, through size and status, historically or ideologically, do so in a vacuum devoid of attention, money, and quite possibly to those from above looking down, purpose.

However, among the clubs and nations that physically cling to the very ends of the footballing earth; are national teams that exist in a twilight world beyond the international scene, thanks to political decisions taken far from any football pitch. Among the teams and their supporters constantly living in the shadow of the games giants, in lowly leagues populated by ageing ramshackle stadiums and dwindling attendances, there exist stories, living histories that better detail all that is captivating and magical about this simple game than that which is offered through satellite television's focus on the biggest and the best.

In a game fast becoming dominated by money, it is those furthest from it that tell the story of football in its purest form, and that can help to re-connect a soul to their first memories of going to their first ever match, or the moment that kicking a ball about a scrap of land or backyard became an obsession. Among the stories of players, clubs, and supporters rarely written about exists the heartbeat and foundation blocks that enables the Premier League and Champions League to be the enormous entities that they are.

Without these fundamental passions and truths that exist, have always existed at the very fringes of mainstream football, at its grassroots, everything that has gone beyond it could not.

It seems apt in a time where the higher echelons of the sport are beginning to lose this understanding of the importance of the game further down the food chain that we begin to explore it more, cherish it. Because in a world where FA Cup replays are being mooted for the scrapheap, and initial matches to be played in midweek to avoid fixture congestion for the bigger teams; where qualification for the World Cup and European Championships could soon be preceded by a pre-qualifying tournament between Europe's 'lesser' nations, so as the 'larger' ones don't have so many 'unnecessary' and 'meaningless' internationals – the world of the minnow needs to be trumpeted like never before.

The riches of the Champions League, and the Premier League seem to be blinding governing bodies to the simple realities that football is such a universal sport because of its inclusivity.

Every young child with a ball can dream of one day playing for their team, their country, of playing in the FA Cup or the World Cup. And if they can't play in the final, then maybe one of the stages preceding it.

As a young boy, the qualifying rounds of the FA Cup felt just as exciting as sitting down to watch the final on television the following May. Salisbury FC's old and ramshackle (even back in the '80s when I was a young boy) and sadly long gone Victoria Park had an extra touch of magic about it on FA Cup qualifying round day.

Sitting down with my grandfather in Victoria Park's only and very basic stand (Grandad had made two cushions out of foam to protect us from the cold concrete seating) the anticipation of a good win, followed by a couple more, that could result in little old Salisbury drawing a football league team in the first round proper had both the supporters in the stand, and the part-time players crammed into their changing room beneath an old, creaking pavilion, dreaming of something special on a blustery autumn afternoon as far from the early summer sun of Cup final day as you could get.

By threatening to devalue the competition by switching it to mid-week, by scrapping replays that could see a minnow team pull off an amazing feat by drawing at home to more illustrious league opposition – setting up a dream return match at a stadium players and fans alike could only dream of – the magic of the competition would be eroded, diluted.

And with it the inclusivity; that any child that dreamt and persevered hard enough could find themselves on a Saturday afternoon running out against Manchester United in the FA Cup third round. That any part-time player could maybe have the chance to do this any given season is what has preserved the competition as the most loved and revered competition on the planet.

It will be, as always, the teams far from the big leagues that suffer the most from these proposed changes and who will lose the slightest of opportunities to mix it with the big time, for just one day.

So too the minnows of the international game will suffer if they are never allowed to test themselves, to develop, by playing against the World's best.

It is what makes the game so special, that the Faroe Islands, Luxembourg, Gibraltar can be drawn to play against Germany and Spain in a qualifying group; that school teachers and firemen and bank clerks can have the opportunity to take on the champions of the world.

It is the connectivity between all abilities that makes football the most watched and loved sport on the planet; it is for anyone, everyone, who can aspire to live out their dreams, no matter from what lowly starting point they find themselves.

It is this seemingly terminal fracturing between the big time and the rest that compelled me to explore and celebrate football that exists way out on the fringes of the game; to check the heartbeat of the sports very essence.

It is, after all, a game that is bigger than the global football entities that run it, that reaches out to more people on a daily basis than any satellite television audience, that enables and gives expression to those that FIFA and the United Nations don't.

Beyond the glamour and money of the elite levels of football there are three things that preserve the game, no matter how remote, forgotten, or forsaken it may find itself: identity, belonging, and meaning.

These three fundamentals have helped keep small teams with no money afloat for more than 100 years and counting. They have helped preserve the histories and stories of the people that once populated them through fading pictures on clubhouse walls, scrapbooks, dusty trophy cabinets, and the passing down of tales from grandparent to grandchild. Without it I would have never learned of the amazing story of Cyril Smith, the kindly old man on the gate at Salisbury selling programmes, whose self-depreciation hid a remarkable past. Thankfully his friendship with my grandfather helped offer up enough of his tale for me to discover after his passing.

Identity, belonging and meaning have enabled communities almost lost to the world to maintain a presence through their love of football. Nations and groups failed by official world bodies survive in an unofficial capacity out on the pitch; shining a light on the reasons for their isolation, as well as celebrating a culture that others would rather have us forget, and a game that they will not be denied.

The fringes of the sport are populated with the obscure, the forgotten, the ignored, the persecuted, and sometimes the taboo that football in the mainstream struggles to deal with.

It is a world of humour, passion, beauty, and wonder. It can also be a world pain, horror, and suffering.

But throughout it all, football way out on the edges of mainstream consciousness maintains a rich vibrancy, a vitality, and a deep-rooted necessity that seems to be able to deal with the ever-greater isolation it finds itself existing in.

Having spent more than a year exploring just a handful of the countless fascinating clubs, players, and nations out there, you can't help but wonder two things: just how many more amazing stories are there out there waiting to be discovered, and exactly who is the poorer for drifting away from the other – those on the fringes, or those that seem to be pulling away from the very spirit of the game?

The following 15 stories from football's forgotten teams; of players and teams mostly ignored by the mainstream media, of people forsaken by politics and humanity, of clubs and nations isolated due to geography helps to reveal a world of diversity, colour, passion, and dedication.

Regardless of size, location, status, the sense of belonging and meaning that every player and supporter in the book takes from their team is every bit as vital and important as that of any fan in the Premier League. In some cases, more so.

Identity, meaning, a sense of self and of belonging cannot be quantified through FIFA rankings, or league tables. And these things don't even begin to consider all those that lay beyond them, containing as they do only nations recognised by the UN and FIFA. Those at the very foot of the football pyramid and on the fringes of the mainstream derive as much meaning from the game as anyone else.

These tales follow European minnows, players surviving in war torn Palestine, clubs at the foot, and sometimes beyond the football classified results service on a Saturday afternoon. Clubs and players whose dedication makes them greater than the sum of their parts, forbidden national teams defying traditional boundaries and refugee teams clinging on to their very survival, they all offer an amazing insight into a vibrant world of footballing humanity that is often overlooked.

After having been on this journey that you are about to read, having witnessed the dedication and passion needed to circumvent a lack of finances, resources, and everything else, you could certainly argue that the real spirit of football truly is alive and well, but not necessarily where you would expect to find it.

CHAPTER I

European Dreaming – F91 Dudelange

LUXEMBOURG, THERE HAS always been something about Luxembourg; a tiny country hidden, both politically, culturally, as well as on the sporting front, between much larger and grander European nations. But despite its size, or, in fact, because of it, there has been that special something that has made Luxembourg stand out where other countries don't; something first initiated by a football programme between England and the world's last surviving Grand Duchy arriving in the post when I was a ten-year-old boy.

My Grandfather, knowing that I loved football programmes almost as much as I loved football itself, had put the word out at the factory he worked in, asking his friends to pick up an extra one for his grandson if they ever happened to be at a match, which is why a week before Christmas in 1982 I found myself pouring over a programme between England and Luxembourg from a European Championship qualifier at Wembley Stadium.

Just like the Panini sticker album from the World Cup of that summer of '82, in which I invested so many hours studying the information on teams from far-away lands, many of whom I had never even heard of before, I would spend an age reading and re-reading that programme. Marvelling at the strange sounding names of the teams that the Luxembourg squad played for back at home, peering into the team photo taken, to the eyes of an excitable ten year old in some exotic stadium, though in reality, and in the best case scenario upon looking at that same picture more than 30 years later, a dank, rain sodden and unfamiliar municipal stadium somewhere in Europe, more than likely long since lost to time and decay.

But to a young boy living in an age before the internet, where the world of football stretched as far as the coverage it received in *The Daily Telegraph*, my parents paper of choice, this programme opened up another world: a world of football beyond a young boy's understanding; beyond the English

First Division and the world football powers of Brazil and Italy, West Germany, as they were then, and all the rest that had played at the World Cup in Spain that summer.

This programme opened up a bigger, or rather smaller world of football outside that inner circle of the world's 'elite', and it was fascinating, intoxicating, exciting, and seemed just as important and necessary, just as vital as that of Zico, Socrates, Tardelli, Rossi, and all the stars of that summer.

Just as I studied the information on the world's best in my sticker album, so too did I the player profiles of that Luxembourg team, dreaming of what the club badges, the stadiums, the team shirts of Red Boys Differdange, Progres Niedercorn, Stade Dudelange, and the other club sides that they played for looked like.

That wonderment captured the imagination just as much as the unbelievable skills of that Brazil '82 side, and for every hour spent staring at the erratically stuck in images of the World's best in my sticker album, wondering about Zico's Flamengo, and Socrates' Corinthians, I spent longer devouring the exotic names and club sides of players playing for countries that I, or anyone else that I knew for that matter, knew nothing about.

To a young boy, the teams from El Salvador, Honduras, Peru, Cameroon, just like that team from Luxembourg, symbolised the unknown, adventure, and all the possibilities that flicking through a box of *National Geographic* maps from the '40s and '50s that my grandfather had kept, offered. Laying these maps out on my grandparents' floor, I couldn't help but wonder at the strange names of strange, far flung places. So, too, that old sticker book.

Joaquin Alonso Ventura played for Santiagueno in his native El Salvador. What did Santiagueno look like? What did the club's stadium look like? The same questions arose for Mauricio Quintanilla, the El Salvadorian striker who played for Xelaju in Guatemala, and Jasem Yaqoub of Al-Qadesseyah, Kuwait, and Ernest Lottin Ebongue of Tonnerre Yaounde, Cameroon.

It seemed that, along with the standard fare of young children idolising the best players in the world, I found myself inextricably drawn to those unknown, 'small-time' forgotten players and teams as well, no matter where in the world. To me they did, and still do, matter as much as the greats of the game; their stories just as valid, as important as those of their more illustrious counterparts, maybe even more so for the tales they may have to tell.[1]

---

[1] Joaquin Alonso Ventura, nicknamed 'La Muerte', The Death, became a fitness instructor and English teacher when he retired, but not before winning the CONCACAF Champions Cup with Aguila,

You can rank teams and nations according to their standard, but you can't rank their importance, the pride of identity, of belonging, to fan and player alike, which remains just as significant and vital at the foot of the FIFA World rankings as it is at the top.

That sticker album and programme helped to open up a rich world of the minnow, the outsider that seemed to strike a chord in me: a shy boy that kept to himself, finding a world of football far from the bright lights and glare of the press, a world populated by the unknown footballer, the unknown fan very appealing. And it was no matter that no one outside of their country had ever heard of them; the players of these teams were competing at the World Cup, or in Luxembourg's case, in a qualifying group for such a big tournament.

That deserved, in my mind, complete awe, irrespective that El Salvador lost ten one to Hungary and came bottom of their group; Ramirez Zapata, who didn't make the cut for selection in the sticker album, and who therefore remains the faceless scorer of that consolation goal, their only one of the entire competition.

But the way they sung their national anthem, played with a passion as if their lives depended on it, even in the face of heavy defeat, only added to their mystique, and made me realise that regardless of their obscurity, their

---

also of El Salvador, in 1976 in an interesting fashion. After routine wins over Aurora and Diriangen of Nicaragua, and fellow El Salvadorians Alianza, they beat Leon of Mexico in the semi-final 3-1 on aggregate. With Leon leading 2-1 from the first leg, the return tie was abandoned after a fight broke out on the pitch, resulting in Aguila being awarded a 2-0 victory and passage to the final where they defeated the wonderfully named Robin Hood or Suriname eight three.

Joaquin's international team-mate Mauricio Quintanilla, or El Chino, despite featuring in the sticker album, narrowly missed out on the '82 World Cup squad, but did go on to earn five caps for his country as well as win the Guatemalan league title in 1980 with Xelaju before returning home.

Jasem Yaquob scored 34 goals for Kuwait and played from 1969 until retiring in 1983 for just one club, Al-Qadesseyah where he won the Kuwait Premier League six times, and the Kuwait Emir Cup four time.

Ernest Lottin Ebongue played in all three of Cameroon's World Cup matches in '82, and was capped eight times in total for his country. His career took him to France where he played a season each for AS Beziers Herault in 1986 and US Fecamp in 1987, before a season with Vitoria Guimares in Portugal in 1988, three with fellow Portuguese side Varzim, and two shorter spells with Desportivo Das Aves and Lamego.

Ernest finished his career in Indonesia where he spent four years playing for Persma Manado and Pupuk Hactim. Preceding all his travels Ernest won the Cameroon Premier Division three times with Tonnerre Yaounde, but arguably his greatest achievements came for his country at the '82 World Cup and the Africa Cup of Nations a decade later where he scored his only international goal in front of a partisan 35,000 crowd in Dakar, in the quarter finals against hosts Senegal.

endeavour mattered, they mattered; and it made me wonder at their sporting lives away from the World Cup, and what that might look like.

It seemed obvious in a way, my love of this hidden, forgotten footballing world, full of possibility and adventure. After all, I had been guided in that direction by my grandfather, first through publications like *National Geographic,* then through the game I loved. It was that Luxembourg programme from Grandad, along with trips to see his team, Salisbury, play in the non-league 'wilderness' of the Southern League, as well as that barely three quarters full '82 sticker album, that ignited my love for the underdog. And if ever there was an underdog, in European football at least, then it was Luxembourg.

The Grand Duchy of Luxembourg totals 998 square miles, making it one of the smallest sovereign nations in Europe. Indeed, it is ranked 179 in size out of the 194 independent countries in the world, and nestles between the borders of France, Belgium, and Germany, far from the main tourist routes through Western Europe. It is the world's last remaining Grand Duchy; an historical anomaly, and a reminder of a bygone era of the Kings, Queens, Dukes and Duchesses that used to rule across Europe before war and revolution changed the political and cultural landscape forever.

After the defeat of Napoleon in 1815, the lands that comprise modern day Luxembourg were disputed over between Prussia and the Netherlands. The Congress of Vienna formed Luxembourg as a Grand Duchy, hovering between the two states that would have equal influence over it, in an attempt to appease both.

In 1839 it became fully independent, and began a relatively anonymous life among its more illustrious and noisy neighbours, with a succession of Grand Dukes as head of state (the latest being Henri).

During World War Two it was, like nearly all of mainland Europe, invaded and annexed by the Third Reich. The government in exile based themselves in London and sent volunteers back to the mainland who participated in the Normandy Landings that helped defeat Hitler.

Given its history and close proximity, culturally as well as geographically, to its neighbours, it is no real surprise that there are three languages used in Luxembourg: French, German, and Luxembourgish, the latter being used by most in general conversation but not until quite recently in the written form.

Luxembourgish is a hybrid language and is classified as High German, though with over 5,000 French words in its vocabulary it often sounds to the untrained ear that those speaking it are flitting between the two larger languages in any given sentence; a glorious eccentricity that I found myself mulling over as I drove through the stunning Ardennes, a seemingly never ending expanse of rich, dense forest that stretches and undulates across Belgium and into Luxembourg, the fresh smell of wet pine courtesy of the rain storms stretching across Western Europe thick in the air.

Dudelange lies at the southern tip of Luxembourg, a small picturesque town that huddles beneath the imposing St. Martin church at its centre, its twin spires jostling for supremacy with a huge water tower that once used to stand among large factories and mines on the far side of town.

This friendly, sleepy place doesn't feel like a natural venue for European football's second largest club competition to begin its ten-month journey to a showcase final in Basel, Switzerland that will be watched by millions worldwide.

But that is what makes the qualifying rounds of the UEFA Europa League so special; long before the big names come along to take the main prize, a glut of teams unknown outside their home town get to participate, get to belong to a prestigious competition, and celebrate the successes that enabled them to qualify – celebrate their pride in their club, their town, their community with an intensity and passion just as great as those that make the final. That Dudelange is a part of this celebration, even though the rest of Europe will take little notice of this, or any of the other first qualifying round fixtures, is what makes these competitions so vital. Just because their club, their town, their community isn't very big doesn't mean it isn't just as important as that of Manchester United, Barcelona, Bayern Munich. It may not seem it if you have never been to such an early fixture in the competition before, but if you had happened to be at the Stade Jos Nosbaum, Dudelange, for F91 Dudelange's match against University College Dublin on a balmy early July evening, or any of the other countless first qualifying round fixtures across Europe that day, then you would know differently.

F91 Dudelange was formed in 1991 when Alliance Dudelange, Stade Dudelange (who were represented in that Luxembourg squad of 1982), and US Dudelange merged in the hope of creating a more financially and sportingly stable club. All three had won the Luxembourg national league and cup in the past, but all had fallen on hard times, and it wasn't until the year

2000 that the new F91 finally put the long-term decline of its predecessors behind it by winning the league.

Given the size of the country and the size of the town, which could be explored in its entirety in a couple of hours on foot, it seems amazing that it could have supported three teams for as long as it did.

From high up on the observation platform beneath the head of the water tower, Dudelange fanned-out around the church and the small town centre, before quickly becoming over-run by the deep, rolling forest that stretched over the hills beyond.[2]

A short walk from the water tower takes you out to where the forest had reclaimed the open mines that once formed a large part of the town's industry. Such a small town surrounded by such verdant woods made you wonder just how many years it would take for it to swallow Dudelange too, if kept unchecked. Not many.

F91's adventures in Europe began in 1993 with a 7-1 aggregate defeat to Maccabi Haifa of Israel in the now defunct European Cup Winners Cup, followed the next year with a 12-2 defeat at the hands of Ferencváros of Hungary.

It wasn't until the first qualifying round of the Champions League in 2005 that F91 finally won a European tie, equalising in the last minute away to HSK Zrinjski Mostar of Bosnia before scoring three unanswered goals in extra time that sent them through to the second round and a 9-3 defeat by Rapid Vienna. Only once have F91 gone beyond the second qualifying round of any of the European club competitions, when a victory via away goals against Red Bull Salzburg in 2012 saw them lose 5-1 to NK Maribor in the third round.

The club are no strangers to European football, albeit only at the early qualifying round stages; their 1-0 defeat to UCD in the first leg the week

---

[2] The water tower housed an extraordinary exhibition of haunting pictures taken during the great depression in the United States in the 1930s. Row upon row of nameless, destitute people, their lives of hardship and struggle etched into their expressions materialised out the gloom of deliberately ill-lit spaces. Their bleak, helpless resignation at their inescapable fate seemed at home in the dark silence of a gallery; these faces lingering as you stepped blinking out into the day on the observation platform at the top. The collection, entitled 'The Bitter Years' was the last exhibition organised by Edward Steichen as director of the photography department of New York City's Museum of Modern Art. Steichen believed them to be 'the most remarkable human documents ever rendered in pictures'. As a gift to his homeland, he requested that the images be bequeathed to the Luxembourg government in 1967.

before being their 47th match in Europe since the club were formed back in '91. But despite the regularity of their appearances in European competition, it was clear to see that the pride in qualifying for it still hadn't waned.

Walking up through quiet, tidy, narrow residential streets the morning of the second leg against University College Dublin, the Stade Jos Nosbaum, which sat on top of a hill overlooking southern Dudelange, hidden by a small wall at the end of a cul-de-sac, was busy with volunteers making the final touches ahead of their big night.

A small army of volunteers, all well into their '60s and no doubt retired, swept the small main stand, an exposed stretch of blue seats that basked in the sun on the far side, and raised the flags of Luxembourg, Ireland, and UEFA as well as a flag promoting respect on four flag poles by the entrance. Others slowly moved the sprinklers that were watering the pitch from spot to spot, or pushed trolleys of food and drink for the kiosks. The place was quietly bustling with excitement at the prospect of another night of European football, and they smiled and nodded as I took pictures, showing me where I could buy my ticket later on, happy to let me wander about their field of dreams.

It is an idyllic spot for a football club, and it is easy to see how such devotion as displayed by this small band of old-timers can manifest itself; the pride in their club, their stadium, their town apparent in the beautifully hand painted club badge mural on the wall above the rows of blue seats, the immaculately tended wooden framed main stand, the carefully displayed photographs, pennants and scarves of previous European fixtures on the walls of the small fan shop. This was their Nou Camp, Old Trafford, San Siro, only smaller, anonymous.

The Stade Jos Nosbaum was not my first Luxembourg football stadium visit. No, the pull of that programme from 1982 had been strong; the fascination of wondering about the likes of Progres Niedercorn, Stade Dudelange, and the Luxembourg national team itself (that had lost that match at Wembley 9-0, which remains to this day the nation's heaviest international defeat) had compelled me to ask my parents if we could make a short detour as we drove across France one summer for a camping holiday near the German border, showing on the map how close we were to Luxembourg and their 15,000 capacity national stadium.

To my amazement they thought that was fair enough, which was how I found my 12-year-old self pressed up against the gates of the Municipal Stadium, peering intently at the patch of seats that I could make out across the pitch, wondering at the thought of England, Germany, and Italy playing here as well as matches between Avenir Beggen, Juenesse D'Esch and Red Boys Differdange. No longer was the thought of these tiny teams an abstract one; here was the home of Luxembourg football, here was their version of Wembley.

I took some very bad pictures with my wind-on camera, trying to take shots between the bars of the main gate, but invariably just taking close ups of the gates themselves. Either way when they were developed the better ones were kept safe; they still are a memento of my first ever taste of football's minnow community.

The thrill I felt standing at those gates, of seeing abstract made real, of having the peace and quiet to experience the scene while my parents and sister sat patiently in the car felt just as intense as when I used to do the same thing at The Dell, Southampton, during the summer months of the off-season.

If we went in to town we would always have to stop off at my spiritual home of football to see if I could spend any of my pocket money on programmes or player photographs from the season just gone, and if there was time I would snatch a few moments pressed up against the locked turnstile gates, trying to catch glimpses of the pitch and the stands through cracks in the old wooden doors; the drone of a lawnmower as the groundsman tended the pitch, the slow rumble of cars creeping past, distant echoes of children playing drifting across the cramped terraced streets beyond.

That quiet moment, where I had the entire ground all to myself, where I could look, absorb it all without the bustle and necessity to keep moving on a match day because of the crowds, those hushed few moments felt special, looking on my first love in a way most people didn't. The rows of old wooden seats beneath the shadow of the West stand, the sun-drenched terraces. For one small moment I got to see them, really see them. They had seen so much through the years, had survived, just, the blitz of World War Two, had been the heart of the town, the community, for more than eight decades.

The fact that I felt just the same levels of electricity, awe, coursing through me in Luxembourg as I did at home helped me realise that, though I loved my team and the big time of the first division, so too did I love the small time teams, the obscure. They felt just as vital, just as important, and I needed them in my life just as much.

If F91 are long in the tooth when it comes to European football, then University College Dublin is still very much taking baby steps.

There can't be very many University teams that can lay claim to having ever played European club football, but UCD's US style scholarship scheme that enables players the chance to combine study for a college degree with playing senior football has enabled a select few to do just that.

Since 1979 when the college scheme was set up upon entry to the League of Ireland Senior Division UCD have made three adventures into Europe, their clash with F91 Dudelange being the third. In 1984 they came away with a very creditable 1-0 aggregate defeat to FA Cup winners Everton in the European Cup Winners Cup, and in 2000 they lost on away goals in the Inter Toto Cup to Velbazhd Kyustendil of Bulgaria.

Their 1-0 home victory over Dudelange in the first leg created history as their first ever European success, despite reports that the team from Luxembourg absolutely battered them looking for an equaliser; inspired goalkeeping by Niall Corbet and lady luck saw them bring a slender lead in to the away leg.

This feat is made all the more remarkable because UCD were actually relegated to the Airtricity League First Division, the second tier of senior Irish football, in 2014, only gaining entry into the Europa League via the UEFA fair play table, and even then, they didn't win that – they came third, behind St Patricks Athletic and Dundalk, but as they had already qualified for this season's European competitions UCD claimed the spot.

It may not be the most traditional way of securing European football, by being successful in domestic league or cup competitions, but as UEFA explain:

> The fair play assessments are made by the official UEFA delegates on criteria such as positive play, respect of the opponent, respect of the referee, behaviour of the crowd and of the team officials, as well as cautions and dismissals.

It is hard not to want clubs that consider such levels of respect to be the norm, to have their day in the sun as a reward for upholding all that can be great about the game. UCD's small but loyal fan base used to include, until his untimely death, the actor Dermot Morgan, who played the wonderful Father Ted in the show of the same name. When asked why, of all teams, he chose to support UCD, the legend goes that he replied, 'Because I hate crowds!'

Whether he would have enjoyed this Europa League qualifier therefore, as 1,200 people began to fill the compact Stade Jos Nosbaum, will remain one of life's great unanswered questions. As the small band of students that followed their team way out to the Grand Duchy began to attach their Irish flags to their corner of the main stand, and sit in the heat of the day drinking beer, you can't help but imagine that he most probably would have.

From the sun drenched blue phalanx of uncovered seats that ran the entire length of the pitch opposite, watching the shadow of the odd cloud undulate across the vast expanse of rolling forest on the hills beyond the water tower, it seemed a ludicrous notion for anyone to not appreciate such a blissful spot. Yes, the 1,200-crowd made this tiny ground seem very full, but the relaxed atmosphere that enabled young children to have a kick about between the milling throng at the kiosk selling beer and sausages, the warm handshakes between UCD and F91 supporters as they huddled around the small fan shop looking at pennants and pin badges, would surely have made even Father Ted at ease.

To be one of the very few UCD supporters that could say, 'I've seen my team play away in Europe', something only a few have the honour of boasting, would have been worth a bit of shoulder jostling while queuing for a glass of Bofferding, Luxembourg's home brewed beer. And as both teams came out on to the pitch the fervour with which the UCD scholars greeted their team suggested they were going to make the very most of this rare opportunity.

On paper, as with the first leg, UCD seemed up against it; a collection of students from the second tier in Ireland playing against a side with four senior internationals in their line-up. Jonathan Joubert, Tom Schnell, Daniel Alves Da Mota, and David Turpel all had lots of experience playing against the world's best for Luxembourg, who were placed 146 in the FIFA rankings.

The team, and the supporters, who shielded their eyes from the sun with a newspaper come match programme given out free at the entrance, seemed very quietly confident of turning the 0-1 deficit around, and their team's composure and skill on the ball in the opening minutes, where they restricted UCD to snatches of possession, seemed to back up everyone's positivity.

Unfortunately for the team and their fans, they hadn't quite counted on UCD's resilience.

After close to 20 minutes of constant pressure, UCD broke down yet another attack by F91 and scurried off on a rare counter. Catching the F91 defence cold they tore down the right wing, and a couple of passes later Ryan Swan, the goal scorer in the first match, swept home another to put the students two up on aggregate. Beer, flags, newspapers are flung into the air like the entire away section have just plummeted down the steep face of a rollercoaster ride, and the students on and off the pitch went ballistic. Stunned silence descended around the rest of Stade Jos Nosbaum, and it is only stirred back into life when a couple of minutes later a UCD defender is sent off for what looked like an innocuous 50-50 challenge.

Suddenly, with more than 60 minutes remaining, and despite their two-goal lead, the tide seemed to have turned in F91's favour. They had dominated play when UCD were at 11, now they were one down it was true backs-to-the-wall stuff from the Irish. Last ditch tackles, desperate clearances, and an ever-increasing string of spectacular saves from the hero of the first leg, Niall Corbet, kept UCD ahead until right on half time when, as the board went up to announce three minutes of added time, F91 midfielder Joel Pedro struck a long-range screamer that no keeper in the world was going to stop right in the top corner: one all on the night, 2-1 on aggregate. And before the home supporters could find their seats, Dudelange tore at UCD from the kick-off, forcing a corner from which Kevin Nakache powered a bullet header into the roof of the net; 2-1, though UCD's away goal still gave them the advantage as the half time whistle went.

But to the fans slumped in the away end and to the UCD players trudging off toward the tunnel with sagging shoulders, that slender advantage seemed as good as useless; UCD had run themselves into the ground trying to make up the superior technique and man advantage of their hosts, and they had conceded twice. Ahead of them lay an entire second half to try and do the same, but this time they couldn't afford to let in any more.

With the sun seeming to be growing stronger, sapping at already tired legs, the students' task seemed almost futile; to the home fans at least, who seemed relaxed once more as they went for more Bofferding, confident that the second half would be a formality.

So what happened next came as a complete surprise. The second half began in a relatively sedate manner, with Dudelange confident that the goal would come, passing the ball about with ease in front of UCD, who would drop all bar one player onto the edge of their penalty box whenever the hosts encroached too far, tackling ferociously to preserve their lead with Ryan Swan, their sole attacking player chasing down any clearance UCD's flat back eight made, trying to take it into the wings until help came.

But as the half progressed and the students tired beneath the hot sun, F91 stepped it up, launching attack after attack, smacking one long range shot against the bar, fizzing others narrowly wide, forcing Niall Corbet into fingertip save after fingertip save.

In front of him the students' tackles became more desperate as the host's advances became more dangerous. UCD bodies threw themselves in front of shots, made last ditch tackles before somehow recovering to hoof the ball down field, praying Swan might be able to latch onto the odd one, and try and take it as far in to Dudelange territory as possible to waste a bit more time.

The minutes ticked by painfully slowly for the visitors as legs began to cramp, and the skill of F91 created opportunity after opportunity. Never, I imagine, had 45 minutes felt so long to the UCD players who knew that if they could hold on, they would create a small slice of European history. History that would create precious few ripples among the wider European football community; but for them, for their club, it would mean everything. However, even among the desperate tackles and lung bursting runs to close down F91 attacks, UCD allowed a little bit of slapstick, a moment of physical comedy that wouldn't have looked amiss in an episode of Father Ted, and would have made their most famous son roar with laughter.

As the clock slowly wound down, and yet another attack had been repelled, UCD found themselves with a throw in on the half way line in the shadow of the main stand. One UCD player slowly retrieved the ball, holding it above his head as if to take the throw-in, before allowing it to drop behind him and he jogged back on to the pitch. A second student took the ball up, held it above his head, looking for a player to throw too, before he too let the ball drop behind him, and ambled back on to the field. With howls of derision raining down from all sides of the ground, the F91 bench gesticulating to the referee, a third UCD player took the ball up, feigned to drop it behind his head too before smirking and throwing it down the line; a tiny moment of magic direct from Craggy Island itself.

The talent of F91, with all its international experience, passed and probed and attacked mercilessly, making every UCD player go far beyond whatever levels of pain and exhaustion they thought possible. Every threatening pass was countered with a lunge tackle and clearance, every run down the wing covered by a student shadow boxing the step-overs and trickery of a Dudelange attacker, every cross powerfully headed away, long minute after minute after minute. And when all that failed there was Corbet in goal to pull off another save at full stretch.

Five minutes of added time at the end added insult to injury, as the students fought off attack after attack, but finally, finally, as the referee blew his whistle one last time those added minutes of excruciating toil only served to heighten the ecstasy, helped embellish the heroism of the UCD ten (14 including the three substitutes and young Sean Coyne who looked to have been sent off unfairly), adding to the legend of the battle of Dudelange. The impossible had happened; through guts and determination they had survived.

As the students celebrated on the pitch and in the stands, some of the backroom staff and various club officials stood in floods of tears, hugging one another in disbelief at what had been achieved, at being a part of the first ever UCD team, a team playing in the second tier of Irish football, to win a European tie. The small band of away fans in the quickly draining main stand jumped up and down, unsure what else to do, and as the sun slowly began to set on this picturesque little ground, in a picturesque little town in this lush, forested spot in southern Luxembourg, they knew they had witnessed their own little European miracle.

It may never be heralded like Manchester United's come back in the Champions League final of 1999, or the miracle of Istanbul that Liverpool instigated in 2005, but this anonymous little fixture, hidden among a great many other anonymous European fixtures at this embryonic stage of the competition, provided a display of heroism and bravery the like of which I hadn't seen for a very long time. That it was only witnessed by 1,245 people is immaterial.

To those who were there, they'll know, no matter how painful it may be to the vast majority, a number of whom sat quietly in their seats, in shock, long after the final whistle, so confused by what they had just seen, their team so dominant in almost every aspect. They had dismantled UCD in every technical aspect of the game, the only thing they hadn't broken was their determination, their bravery.

As the supporters drained away beneath a setting sun, slipping away into the quiet streets, only a couple of turns of which and the compact Stade Jos Nosbaum disappeared from view as if it had never been there, those same old-timers from the morning began to lower the flags, empty bins, sweep the stands with far less vigour than they did earlier, their European adventure over for another year.

It's not so much defeat that hurts these long-time volunteers of F91, after all supporting Dudelange, supporting Luxembourg, being the peren-nial underdog, you must grow accustomed to losing; it's more that this year, this fixture, for the first time in a very long time they weren't the underdogs. They had been the bigger and better team. But it just wasn't to be.

At least there would be next year, though no consolation right now, because surely this team would be good enough to remain at the top of the domestic league, ensuring another crack in a year's time. As I wandered about the now near deserted Stade Jos Nosbaum, watching the old-timers at work, I certainly hoped so.

For F91 Dudelange there would hopefully be next year. For University College Dublin there would be, probably against even their wildest dreams, next week, and a trip to Slovan Bratislava in the second qualifying round, where they would ultimately lose 1-0 before a 5-1 defeat at home sent them out.

But for now, for one night, they could allow themselves a moment of celebration. A celebration their supporters embrace fully, as a group of four students weaving away down the street drunk on success and Bofferding ask each other two questions in broad Irish accents:

'Where the hell is Bratislava?', and 'Where can we get some more of this Bofferding?'

For them it was going to be a long night. For their club it was a night that will never be forgotten.

And that I think is the point.

Great stories aren't just the preserve of football's elite. The soul of foot-ball plays itself out wherever there is a scrap of land, a battered old ball, or 1,200 people in a small stadium in southern Luxembourg. In fact, the soul of football can be far more easily discovered the further from the elite level you travel, where barriers between player and supporter, clubs and those that love them don't exist. It is a vibrant, exciting place, and how many other stories like UCD's would be played out across this one night of Europa League first qualifying round football? How many more acts of devotion by untold volunteers in preparing their spiritual homes for its big day; how many more tales of die hard supporters travelling to far flung regions of the continent all in the name of the club they love?

We will never know. But out there a precious few do, and that is what really matters. And thanks to one old programme from 1982, given to me by my Grandad that set me on my way, I felt very happy knowing that I had, finally, become one of them.

CHAPTER 2

If Football Shirts Could Talk – Palestine

Part One – back to 2003

IF FOOTBALL SHIRTS could talk what stories might they be able to tell? Potential answers to the sports eternal mysteries that seem destined to remain locked within the confines of dressing room walls, turning to myth with the passing of time.

If they could what might they be able to say about the goings on in the Colombian dressing room minutes before their last group match at the World Cup in 1994? What could they tell us of rumours of threatening phone calls from drug cartels, an unfortunate own goal resulting in the South Americans early exit from the competition, and the subsequent assassination of Andres Escobar, the scorer of that own goal?

What of the goings on before the World Cup final four years later? What really happened to Ronaldo? Did Nike force the Brazilian management to play him regardless of him having a seizure?

What could they tell us of the dynamics and power struggles between countless big name players and managers throughout the decades?

But personally, a far more important story that had haunted me for more than a decade, a story far from the bright lights of the World Cup, a story with so much more to tell, if the shirts could only tell me, would be what became of the wearers of an old amber and black kit, liberated from a life destined to fester in an English attic in 2003, and re-invented as the training kit of the Palestinian FA's Gaza based under-15 team?

All these years later, after well over a decade of war, deprivation and suffering, where might those shirts be now, and more importantly, what became of the young boys that wore them?

But first, how did a football kit that had long been forgotten in a loft on the outskirts of Southampton get there, to Gaza, one of the most dangerous places on earth, in the first place?

In 2001 I began raising funds to start a team that would be called Druk United in the little known and very poor Buddhist country of Bhutan, high up in the Himalayas. Short on resources and money, it proved a rewarding experience providing children with a chance to access kit and coaching, to play the game they loved, and which resulted, 14 years on with one of the team's players representing his country in their first ever World Cup qualifier in Sri Lanka, before going on to captain the side against Hong Kong and The Maldives.

With all the extensive fundraising I managed to accumulate bags and bags of kit that enabled even more groups within Bhutan the chance of having a kit of their own. Some also found its way to Montserrat, Bhutan's opponents in an international friendly played in 2002 and captured in the inspirational film *The Other Final*.

And then there was a bag of old amber and black kit, won for a couple of pounds on eBay, left over after all the other parcels had been sent on their long Himalayan or Caribbean treks. What to do with that?

Palestine, like Bhutan, was, and still is, a country desperately lacking in sporting resources. But unlike Bhutan, whose geographical isolation bars easy access to facilities just as much as its economy; the eternal Arab-Israeli conflict, with economic blockades into Gaza and aggressive Israeli incursions in response to mortar fire from Hamas positions into Israel, (that in turn are retaliations to oppressive Israeli policies that can all too frequently descend into all-out war) keeps the football community of Palestine, and especially those of The Gaza Strip, living off of scraps and in horrendous conditions.

Regardless of political leanings and thoughts on one of the most divisive issues in the world, the simple bond of empathy that can be created between one football fan and another can often elevate itself high above the realities of centuries of unrest. Knowing the joys that our game can bring into our lives, the escape from the everyday, the ability to dream, to live out our dreams, it is easy for someone that has it all to want to help those with precious little, and the people of Gaza have exactly that. A set of old, unwanted shirts, though very small and insignificant in the scheme of things, well it was something where often there could be nothing.

Palestine and all its hardships seemed as good a recipient for this old kit as any, and after some very vague emails to the only contact details of the Palestinian Football Association that I could find, I received a reply from Jamal Zaquot, General secretary of the PFA, who said the boys' team from Gaza would be very happy to have it, providing an address in the Gaza Strip where the kit could be sent.

Looking at those lines of text that made up the address I wasn't entirely confident that any parcel sent to it would make it through the various borders and check points and blockades that separated Palestine from the outside world. But send it I did, and a couple of weeks later came back a letter of thanks confirming it had arrived safely, and a number of small photographs, indistinct and hazy, their contents fragile, washed out, like partially developed Polaroids that only hinted at the larger picture around them. They were photographs of the boys training in the kit at a deserted, sun bleached stadium somewhere in Gaza.

Despite having received similar pictures from all over Bhutan and Montserrat in the previous months, it never stopped feeling surreal to witness shirts that had been piled in one corner of a spare room having new life breathed into them by grateful recipients across the globe.

That a set of kit that had been sat in someone's loft for who knows how many years had found its way to one of the most war-torn spots on earth, and was enabling children that had to survive among it all to play the game they loved is a hard notion to fully absorb, to properly comprehend. And like the pictures from Bhutan, these photographs from Palestine found a safe resting place in an old scrapbook, to help keep their meaning, their contents safe.

And there they stayed, though the faces that looked out from them endured, and kept coming into sharp focus every time another news story appeared about the tensions in the Middle East.

With the significant language barrier (Jamal had communicated with me using his broken English, my Arabic being non-existent), as well as the extreme lack of resources, limited windows of communication, political tensions that closed borders and shut off basic amenities, and the almost constant threat of all-out war, something as simple as a list of the boys' names that featured in those photographs, where they lived, what they hoped to become, seemed all but impossible in 2003, and even more so now, all those years on. That a few grainy photographs existed of their training match on a water starved patchwork pitch, a 90-minute respite from the realities of living on The Gaza Strip, seemed miracle enough, and was proof of who they were, and what they loved to do; a permanent testimony for nameless faces of their love of football.

If they could talk, what could those old donated tops have told us about their owners? Could they answer the question that stuck with me over the years since: whatever became of those boys that looked out from those photographs?

Since 2003 when those shirts made their way to Gaza, Palestine, and Gaza in particular, has been through hell; surviving through an eight-year economic blockade, three Israeli offensives in five years, the last of which in 2014 causing damage to 60,000 homes, 20,000 of them now deemed uninhabitable. Indeed, Beit Hanoun, a city on the north-east edge of the Gaza strip, lost 70 per cent of its homes to bombing raids, leaving the entire city virtually unfit for human habitation.

The charity Oxfam estimate that it will take a century to rebuild Gaza back out of the dark ages, with 273,000 people having been displaced by the attacks, 1.8 million affected by water shortages, 138 schools damaged, and over 300,000 children in need of psychological support after everything they had experienced.

It is impossible to tell just how many people died from the 2014 incursion alone, never mind those that went before it; aid agencies believe that 551 children perished, and that 142 families in Gaza suffered the loss of three or more relatives, but it is easy to concede that such profound devastation to Gaza's infrastructure came at a significant human price (one estimate has the total of fatalities during the 51-day attack of Gaza in 2014 at 2,145 and with more than 10,000 injured).

In its aftermath, those that endure live with a 45 per cent unemployment rate after 220 factories were destroyed, including one that made carpets, and another that made biscuits and sweets. Dairy farms, livestock, orange groves, mosques and television stations were destroyed, leaving two thirds of the population existing in extreme poverty, and with the most basic medical, educational, and social facilities. So basic that it must feel like an insult to the people that have to use them to call them that, people like those boys from 2003.

With just vague photographs, no names, no addresses, an indecipherable language barrier that made what little records there were in such a devastated infrastructure virtually meaningless, it would surely be impossible to learn of those boys' fate during the incursions. All there was to go on was hope, and fear.

Certainly, Palestinian football suffered as greatly as everyone else in Gaza.

Thirty-two sports facilities were laid waste by bombing campaigns in 2006, 2012, and 2014, including 20 football pitches. Gaza's main stadium, the stadium in which the photographs of the boys were taken was destroyed in 2006. FIFA funding helped build it again, only for it to be bombed once more in 2012, and again in 2014. In 2015 FIFA once more agreed to fund its reconstruction, and so the circle of sporting life in Gaza continues.

Along with the sports infrastructure, many members of the football community lost their lives. Palestinian football legend Ahed Zaqout was killed in the 2014 attacks by a bomb strike while he slept. Four young boys from the same family were killed while playing football on the beach near Gaza City's fishing port. Ismael Mohammed Bakr, nine, Zakaria Ahed Bakr and Ahed Atif Bakr, both 10, and Mohammed Ramiz Bakr, age unknown were targeted by a gun ship out at sea. Jawhar Nasser Jawhar, 19, and Adam Abd al-Raouf Halabiya, 17, were reportedly shot by Israeli snipers in the relative calm of the West Bank, having finished a training session with their team Abu Dis FC. Medical reports reveal that Jawhar was shot 11 times, seven times in his left foot, three in his right, and once in his hand. Adam was shot once in each foot; neither are likely to walk again, let alone resume playing football.

Before them in 2009, three national team players: Ayman Alkurd, Wajeh Moshtahe, and Shadi Sbakhe were all killed during the Israeli 'Operation Cast Lead'. All three died in separate incidents, in their homes, in a devastating 72-hour period. In total, it is believed 32 active sports people lost their lives during the 2014 incursion alone, and countless fans. And among all that, among everything that went before it, those boys of 2003, where were they among the constant images of bombed out buildings, streets, entire communities completely gutted, rushing ambulances and cars carrying more and more injured and dead to already overcrowded hospitals. If only those shirts could talk, and tell us of their owner's fate.

However, despite all the devastation there are shoots of recovery, no matter how fragile.

International aid charities continue to do what they can to help the suffering in Gaza, and in January 2015 FIFA pledged $1 million, for a second time, to help rebuild the football stadiums damaged by the 2012, and 2014 attacks, and in this war-ravaged state that totals just 360 square miles, football, such a vital social outlet for the people in Gaza just as the world over, somehow still survives.

Played on the five stadiums that survived the bombing campaigns, Gaza boasts a three-division football league containing 56 clubs that has managed to compete every year since 2010, with Ittihad Shojaeyya running out premier league champions for the season just gone, replacing Shabab Rafah who had won it the two previous seasons.

The players of the Gaza Strip League still dream of a freedom of movement that they are currently denied, which would enable them to travel to The West Bank, where the Palestinian National Team is based, a national team that is holding its own in international football despite the catastrophic setbacks it has had to overcome. One glimmer of hope for these players came in 2015 when the Palestine Cup, a match over two legs between the champions of Gaza and the West Bank, was able to take place for the first time this century.

Watched by 10,000 spectators in Yarmuk, Gaza, Ittihad Shojaeyya played West Bank champions Ahli Al-Khalil before the team were allowed to cross into West Bank for the return match a few days later.

It was a small concession from the Israeli FA after threats of sanctions by FIFA, however it meant everything to the Palestinian people that have been denied so much. And maybe among those 56 clubs in the Gaza football league, maybe among their squads, or among their supporters in the stands, maybe even at that historic match in Yarmuk, on or off the pitch, were those boys of 2003. They would be, more than 12 years on, in their late 20s.

Maybe, despite everything that they must have endured since that training match one hot day all those years ago, they are still taking up their boots and heading out to play. You can't help but hope, very, very much that that is the case.

If only those shirts could let us know, what a tale they might be able to tell. But they couldn't. In all reality they were long gone, lost among a hellish rubble that is life and death in Gaza.

But even if they couldn't talk on behalf of the boys that wore them, thankfully, amazingly, one man could.

Part Two – Twelve years later

IT IS A BEAUTIFUL sunny day, unseasonably warm for early October, the fog that had been lingering over the still waters of West India Quay and Canary Wharf in the heart of London's business district burning away.

A small huddle of food stalls stood by the waterfront, basked in the sun trap that had been created by the large corporate skyscrapers around them. Huge skeletal cranes, a last reminder of the areas dockland past loomed over them, their newly painted black frames stark against the brilliant blue sky.

It is a towering and imposing testament to the city's ever evolving skyline, where old and new intertwine seamlessly. People just passing through, people like me, stand slack-jawed, looking up at the scale of it all, much to the annoyance of the traders and office workers bustling their way past and in to the pristine tower blocks.

It seems an unlikely setting for any part of a story about a Palestinian boys' football team from 2003, unlikely in the extreme. So how did I come to be here?

Even in this age of technology and communication the thought of trying to track down nameless faces of a 12-year-old photograph from one of the most war ravaged and deprived states on the planet, a state that speaks a language that I have absolutely no knowledge of, a state that has been bombed into the dark ages and has limited electricity, limited anything, well it is a daunting one.

Vague emails to the Palestinian FA and addresses that I still had from way back in 2003, requests on social media channels for any information, even vaguer searches on the internet resulted in not even the most insignificant of leads.

It was only after posting a blog about those experiences of 2003, of putting my requests into some kind of context, handing over what little information I had, did some tiny morsel of news surface.

One of the few English language blogs on Middle Eastern football sent me a link to a Facebook account for Jamal Zaqout, the General Secretary of the Palestinian FA back in 2003, and who had sent me the photographs of the team in the kit more than a decade ago. Finally, finally a breakthrough, though it came with the warning that this Facebook page could remain dormant and unused for vast periods of time.

Either way it was a lead, my only lead, and I duly sent a copy of the blog, the photograph, the initial letter I received from him, as well as a request for any information on these boys of 2003 to Jamal. And then I waited. And waited. And waited.

As time passed, various explanations to the deafening silence that confronted me came and went. Maybe Jamal communicated back in 2003 through an interpreter? Maybe he didn't read English? Maybe he no longer used Facebook? Maybe something had happened to him? From there I didn't want to continue along that line of 'maybes', considering all the potential fates that could befall an inhabitant of Gaza, so I set about on an altogether more positive footing translating everything into Arabic using translation programmes on the internet. And with some trepidation I re-sent everything again, hoping that the message wasn't completely incoherent. Nothing.

Months passed, and while I still tried to find other leads (English language records of anything in Gaza, understandably, being non existent), I began to reconcile myself to the fact that these faces, looking out at me from a small, grainy photograph, may never have names put to them, their fate may well never be known, to me at least.

A state that had endured and suffered so much, had nearly been raised to the ground on numerous occasions by invasion and war, whose medical, educational, and economic infrastructure had been brought to its knees, would surely not be able to give up the names of a few young boys that had loved to play football a long, long time ago. With more than a little sadness, those photographs that Jamal had sent me went back into their scrapbook with faces still nameless.

And that was that. Or so I thought.

It came completely out of the blue, during a mind numbingly tedious work training day. During a five-minute break between sessions I found myself idly checking emails and social media in order to not have to chat 'work' to my colleagues, when a notification appeared. I had a message. Thank God, I thought, relieved to genuinely have something to take me out of this drudgery for a few seconds. The second half to that training day slipped from my mind when I realised that the message was from Jamal apologising for not getting in touch sooner, that he didn't get the opportunity to use the internet very often.

He was no longer a part of the Palestinian FA, but he still lived in Gaza, and he remembered me, and the kit, and he remembered the photographs he had sent. Attached with his message was a photograph of the boys from the same year, a bigger and clearer official looking team picture of the boys in their national team kit. Attached with it was a six-page document containing the names of the boys, and as much information as he had on what had happened to them.

I sat quietly during that break in more than a little shock, reading the fate of the 14 boys from the picture, a fate that mirrored their country.

This team and their individual stories were a microcosm of their homeland, and their short biographies contained all the horror, pain, suffering, anger, despair, the odd glimmer of hope, and snatches of some kind of normality that news reports that covered Gaza often detailed.

The more I read the more I thought of the two photographs Jamal had sent, the one back in 2003, and the one now. It was only on seeing the second that it really hit me, the ashen shadow that seemed to haunt their expressions in both. I thought of my two nephews and their school photographs, George's rugby team picture, old football squad photos from my youth, indeed any team photo I had ever seen. All had a smattering of smiles, grins, smirks, the odd serious look, but rarely, if ever did I see haunted. But here, in both photographs from Palestine, the hardship of their environment betrayed their appearance; the horrors they had been forced to grow up with laid bare. It was uncomfortable viewing.

All of a sudden I felt a sense of dread, afraid to start connecting names and biographies to their place in the photographs, apportioning fates to faces that I had looked in on over more than 12 years, defining them forever...

For some a life of relative normality, or what would pass for that living in such an extraordinary environment as Gaza, played out across the pages of Jamal's notes. Mohammed Hinnawi carried on playing football for Al-Shati, but then left football altogether to become an entrepreneur, of what Jamal didn't say and the internet wouldn't elaborate. Mahmoud Asiqala carried on playing football until 2009, and it is believed he now works in a sweet shop, though from the list of targeted factories during the 2014 attacks, even such a benign living cannot isolate you from the dangers of life in Gaza. Moataz Ghazi Buhaisi played in the third tier of Gaza football with Deir al-Balah until 2012, and he is now an engineer in Qarara. All that was known of Yasser al-Batneeji was that he played as a goalkeeper until 2004; for Yasser it would seem, his fate will remain unknown, as will Ahmed al-Haddad who left football in the same year, 2004, and emigrated to Pakistan, beyond that Jamal had no clue as to what life had in store for him. Omar Fares Abu Shawish, a young face in the bottom right hand corner of Jamal's picture also stopped playing football in 2004. He is now a celebrated writer and poet with the Afaq Association in Nusirat.

Unsurprisingly for a photograph of a national teams under-15 side a number of the players remained, and remain in football. Hamada Ayedi plays with Al-Estqlal, a team at the top of the second tier of football in Gaza. Abdullah Abu Suliman plays with Al-Tufah, Mohammed Boreis for Al-Shafe'i; a simple description of a part of their lives, the drama and struggle of daily life in Gaza for them remains unknown.

Of all 14 boys from the photograph two have made a career in football for themselves outside Gaza. Hamada Rikhawi left to play in the much safer West Bank, plying his trade in the Premier League, where Jamal considers him to be one of the best Palestinians currently playing. But of all the boys in that photograph, Khalid Mahdi climbed the highest within football. One of the best defenders in Palestine, Khalid helped the national team win the Asian Football Confederation Challenge Cup in 2014, and featured in three world cup qualifiers for the 2014 finals in Brazil. Khalid, like Hamada, moved to The West Bank to further his career and currently plays for Markaz Shabab Al-Am'ari in the Premier League.

For all of these boys we have just a snapshot of life. It does not take into account the complexities, hardship, and horror that life in Gaza often brings. What life has befallen them around these little snippets we will probably never know, however the stories of the final three boys from that photograph from 2003 may help to paint a bigger picture of what a life in Gaza can offer, and may help to flesh out the realities this young football team have faced.

Alam Shabbir currently plays for El-Jalaa club in the second tier of football in Gaza and works as a police officer. Jamal's notes then went on to explain that Alam's family home was bombed during one of the many wars that Gaza has endured, and his young nephews were killed.

Mohammed Zash's entry in Jamal's notes was even shorter:

> He martyred in 2007 in result of the Israeli aggression, and Israel bombing and destruction his home in the 2014 war (I believe Jamal meant to type 2004).

Mohammed, the young boy bottom left in Jamal's picture, knelt next to Khalid the successful international footballer, was dead. He would have been no more than 19 years old in 2007.

Due to the vast numbers of Palestinian dead, the language barrier, and the severely damaged and depleted records within Gaza, the lone statistic of Mohammed's death, the story of what happened to him in life since that photograph of him with the Palestine under-15s appears lost among a vast firmament of untold tragedy and suffering. Jamal's simple notes on Mohammed's life asks more questions than it answers. Was he a victim of an Israeli attack in 2007, or was he martyred during some form of retaliation? If Jamal's typo really is meant to read 2004 and not 2014, did Mohammed die in 2007 avenging whatever terrible event befell him not long after he turned 16 years old? Or is it a case of a simple loss of meaning in translation, and Mohammed died in 2007 as a result of a second assault by Israeli forces into Gaza, three years after his home had been destroyed?

The term 'martyr' means different things to different cultures; Western press coverage commonly reads martyr as a combatant killed in some form of action, while Palestinians use the term to describe anyone who has lost their lives through the seemingly endless troubles.

When pressing Jamal for any further information that he might be able to find on Mohammed, the pain and suffering that reverberated through his answer hinted at the unfathomable horror, chaos and confusion that must result in surviving in such unimaginable conditions:

> I am sorry but I can't help you getting any more information because I stopped working at the Palestinian Football Association. Also, I spent almost all the ten passed years abroad. Also, I do not have any information about Mohammed Zash because the time he martyred was very difficult and full of stress, there also was the conflict between the Palestinian detachments. I do have Motaz Albhaisi's contact details, one of the boys from the team, if that will help? He may have a little more information?

Thankfully, there was no need to wait months for a reply from Motaz – only days – though he still apologised for the delay in responding, citing the 'electricity conditions in the Gaza Strip' that effect the Deir El-Balah refugee camp in which he lives.

It is still called a camp, referencing its initial hastily constructed sea of tents and mud brick buildings for 9,000 displaced Palestinians at the end of the Second World War. However, the Deir El-Balah camp that Motaz recognises today is now built from concrete, a process that began in the early '60s when it became clear that there would be no resolution to the territorial dispute between Palestine and Israel.

This camp that was hoped would be a temporary home until its inhabitants could return to the houses they were forcibly removed from in the '40s is now in its eighth decade and contains eight schools, a sewer system, and other municipal services for the 12,000 people that live there. Despite the number of people that it houses, the Deir El-Balah camp is the smallest of the many camps that scatter the Gaza Strip.

Motaz Albhaisi, the young boy on the far left of the middle row in Jamal's photograph, standing immediately behind the crouched Mohammed Zash, told of his life in Gaza, where he had graduated with honours from the College of Engineering Department at the Islamic University of Gaza, receiving high marks for his degree in Civil Engineering.

'One of my hobbies is playing football and one of my dreams was to represent the Palestinian National Team. I was playing in Deir El-Balah in Gaza and graduated through its age groups.

'I was playing on the Palestinian National Team under the age of 15 in 2003', he went on, 'and I was called up to play on the Palestinian National Team on 2004 and 2005, but the educational conditions and the difficult situation we are living in the Gaza Strip prevented me from continuing to represent Palestinian team several times, and limited my practice to play football. I wish I could be more satisfactory in the scientific and practical career and get a scholarship in the near future to complete my master's degree, and then a PHD'.

As for Mohammed, Motaz's information on his former team-mate, though far from detailed, helped put some semblance of a story to this young man's life. No matter how vague, it felt like a treasure trove by comparison to what had gone before it; where a young man's life and death had seemingly become lost amongst an ocean of unspeakable horror and hardship.

'Mohammed was born in 1987 and grew up in a simple family, his hobby was playing football since childhood, and was included in the age groups of the Alzytoon Club in Gaza. He played in the Palestinian National Team at under-15 and under-18 level', he went on, 'and he also played for the Palestinian Olympic Team and the first National Team.

'Due to the difficult economic situation of the people in the Gaza Strip, where the difficult conditions experienced by Mohammed did not serve him to continue playing football, and practice his hobby, which forced him to look for jobs covering the initial family needs, and he worked as a painter and in construction.'

The next sentence Motaz wrote about Mohammed became a little lost in translation, though this young man from Gaza's English was as impressive as it was descriptive in his attempts to convey Mohammed's ambitions and dreams; which is why I have left it just as Motaz wrote it, as its sentiment expresses beautifully a young man's hopes for a future that would never materialise.

'One of Mohammed's dreams of becoming a house in the future where this dream is one of the elements of marriage in the Gaza strip, and almost his dream to be achieved, but the oppression and injustice and aggression on the conditions of the people in Gaza prevented him from seeing this dream where he was martyred on 16-06-2006. That's all I know about Mohammed.'

The hints at a simple dream of owning a home so as he could get married were as universal as they were heartbreaking, knowing that those dreams came to nothing. Motaz's new date of 16-06-2006 differs to Jamal's understanding of when Mohammed died, but one can't help but defer to the detail that Motaz could provide.

It still gets us no nearer to understanding the circumstances of Mohammed's passing, as even searching for records of a particular date, a particular person among the virtually non-existent Arabic or English language online records on Palestine, and Gaza in particular, is a hopeless and fruitless task. But at least this date of 16-06-2006, the day Mohammed died, can allow us to find a little context to the situation in Gaza at the time, and the conditions these boys from the team photograph lived and died in.

In June 2006 Gaza existed in the aftermath of the second Intifada (the second Palestinian uprising against Israel) as well as through the first weeks of the Israel-Gaza conflict. The United Nations Office for the Coordination of Humanitarian Affairs' report 'Israeli-Palestinian Fatalities since 2000 – Key trends' published in August 2007, detailed life in Gaza in 2006. The report details that of the 650 or so Palestinians to die as result of the conflicts, 78 per cent came from Gaza. It goes on to report that of the roughly 100 children to die in Gaza, 31 per cent were under-12, and that:

The vast majority of children died as a result of injuries sustained either to the head, chest or to more than one place of their body.

The report went on to detail further conditions that the people of Gaza, Mohammed Zash, Motaz Albhaisi, and the other boys of their under-15 team lived and died in during 2006.

At least 284 Palestinians have been killed for moving within 150 metres of the perimeter fence with Israel, 117 of them civilians, including 23 children.

During 2006, Israeli Security Forces fired some 14,000 artillery shells into the Gaza strip which were responsible for killing 59 persons, almost all of them civilians.

Extra-judicial or targeted killings are illegal under international law, unless the perpetrator acted in self-defence, there was an imminent threat of death or there is a clear case of armed hostilities occurring. In the vast majority of Israeli Defence Force targeted killings of Palestinians, the victim was driving when killed or killed by fire from a helicopter.

The report also details the loss of life in Israel from rocket fire launched from within Palestinian territory. However, the numbers, no matter how tragic, are miniscule by comparison to the lives lost in Gaza – among them that of 19-year-old Mohammed Zash: footballer, painter, with a simple dream of a house to call home.

As with so much to do with Gaza, isolated as it is behind blockades, closed borders, and an infrastructure damaged beyond belief, it may be that this is all that we will ever know of Mohammed's life; that Mohammed's tragic story, and the circumstances around his death, never becomes completely clear, at least to me, and possibly even to those that knew him, that played football with him. At least there is something, some knowledge of his life, his football career, no matter how frugal.

Martin Luther King once said that 'riots are the language of the unheard', and whatever fate befell Mohammed, those of us lucky enough to live where peace, equality, and freedom are the norm cannot fully understand the frustration and anger of enduring the unbelievable deprivations in Gaza. We can empathise, but until it is our family, our home, our future being threatened, we can have no way of knowing how we might react. For what it is worth, and from the scant information at hand, the picture that it paints of Mohammed is of a football mad young man with dreams of a family life, and nothing more. Either way the death of the boy from Jamal's photograph is, no matter how you look at it, tragic.

However, if Mohammed's story is tragic, the story of Mahmoud Sarsak, the last of the 14 boys in that picture is simply horrific.

Mahmoud was born into a football mad family; his father played semi-professional football in Egypt in the '70s, and Mahmoud was one of five brothers who played professionally in Palestine, graduating from playing with whatever scrap of a ball he could find on the streets of the Al Shabora refugee camp in Rafah, where he grew up.

Mahmoud quickly moved up from playing for the under-15s to appearing for the Palestinian Olympic team, playing regularly in qualifying competitions. He then went on to appear for the full national team in matches against Iraq and China, all the while increasing his reputation as a prolific striker with club side Khalamat Rafah. It was such progression that earned him a two-year contract with Balata Youth, a team playing in the virtual serenity by comparison to life in Gaza, of The West Bank Premier League.

But just as this new life in The West bank, complete with a chance to further his career was about to begin, it all came crashing down.

In July 2009, as Mahmoud reached the Erez Border checkpoint into Israel on his way to meet up with his new team-mates he was arrested and detained on suspicion of being involved in an attack on an Israeli soldier the year before. Despite his strenuous denials, and the lack of any evidence (none was ever presented, or any charges made against him) he was detained and imprisoned for three years.

During this period of 'administrative detention', Mahmoud was subjected to a string of horrific and seemingly never ending forms of torture. In an interview with Amnesty International he explained how he was hung from a ceiling by handcuffs, tied to a chair in a refrigerated room where the cold would make him lose consciousness. He was left in a dark room with no natural light, then one with a light so bright it wasn't possible to sleep. If he ever did fall asleep he would be beaten, losing his two front teeth in this way. He was subjected to a barrage of deafeningly loud music for 12 hours at a time.

Mahmoud would be moved from prison to prison so as he would never really know where he was, let alone his friends and family. Sometimes he would find himself in a metal shipping container somewhere in the desert, crammed in with many other prisoners, where the heat would become unbearable.

Despite all this Mahmoud, kept his hopes up of being released, as he explained to Amnesty International, because he knew he was innocent. But even this strength was tested when his detention was extended by yet another six months in early 2012.

Unable to carry on like this, Mahmoud began a hunger strike that would last for 101 days and nearly cost him his life. At points during that time he lost his sight and hearing, as well as over half his body weight, intravenous drips kept him alive. All the while international condemnation of his treatment aimed to keep his name and his story from slipping into obscurity like so many that had been imprisoned before him. Eric Cantona and film-maker Ken Loach were just a few of the celebrities that, along with human rights organisations, called for his release.

Unaware of this the boy from Jamal's photograph resisted, fought, lost deep within the Israeli prison system, until finally, on 10 July 2012 he was released. Released into a world where the injuries sustained from three years of imprisonment and torture, and more than three and a half months on hunger strike made returning to a life as a professional footballer almost impossible; released to the news that a fellow Palestinian international footballer who he had been detained with, Zakari Issa, who had been suffering from blood cancer and had been denied treatment whilst under arrest, had died a month after his own release.

Once free, Mahmoud set off on a speaking tour of Europe to highlight the plight of those he had left behind in administrative detention, and it was on that tour that he met, fell in love with, and ultimately married Victoria, the daughter of a Palestine Solidarity campaign member from London.

A new life began for Mahmoud, a life to replace the one that had been taken away from him in such brutal fashion. If he couldn't live in Gaza anymore, then, he decided, that he would have to bring Gaza to London. With the help of his wife he set up a food stall that provided a taste of Palestinian cuisine, with falafel as its speciality, to markets across the capital. It was a stall that, on a bright sunny morning in October 2015, stood nestled in among plenty of others on the banks of West India

Quay. In front of it stood an awkward looking man with a picture frame in his hand, who asked meekly to the woman on the stall, 'Is Mahmoud working today?'

The woman, it turned out, was Victoria, Mahmoud's wife, and as I explained what on earth I was doing she told me to stay there, that she would find him, that he wasn't far. She slipped in to the nest of stalls and bodies busily preparing for the lunch hour rush, and I quickly lost sight of her.

Then, after a short while, a man began to approach me from across the way, smiling, and, before I knew it, there stood Mahmoud, the young boy from all those years ago, from that photograph, shaking me warmly by the hand. I offered him up the frame, with the four small pictures that Jamal had sent me 12 years earlier, and explained that they belonged to him. Mahmoud stared at them and traced his fingers gently over the faces looking up at him; faces from another world, another life.

I explained that I had sent that kit back in 2003, and I had been trying to find out what became of the boys that wore it, that Jamal had helped me out, had helped me on my way to finding him.

He shook his head, pointed himself out to Victoria, then the five or six that he knew were still playing in Palestine.

'A few I think, they are dead,' picking out the boy in the bottom left hand corner, he said quietly, 'Mohammed.

'I remember this kit, this photo', he said, and went on to explain that their main kit was white and green, but that they had used the kit I had sent for training matches, and they had also played in it on a tour of Norway. 'I have a picture of me wearing this kit, here with me in London! Most of my photographs of that time are still back home in Rafah'. He would contact his family to see if there were any more but it was very hard to get through these days. There was often no electricity, no phones. Speaking to them was not easy.

Mahmoud stared at the pictures then showed them to Victoria, the others showing a training match in progress, a few people sat in a stand beyond. 'This ground, where these were taken, it was bombed by Israel, completely destroyed. They are trying to rebuild it.'

For someone who had been through so much there was an absence of anger in his voice. Maybe the nostalgia of a time where football had been his life, as a young boy playing on the dusty streets of Rafah had taken over. Maybe after so much suffering he had no time for bitterness, for hatred, instead possibly focusing on the here and now, on Victoria, on his stall. Who knows. Who knows what demons, nightmares such an experience may bring during the long dark hours of night.

'Thank you,' he said. 'Thank you for this,' as he held up the frame and smiled, glancing at his stall, at the work still needed to be done to get ready for a busy afternoon's work making and selling food from his beloved homeland. It was only a short couple of minutes of conversation, but after everything that it had taken to reach this point, it was more than enough. It was more than someone, a complete stranger who had once sent a football kit into a warzone for some anonymous young boys to use, could have ever dreamed of experiencing. It was enough to see him well and happy after everything that he had been through, clutching the picture frame full of memories to his chest.

And then, it was time to let him get back to it, but not before we shook hands once more, and said that we would keep in touch, hopefully talk some more some time. Then, as the early lunch crowd began to file out from the tower blocks around us, milling about expectantly as the intoxicating smells of the food stalls lured them in, we smiled, and said goodbye.

From the bridge that crossed West India Quay, Mahmoud's frame quickly became lost among the bustle of bodies around the food stalls, but his warmth, his smile, his gentle demeanour lingered on through the photograph that Victoria took of us both. And as I looked down at it on my camera it was such a contrast to the serious face, to those serious faces that looked out from Jamal's picture of 2003, a picture that now had depth and context. It didn't matter that it was a short meeting, a short conversation; it spoke volumes and told me more than I had ever hoped for. Meeting one of the boys from that grainy picture, having them stood, smiling, right in front of me if only for a few minutes was more than I had ever dreamed possible.

And there, as I watched the throng of the food market beyond, after such a long time, that photograph was complete.

Those boys of 2003 finally had names, lives, stories, even if they were far from comprehensive; some heartbreaking, some inspirational, some joyfully mundane considering the world that they lived in.

And if those shirts that they wore had been able to talk, if they could have detailed the stories of their wearers, then they would have been able to paint a broad picture of what it is to live in Palestine, to be a Palestinian in the 21st century. From the tragedy of Mohammed Zash, and Alam Shabbir's nephews, to the horrors of Mahmoud's unlawful detention, to the successes in the national team of Khalid Madhi, and in the world of poetry with Omar Fares Abu Shawish. From Mahmoud Alsiqala, working in a confectionary shop that hopefully avoided the bloodshed, to Moataz Ghazi Buhaisi's job as an engineer, Palestine's story is that of the 14 boys of the under-15 team from 2003.

I am glad that, after more than 12 years, and even if it is only to a few, theirs is a story that has finally been told.

CHAPTER 3

The End of the Classifieds and Beyond – Llanelli Town

AS A YOUNG BOY, the classified football results on a Saturday evening were compulsory viewing.

So too was the vidiprinter that would chunter along the bottom of the screen while Grandstand was on air during the afternoon; necessitating having to sit through motor cross, wrestling, rugby union, and rugby league to catch the latest score from wherever Southampton were playing.

Although I had no interest in any of these sports, I can't begin to imagine how many matches, bouts and races I must have sat through, I did by default become an apathetic expert on them all, all in the name of a snatched glance at the latest football scores.

Once all the results were in, there came the excruciatingly drawn out classified results service, that would reel off a seemingly never ending stream of scores from a never-ending list of leagues, before the updated league tables could be displayed, and for a few short moments you could digest where this latest win, loss, or draw had left the Saints in the table: Football league Division One, Football League Division Two, Three, Four, The Gola League, The Scottish Premier Division, Scottish League Division One, Scottish League Division Two, Three, The Welsh League, The League of Northern Ireland – all had to be read out before the long trawl though the league tables could begin.

And just like the sports I wasn't interested in, I became an unwitting expert on league positions of teams that I knew nothing about, way down the long list of divisions that would be paraded in front of me on a Saturday.

Among these lists of team names some captured my imagination more than others, as mysterious and exotic sounding as they seemed to a young boy: Stenhousemuir, Tranmere Rovers, Ebbw Vale, Forfar Athletic, Afan Lido. It was another world, a hidden world that remained so in an age before the internet; the only further information that could be gleaned being through the columns of results and tables in my parents Sunday paper – the obscure names of goal-scorers and the paucity of supporters that saw them only adding to their mystique.

And just as a match programme from an England v Luxembourg fixture sparked my imagination, and piqued my interest in national teams far from the bright lights of the World Cup final, so too did these obscure, unknown teams way down the classifieds.

A year or two later and a world beneath even the classifieds would open up to me when I was old enough to ride my bike down to the Rec to watch Blackfield & Langley in the Hampshire League play on a roped off pitch, and my Grandad started taking me to see Salisbury in the Southern League (on very rare occasions the odd Salisbury result would flash up on the vid-iprinter, sending me into raptures). Just as the four-page programme at Blackfield, and the more comprehensive *Victoria Line* at Salisbury would be devoured for information, on the teams playing, and the others in the league tables, so too did programmes from these mysterious teams of the classifieds help bring a new, fascinating world to life.

Before the internet and club websites, before newspapers dedicated to the lower and non-leagues existed, the only way that I could find out any-thing about these obscure teams on the fringes of the classifieds would be through *Steve Earl's Football Programmes*, a mail order enterprise selling football programmes from all over the country, and sometimes even further afield. It was an amazing resource, and one that is still going strong today out of a small shop in Bungay, Suffolk, where it still advertises in the back of football magazines with the same cartoon character programme seller.

By sending a few stamps to this address you would, and still do, receive a catalogue containing thousands upon thousands of programmes.

Pocket money saved up and passed on to mum, who would then write out a cheque and send it on with my list of wants, would be followed by an excruciating wait of a couple of weeks until a brown parcel would fall through the letterbox. Inside, teams like Tranmere and Forfar and the leagues they were in would open up through their match programmes, revealing the same passions and devotion as was expressed through the pages of England's and Southampton's. Just as I was witnessing with Salisbury and Blackfield, the world of football was far more rich and captivating than just the very top of the game.

My fascination with the world of football far from the bright lights flourished among the pages of the ever changing Tranmere programmes of the '80s, that began as a single card sheet folded in three, before expanding into a newspaper style, then reverting to a more familiar programme look with a smart cover. My interest in the overlooked taking shape through the sleek two tone blue and white Forfar programmes of the same period, all sporting strange but captivating club badges that I had never seen before. Through the black and white team photos of the visiting teams and the player pics detailing countless journeyman footballing lives a long way from the top of the classifieds, through action shots of previous matches capturing a moment frozen in time – spectators, few in number by Southampton's standards, looking on expectantly from unfamiliar stands and terraces as far removed as you could get from FA Cup finals, Division One Championships, European and World Cup finals.

Through the pages of these programmes, the importance of Forfar, Tranmere, Newport County and all the other teams populating the lower reaches of the classifieds, to the small crowds captured in these action shots that supported them on their anonymous journey, they were everything. These little clubs meant to their supporters what Salisbury had quickly come to mean to me. Irrespective of status, they were as important to the few that followed them as Manchester United or Arsenal. This forgotten world at the foot of the classifieds, thanks to the catalogue of programmes from Steve Earle, was beginning to reveal itself to a young boy to be as exciting, passionate, and as worthy of discovery as the very top of the game.

Which is why, more than 30 years after first discovering Steve Earle, Luxembourg, El Salvador, Salisbury and Forfar Athletic, I found myself trying to find a match to watch while on a February half term holiday in St. David's, Pembrokeshire, on the very far reaches of west Wales.

Annoyingly, it turned out the opportunity to watch a match at the foot of the current classified results service would be a few hours too early to catch as we drove up: Haverfordwest County and Bangor City of the Dafabet Welsh Premier League, the second to last league to be read out, kicking off at half past two.

Haverfordwest really did represent the end of the football trail in one of Wales' most remote counties. Beyond it, roads grew ever smaller as they snaked their way to the rugged coast and a storm tossed Atlantic Ocean. Only Solva, a team from the Pembrokeshire League Division Two, a league so remote their top teams rarely take up the offer of a play-off that could take them up to the Welsh League Division Three because of the travel that would incur, lay beyond Haverfordwest; their mud-covered players battling valiantly in failing light as a storm rolled in across their exposed pitch. As corner flags whipped violently, and whitecaps crashed against the black rocks of the bay beyond, the dull boom of wave on cliff-face like a distant cannon, the end of what looked to be a challenging match played out as we drove past.

So, to catch a game this week from such a remote location, we would need to leave the classifieds behind, and head out into the little known, to me at least, Welsh leagues beyond.

Welsh football, to those outside of Wales, is often considered to begin and end with the Welsh teams that play within the English football Pyramid. Swansea City, Cardiff City, Newport County, Wrexham, Colwyn Bay, and Merthyr play, to varying degrees of success within the English game; and, bar a passing reference to the Dafabet Welsh Premier League in the results service on a Saturday afternoon, that is it.

However, look beyond the Welsh teams playing in England and you find a football pyramid teeming with clubs all competing beneath the banner of their own Football association.

But why, when the ceiling of expectations is the Welsh Premier League at the foot of the results service, don't teams follow Colwyn Bay and Merthyr into the English system, and the potential to move toward professional football and the riches of the upper echelons of the English game?

The Welsh football pyramid offers a refreshing answer: because sometimes money isn't everything. Identity, pride, and belonging all chime louder to some than the lure of whatever lays beyond the border.

Wales is a country proud of its roots. Its language stands alongside English on street signs and buildings, its history lovingly preserved, its countryside protected, its industry celebrated and defended as best as it can by the Welsh Assembly. Being a part of the Welsh football pyramid is an extension of that pride, of that belonging, and helps to cement an identity, a sense of nationality that joining the English leagues could potentially betray.

Only outside Wales is the Welsh Premier League not given the full respect it is due. Yes, it is a league that sometimes struggles from a lack of support, with Bangor City, who achieve average crowds of 700, being the best supported team and all of the league's clubs suffering from some football lovers in Wales preferring to cross the border to watch the giants of world football in Liverpool, Manchester and London rather than the teams on their doorsteps. However, despite that, it is also a very competitive league that offers one team the chance to be called Champions of Wales. In a country so proud of its identity and culture, that is a great honour – even if the football community outside of, and indeed sometimes within, Wales doesn't always notice its significance.

Being a part of the Welsh football pyramid can also open a pathway into competing in Europe with the Premier League champions, and the Welsh Cup winners joined by the second placed team and the play off winners in the qualifying rounds of the Champions and Europa leagues. Whoever represents their club and country never lets it down, cherishing what is clearly a very proud moment. Having witnessed Bangor City go toe to toe with, at the time, the Champions elect of Iceland in Stjarnan FC; a team that went on to beat Lech Poznan of Poland and Motherwell of Scotland before coming up short against European Giants Inter Milan at the San Siro, it was clear to see that the passion and pride within the Welsh Premier League can take teams far beyond what the outside world might expect of them.

Because Bangor never looked out of place on the same pitch as Stjarnan, the champions of a nation that would qualify for the European Championships the following year, before shocking the world in reaching the quarter finals.

The validity of the Welsh Premier League and the pyramid beneath it is only questioned by those that know nothing about it, that only see its lowly status on a Saturday afternoon in the classified results. Just because, like Luxembourg, the Faroe Islands, or countless other leagues around Europe and the world, it isn't one of the big European leagues, doesn't mean it isn't important. Sometimes the power of identity and belonging, and the pride and worth that that brings outweighs the potential riches of the English game, and makes leagues like the Welsh Premier just as vital.

It is a competition that has bound every corner of the Welsh football community together. From Haverfordwest County in the most remote south westerly part of the country, to Aberystwyth on the Atlantic coast, to Bangor just north of Snowdonia. It is a league that not only helps to cement the identity of Wales and the pride of the Welsh, but one that also helps to preserve the national language with its highlights shows aired in Welsh on s4c It is a league, with clubs rooted in their community, run by the people, for the people, that many disenfranchised supporters of English Premier League teams may actually be a little envious of, if they knew anything about it. It is a league that many teams in the pyramid beneath it aspire to; teams like Llanelli Town and Pontardawe Town.

Stebonheath Park, Llanelli, is no stranger to storms. From the one battering the Atlantic facing coastline of Western Wales an hour or so further down the road, and is creeping menacingly toward us under the veil of darkness, to the financial one that forced the then Welsh Premier League Llanelli AFC into liquidation as the 2012–13 season came to a close.

For those hardy souls cowering beneath the floodlights' glare on a bitterly cold night that promises worse, the looming storm is an apt metaphor to what life as a Llanelli supporter has been like in recent times.

From European nights as Welsh Cup holders and Premier League play-off winners against the likes of Motherwell, Dinamo Tbilisi and most recently Kups of Finland, to the newly reformed Llanelli Town finding itself in the Welsh League Division Three (the fourth tier of Welsh football and lowest you can go before you enter regional park football leagues), the supporters of this club that dates back to the late 19th century have seen it all.

But promotion from Division Three as champions last season, and a solid mid table position in Division Two, in what is only their third year in this current incarnation, sees their long-suffering fans in a positive, if not self-depreciating state of mind. As a number of the old-timers, decked out in Llanelli scarves that looked like they too had seen many a long season, climbed the steep steps up into Stebonheath Park's main stand and looked out at the sea of empty seats before them, they couldn't help but ask to those already in their seats: 'Is there room for one more?!'

Those of us already in situ smiled and chuckled with each new face appearing at the top of the steps and their little outburst, for it was their club to mock.

There is no doubt they must have seen it all at this ground, good and bad; full houses and European nights beneath the lights, cup wins and league championships, relegation, financial meltdown, the crowds of old slowly drifting away (a malaise that every non-league club can identify with). Indeed, a page in the match programme entitled 'Meet the Committee' offers an insight into life at Stebonheath Park, when Keith Thomas, chairman of the supporters' association, and whose first Llanelli match came at the end of the Second World War described his first experiences supporting 'The Reds':

> The long trek up Glenalla Road seemed never ending for a five year old boy until we eventually arrived at the Evans Terrace entrance. On entering the ground I took up my position on the large covered terracing which stood at the town end. I was almost swallowed up by the magnitude of Stebonheath Park, it was awe inspiring.

Walking around the same ground now one can only imagine how things have changed since the '40s. As you walk behind the goal nearest the entrance, and closest to the main stand and the tea shop, it is clear that neither end have had any terracing, covered or otherwise, for quite some time. Old turnstiles and exit gates that look like they haven't been used in an age stand locked up and dormant in the shadows beyond. You can't help but wonder if you might find Glenalla Road, a faded Evans terrace sign, and a sea of memories the other side.

Regardless of the changes, and regardless of the biting cold on a bleak night and the potential lure of the Champions League on the television at home, these self-depreciating old-timers begin to rattle through the turnstile behind a strip of uncovered seating and a small open terrace on the far side of the pitch, and slowly make their way round to their seats in the main stand. This is after all their club, no matter what league, and no matter who else is interested in it. They would rather be nowhere else but here.

As it drew on to kick-off the stand began to become a little more populated, topping out at 160, as announced over the tannoy during the second half. Teas in hand this hardy band congregated at their usual spots; a few souls lost in a sea of coats and hoods huddled on the open seating beyond, an even lesser band of eight took to the terraces ready to offer chants and cajoling to their heroes in red, and mockery to any Pontardawe winger that came too close.

Thankfully the assembled Llanelli ultras missed an opportunity to lay abuse at the door of the visiting goalkeeper when, during the warm-up a ball he thought had strayed beyond the far post actually cannoned back off it and into his groin, much to the hilarity of the strikers taking pot shots at goal – the next five or six going uncontested as the winded keeper remained bent double, wishing in his prone position for the pain to subside.

Pontardawe Town, like a significant number of the teams in Division Two of the Welsh League, could consider this match to be a local derby, with all the teams stretching no further east than Chepstow Town and Caldicot Town each side of the Severn Bridge, and Croesyceiliog who are from just south of Carmarthen, 30 minutes to the west. The Welsh Premier League is the only fully national division. Beneath it The Welsh leagues service the clubs along the southern coast of the country, and other leagues feature teams from the north and mid-Wales.

The fair number of Pontardawe fans that have made the short trip from the other side of Swansea aren't just here because it is a derby. A win would see them move top of the table and set them up for a swift return to the league they were relegated from last May, and from there they would be one step away from the promised land of the national league.

I cannot remember the last time I saw a match where both teams ran out onto the pitch separately, so institutionalised have I become to the obligatory walk out of both teams before conducting a line of handshakes that precede English and Scottish League matches. Even in the lower reaches of the English non-league game is this norm, so it was a real throw back to my youth to see Llanelli in their red kit run out, followed a minute or so later by Pontardawe in the black and white stripes, finally the referee and linesmen a short while after. It looked more like a scene from an old Pathe newsreel from a Stanley Matthews match in the '50s.

However, once the referee blew his whistle and the first strong tackles began to slowly escalate into more agricultural ones, you could maybe understand the lack of need for handshakes.

Despite a number of players from these opposing teams warmly embracing each other during the warm-ups; a league so condensed into a relatively small geographical space can only ensure that many have played on the same side in seasons past, once the match had started there was no love lost. It was clear from the off that this is a hard league, populated by tough players. Strong tackles peppered what was also a decent spectacle, with both teams trying to pass the ball around neatly to break each other down.

Bruno Forkuoh, an Italian, who found himself out on the wing for Llanelli via spells with Seaside and Garden Village, broke away and smashed the ball home under the body of the Pontardawe keeper for his second spot of bad fortune of the night. Rob Shannon, a recent signing for Pontardawe from West End equalised with a header at the far post before the Pontardawe keeper's third spot of bad luck in spilling a cross resulted in Llanelli skipper Lee Bevan putting them back in front.

Considering the weather and the heavy pitch it was an entertaining spectacle, with the old-timers in the stand applauding a good pass, and lambasting one of the opposition as they rolled around after being scythed down; a similar tackle however from a Pontardawe player had them baying for blood: 'Straight red ref, that's what that was. Bloody disgrace!'

Stebonheath Park beneath the floodlights and the darkness beyond is a special place to watch some football. It sits in a dell with a steep grass bank rising up above it that is topped off with a row of houses that curve round and down to a large church; its black silhouette almost lost in the shadow, only revealing itself deep into the first half when eyes had become accustomed to the scene. Whether man made or natural it is a perfect amphitheatre for football, and as the old-timers took off down the steps at half time for a cup of tea, satisfied with their team's efforts, it was easy to imagine the Stebonheath Park of Keith Thomas' childhood rising up out of the darkness, it too cowering beneath dark, ominous skies, the lights of what could well have been Swansea twinkling away in the valley beyond.

Despite it 'only' being a Welsh League Division Two match in front of 160 people on a freezing cold Tuesday evening in February, the importance of this game and this stadium was tangible among those in attendance. It may not be a history that carries much weight beyond the borders of Llanelli, let alone Wales, but the full page of club honours listed in the programme, dating back to a first Welsh League Division One Championship in 1913–14, along with the ghosts of big European nights are easy to imagine on the now deserted, floodlit pitch, and across those long lost terraces.

The old men queuing for a hot drink in their equally old football scarves ensure that that is the case; witnesses as they are to great moments and matches in front of thousands that took place here at their second home, known affectionately as 'Stebo'. The glint in their eyes as the match played out, the passion and love for their club making it easy to feel the history, the importance of their team made flesh and blood. As custodians of their football club and its history, both good and bad, they have the gift of perspective when things begin to go wrong in the second half. A well worked equaliser for Pontardawe, followed by a defensive mix up to give the visitors the lead is met with a shrug of the shoulders that seems to say 'yes but two years ago, we didn't even have a team left to support'.

Another error and another goal for the away team, ensuring the points went back east, beyond Swansea to Pontardawe was met not with vitriol from the stands but only a little frustration. As Llanelli tried desperately to get back into the game, pumping the ball forward at every opportunity, a few anguished shouts from the old-timers as time and again it didn't work: 'Why always with the long ball now? Why not keep passing it?'

With the gift of insight and experience in losing their team when it was liquidated back in 2013, a single defeat was far from the end of the world. And if defeat was coming, those swaddled in their decades old red scarves seemed to prefer defeat playing the Llanelli way, rather than fruitless long balls that only served to frustrate the reds striker to the point of lashing out at a Pontardawe player and getting himself sent off a minute or two from the end.

When the end finally came there was little in the way of dissent from the faithful, instead handshakes between one another, slaps on the back, waves as they began to drain away until next time and the next game, where they would all congregate once more in the same seats, with the same scarves, ready for whatever their team could muster.

Despite the following days papers not even listing the score (only the Llanelli Star mentioned it) it would be a mistake to disregard this third-tier match in Wales as meaningless. To the travelling Pontardawe supporters who cheered their players as they celebrated on the pitch, the win taking them top of the table, to the Llanelli fans making their way slowly to the exit past the vast expanse behind the goal where Keith Thomas' terrace once stood, this match symbolised an awful lot; for the present, past, and future were all in attendance.

History, community, belonging, friendship; everything that makes football clubs an integral part of the area they inhabit were on display around Stebonheath Park. The fact that both teams, and the league they play in remain lost, far beyond the end of the classified results on a Saturday afternoon is immaterial. It is the classifieds loss, as it is the loss of those who preferred to stay in and watch the Champions League on the television, or travel to see 'bigger' matches in 'bigger' leagues across the border. Because the television can't give you everything that Llanelli and Pontardawe gave their supporters. It can't give you the feeling of belonging, of being a part of something. And neither now can the top teams in England, where fans are treated as little more than customers, far removed from those that represent them, their community.

A few days after the match, on a remote beach a stone's throw from St David's, a young girl stood on a rock watching the storm-tossed sea crash against the cliffs at the mouth of the bay. Arm outstretched, hand raised she stood as the powerful waves rolled in toward her, scrabbling for cover when each one broke and hissed over the shingle, submerging the rock she had been standing on.

Once each one had subsided she jumped back on her rock, stretched out her hand again and shouted 'halt' at the angry surf. Finally, after about a dozen attempts, and a dozen last minute dashes to safety, one wave fell short of her rock, lingering a foot or so away, before receding.

'Look' she shouted back to her Dad and sister who had been beach combing. 'I made the wave stop!'

For the teams at the foot of the classified results, and those like Llanelli and Pontardawe far beyond, this is their life, railing against the powerful tide of the Premier League and the Champions League. It is a life they are used to, and as long as they have their faithful support, their purpose, it is a rich life well worth living. And every now and then, hand outstretched, the tide falls a little short for these teams, and for a moment they remain atop their rock. For Pontardawe, the chance of promotion looms large, for Llanelli the Welsh Premier League and European nights remain a little way off. But while they keep jumping back on that rock like that little girl, while they have hope, they have everything. Good luck to both of them.

CHAPTER 4

Neither Here nor There – Berwick Rangers

'JESUS, WE MUST BE MAD', a ruddy faced Clyde fan long past retirement muttered as he crumpled into a chair in the Berwick Rangers supporters' club bar. Taking a sip from his pint and shifting awkwardly after a cramped two-and-a-half-hour journey from Glasgow in a small white mini-bus parked up outside, he waited for his fellow passengers, all of whom were some ways past pensionable age. One by one as they were served they tottered from the bar on stiff joints, drink in hand to join him.

He shook his head and repeated himself, a look of shock, of exasperation at their self-inflicted plight writ large across his face; nods of agreement from his companions as they sipped at their drinks and considered the decisions and acts of blind faith that had brought them to this point.

No-one mentioned exactly what was the cause of their apparent insanity; it was just taken as read. Was it the long trip in what looked like the most uncomfortable and oldest mini-bus known to man? Was it that their reward for such a journey was to sit for the best part of two hours out in the biting cold watching a Scottish League Two match, the fourth tier of the Scottish game? Was it their devotion to their team, known as the Bully Wee, and their nerve shredding tilt at the championship title?

'I tell you,' our man confessed to any that would listen, 'I died a thousand deaths last week. It was just awful, when they scored in the 82nd minute! Oh my God!'

A few nods of affirmation at last Saturday's three all draw with second from bottom Montrose, which had tested the frayed nerves of Clyde's septuagenarian travellers, and handed their title rivals East Fife a four-point advantage at the top of the table. Or was it something else that had caused his initial outburst? Because this long trip to follow their team is unlike any other in Scotland. In fact, it is an almost unique feature in all of world football, this journey that they and their little white mini-bus had just undertaken. Because who else has to travel to another country in order to see their team play a league game?

Well any team in the same league as Berwick Rangers for a start.

When it comes to a team that could truly be described as 'out-there', that are truly out on the fringes of football, Berwick Rangers are a perfect fit both sportingly, being an English team playing in the Scottish leagues, but also geographically, existing as the town does among the vast and isolated tracts of farmland and hill strewn wilds between England and Scotland.

The town of Berwick straddles the mouth of the river Tweed some two and a half miles south of the Scottish border. This small market town, population around 12,000, is closer to Edinburgh than it is Newcastle, and over a period of 400 years through the Middle Ages, when England and Scotland fought one another for supremacy, Berwick changed hands between the two nations 13 times, so important was it as a frontier defence.

Indeed in 1305 the arm of William Wallace was displayed in Berwick after his execution and quartering on 23 August, a powerful symbol of supremacy, at least for a short while. In 1482 Berwick changed hands for the last time, becoming and staying a part of England, and the 1707 Act of Union between England and Scotland ended any contention as to which country it belonged to.

The long train journey up to Berwick however, helps to paint a picture of a small, isolated town, far removed from anywhere; unique in its need for both Scotland and England. It is a town with an identity unlike any other in mainland Britain, an identity most likely inconceivable to the nationalist pride displayed in almost every other village town and city north and south of them, at least when it comes to sport.

From Darlington, where two old-timers sat on a bench overlooking their allotments, basking in a rare patch of sunlight, to the cathedral city of Durham, to the bustling metropolis of Newcastle, the train snakes on out into ever increasing tracts of pastoral farmland. The unpredictability of April plays out in the skies above as densely bunched storm clouds trail dark veils of rain, before giving way to vistas of wispy clouds with sunbeams breaking through, plunging to earth like anchor lines, digging in to desolate hillsides. On and on the train ploughs through remote countryside, and as we pass Morpeth, then Alnwick, the coast and the mystical Holy Isle and Lindisfarne Priory appears faint out at sea through the fog of yet another rain storm, the priory perched, impossibly it seems, on high, treacherous looking cliff-tops and rocks. On and on until finally the train begins to slow and as it banks right the picturesque town of Berwick comes in to view, tucked beneath 400 years of fortifications and sheltering from the slate grey sea behind a great sea wall known as Berwick Pier.

As people disembark onto the station platform, those arriving for the first time truly feel like they have happened onto the middle of absolutely nowhere, neither here nor there; a couple of miles shy of a Scottish border populated only by fields of sheep and monitored by windswept hill tops, and far from anywhere in England.

However, it doesn't take long to realise that that isn't how the town of Berwick sees things.

Identity is a powerful thing, often promoting pride and prejudice in equal measure. Never more can that be seen between Scotland and England, where the contradiction of animosity between two countries so close is as unfathomable in its complexity as anywhere else on earth.

More than a millennium of history, conflict, and alliance can offer up a world view of your choosing, and can create an individual or national identity to represent your understanding of that.

For two countries so closely tied to one another, whose populations intermingle and co-habit north and south of the border peacefully, the spectre of national identity can bring all that crashing down.

Politics and sport are the main offenders, with the national football teams of both countries the zenith of nationalist ferment. Like local derbies between neighbouring towns can divide work colleagues, friends, families, turning two sets of fans that have so much in common outside of football into bitter enemies, so to the national teams of these two great nations fractures mainland Britain, for 90 minutes at least, completely.

It is something I have always struggled with.

I was born in Southampton, England. I grew up in Southampton, England. My parents were born in Salisbury and Worthing, both in England. My mother's parents were born in Salisbury, as were their parents.

But my father's mother was born in Banchory, between Aviemore and Aberdeen, Scotland and her parents hailed from the Orkneys, Scotland. Growing up I was proud of both sets of lineage, finding a pride in my one quarter Scots heritage as much as I did in my history among the Wiltshire farming community, and because of that when it came to football I supported both national teams.

During the 1982 World Cup I cheered on Scotland against New Zealand and Brazil just as much as I did England, though at the time I had never even been to the country of my grandmother's birth.

My mother found a Scotland jersey in a sale that I wore religiously, despite it itching something awful.

While on holiday in Aviemore as a child, watching Shinty (a kind of extremely aggressive form of hockey) at a nearby pitch, and a Highland Games in Inverness, as well as a couple of hours left on the banks of Loch Ness, monster watching, I felt just as home as I felt some 500 miles away, back home, even though it had been my very first visit to Scotland. It felt right, comfortable, so much so that on the last day of the holiday I had to wander off while mum and dad were packing the car so as they couldn't see me crying.

It was a hybrid identity that I had to keep quiet, especially at school, where any tiny fragment of difference to the norm usually resulted in a beating, and remained muted in later life where it didn't seem an option to have an affinity with both sides of the old enemy, at least in footballing terms.

As the last of the train doors slammed shut, and a shrill whistle pierced the air, a jolt, then the carriages slowly began to slip away on their long journey up to Inverness and the ghosts of long finished Highland games, I turned and stepped out into a town that would reveal itself to have an identity as unique as its history. It was a town that, rather than being 'neither here nor there', was in fact a community 'from everywhere and anywhere'.

Its bustling high street sported two banks: The Royal Bank of Scotland and the Bank of Scotland, and despite being two and a half miles inside England there was a gift shop dedicated to all things north of the border. Scottish accents mingled with broad Northumberland, and a third, an amalgamation of the two, that drifted from one to the other in the same sentence added a little spice to overheard conversations on narrow streets that nestled in the crook of this beautiful little town's medieval fortifications. Ramparts that had become grassed over, either by design or by nature, and had in turn attempted to keep both the English and Scottish out, overlooked all; the fortification's well-tended paths and handrails up to its numerous summits now welcomed everyone. On a steep street that sloped down to the River Tweed and a chandlery shop with small fishing boats moored alongside, a young boy with a broad Glaswegian accent raced to a red phone box and opened the door and stepped inside.

'Look at me, maw, I'm in London!' he yelled back at his parents, the novelty of it making it seem, to one little boy at least, like despite only being two short miles from his homeland, he may as well be all the way south in London.

Geography meant that there was a sense of Scotland in the large red stone townhouses that dominated the old town; the reds faded a pale pink on the sheltered sides of the street, those facing the North Sea turned a dusky colour by decades of winter storms. These large hewn stones would have come from similar quarries to those that supplied Edinburgh and beyond.

Sitting on a bench on Berwick Pier at high tide, a perpetual swell rolled in against it and on all the way in to shore. The distant outline of Holy Isle appeared faint on the horizon, whirlpools and breakers exploded over treacherous black rocks just beneath the waterline that would reveal themselves at low tide as possible remains of some older pier head whose body had long since been dismantled or eroded to away to nothing. Sitting in the sun reading the history of Berwick Rangers Football Club, a seal bobbed in the water on the sheltered side of the wall not far from me, blowing what sounded like a raspberry in disgust when it realised I had been watching it and dived out of sight. It returned the following day at low tide, beached on a sand bar on the far side of the Tweedmouth to the pier, keeping a wary eye on beachcombers that wandered and batted away sand flies that blighted both pier and the beachfront when the North Sea was at ebb. Vast rafts of kelp shimmered and undulated at the mouth to a small inlet near the old, now exposed pier head as Berwick's footballing past came to life.

Just like the town's history, the Wee Gers story straddled both England and Scotland. And like the town they were from, their football team were inextricably linked and connected to both.

The town's first forays into football were in the Scottish Border league and the Amateur Border League. The club had made several attempts to join the North Northumberland League within the English football system, but had been turned down every time. Presumably its members didn't like the idea of having to travel to the far extremes of their county to play Berwick. So, by necessity and rejection the English town of Berwick had to continually turn to the welcoming arms of Scotland in order for its football team to survive. And for much of the Wee Gers history survival seems to have been its main sporting triumph, though they have enjoyed promotions and cup giant killings along the way.

Joining the Scottish Football League in 1951, and settling at their Shiel-field Park home in 1954, Berwick's geographical isolation with both England and Scotland, coupled with the small population of the town meant that the club existed, and still exists on small attendances and with the need for prudent financial management. Taking the eye off the financial ball can be disastrous for a small team without a wealthy benefactor, and, like many small teams, Berwick has sailed very close to the edge in the past.

Throughout Berwick's football history: Border League football, rejection by the North Northumberland League, Entry into the Scottish Football League, the club has trodden a path through two countries, both of whom having a strong identity – especially when it comes to football.

The geographical certainty of being an English town, its inextricable links to another country just a few short miles away, its sporting connection with one, yet its governance by another is a dizzying array of contradictions and confusions, especially when considering the often black and white simplicity of football allegiance on both local and national levels.

The English town of Berwick's first team squad at the time of my visit were made up of all but two players from Scotland. Only team captain Jonny Fairburn and Dwayne Coultress, who was out on loan to Scottish Junior side Newtongrange Star came from south of the border. Yet despite playing in the Scottish Football League, these Scottish players, and their two English comrades are registered by the English FA. A player can get sent off in Scotland, but will be punished in England.

It is a unique situation, and given the certainty of identity within football allegiances, it seems hard to fathom how a club that straddles that great divide between the old enemies of England and Scotland can exist at all, let alone survive and attempt to prosper.

A club that is neither here nor there, caught between two eternal sporting enemies that were once eternal warring enemies; what sort of an identity can come from such a seemingly hostile environment? As it turns out, something that seems to defy the perceived logic of everything that went before it, combining proud symbols of identity to create an entirely new and unique one. It is like the notion of two atoms colliding, the club badge of Berwick Rangers. Surely it can't happen without some kind of catastrophic event occurring? Where else but on the club crest of this small border town's football team could the Scottish lion from its royal standard and national football team's crest be joined by the English lion from the equivalents south of the border?

The scarves made by the supporters' club to help raise money for their team carries both the Scottish Saltire and the English St George's cross. It is a union that for many could appear completely unpalatable; but when you are between a rock and a hard place, when your existence is forged upon two proud nations not one, the clear-cut notion of 'them and us', just as I experienced growing up, simply doesn't carry any weight. Berwick Rangers' fan base is split roughly 50-50, Scottish-English, even if the squad, the fixtures, and the club's governance isn't.

Berwick is a town that doesn't necessarily see what everyone else sees, but instead forges ahead with a self-built sense of identity and being, with their football team a proud, if not small-time symbol of who they are. Though this hasn't come with the occasional hiccup, as witnessed in 2011 when Stranraer, another team close to the border, but north of it, and some hundred plus miles to the west of Berwick (matches between the two are jokingly referred to as border 'derbies' despite the distance between them) called for Berwick Rangers fans to be banned from bringing flags and scarves with the St George's cross on them to matches as they believed there had been an escalation of tensions with their presence.

In a league where attendances rarely top 600, and supporter segregation is often unnecessary, it seems a little over the top to demand banning Berwick's supporters from displaying their unique identity, but it does highlight just how unique, and misunderstood it can sometimes be.

Though Alec, another old-timer from the mini-bus from Clyde doesn't seem to have a problem with it. As he gingerly walked from the bar, leaning on his stick while nursing his double shot of whiskey, Alec asked if he could sit in the seat next to me at my table. The sofas that were free, he explained, were too low for him.

I had witnessed him struggle to get out of one when he first arrived, preferring to sit while the mini-bus rush at the bar calmed down. Even in a higher, firmer chair he tentatively, shakily aimed to sit, his legs unsteady without the support of his stick that he had crooked over the back. Finally down he took a breath, then a dram, and settled into his seat. With one eye almost closed up, and a cap pulled down over the other, a stooped back naturally leaning him in to his drink, Alec looked all of his 80 plus years.

'Long trip?' I offered, nodding at his mini-bus.

'Naw', he said 'just over two and a half hours. Not too bad.' When asked if he begrudged having to come to England to see his team play in the Scottish League he shook his head. 'Naw, we've been doing it long enough now it's no bother. Plus', he said with a wily smile, 'I count this as seeing my team play in Europe!'

Alec had been watching Clyde play for 70 years.

'Though I've only been regularly coming to away games since I retired. Although that was 25 years ago mind.' He had worked for Weir's, a big engineering company in the heart of Glasgow's industrial hub his entire working life. 'Have you heard of it?' he asked, and when I shook my head he sighed a little, a sign that the world he had grown up in and knew was slipping away. 'We were respected all around the world for the work we did. We had offices all over. Now a lot of it is closed down, gone.' The sadness at its decay palpable in his voice.

His team, Clyde FC, or the Bully Wee were formed on the banks of the river Clyde and grew up among the chemical, engineering and textile works and the crowded population that worked them. The club was and is as much a product of its environment as its fans such as Alec; it is a bond unbroken by the club's relocation to Cumbernauld, 13 miles east of Glasgow in 1994, that compels very old men and women to take such journeys every other weekend, even into England.

Once the mini-bus had decamped fully, and everyone had got their drinks, fanning out on tables around me it was clear that the madness suggested by the ruddy faced old man was not at their current location, but at the nerves that following your team on a faltering promotion push can cause.

It was clear that Berwick was just another destination, no matter whether in England or not, a permanent fixture that some of them had descended on since the Wee Gers had joined the league 65 years earlier. Indeed, it is testament to his loyalty and passion for his team that Alec had been following Clyde for a good five years before Berwick joined the ranks all those years ago, though his team have fallen on hard times of late, which must be why this tilt at success is playing on its supporters' nerves so.

'We got relegated two seasons in a row,' he said shaking his head, 'It went bad very fast. People forgot about Clyde. They forgot that this club has won the Scottish Cup three times.' Alec is clearly a man who supports his team through thick and thin, his dedication to the cause is unquestionable.

No matter how fast they have fallen, or how far they have to travel, health permitting he will be there.

The lot of a Clyde fan was, is, and probably always will be the lot of Alec and his mini-bus of companions. No matter what they do they are dwarfed by their city and old firm rivals of Celtic and Rangers. Indeed, even their city contemporaries of Partick Thistle (who they traditionally hold the most lower league derby hostility towards), Hamilton Academical, and St Mirren are all doing considerably better than the Bully Wee at the moment. At the moment, Clyde are the Berwick of Glasgow, ploughing their own furrow much to the indifference of everyone else.

Leaving Alec to his drink with a warm handshake and a hope that he enjoyed the game, 'Aye, you too,' he said with a wave, it was time to head in to Shielfield Park for a first taste of Scottish League football in England.

The home of the Wee Gers sits across the river Tweed, and is dwarfed by the shadow of a large aggregate plant. A rare example of big industry in this small market town, towering silos with interconnecting platforms loom over the main stand that is cut adrift from the pitch by a large red clay track. Once used for Greyhound racing it operates now as a speedway circuit, which helps to explain the heavy crash mats that line the perimeter as it bends round behind each goal. Like a number of lower league clubs both north and south of the border, this secondary use of a stadium has helped keep the wolf from the door for many a long year; supplementing dwindling crowds and ever increasing overheads.

For Berwick, average attendances tend to top out around the 500 mark, as evidenced by a page in the match programme reminiscing on past matches that had been played out on this day. The attendances of the three selected home fixtures going back 50 years all hovered just above or below the 500 mark, the club forever living a hand to mouth existence given the expense and distances needed to travel to play in Scottish League Two as a team from just south of the border.

The round trip from Berwick up to former Highland League stalwarts and current League two contemporaries Elgin City takes nine hours and 472 miles to complete; club officials, fans and players must have sighed with relief when Peterhead, a similar distance away on the remote east coast of Scotland gained promotion to League One! Even the shorter trips in League Two will take up the majority of their supporters' day in order to support their team, and, as friends met up on their usual spot on the terraces on the far side to the main stand, one supporter scolded another when he shivered and commented that it was cold.

'Cold?' His hardened friend scoffed, 'Man you haven't even watched football until you have stood out on a bitter Tuesday night in December at Arbroath! The ground is right on the coast, and the wind comes direct in off the North Sea, and there is no shelter. It blows all the way from Norway and doesn't stop until it has cut you in two! Now that is cold.'

Supporters decked out in their gold and black Berwick scarves mingle about the tea bar, an even split of Northumberland and Scots accents among them. In the stand a dad and his two young boys, both sporting Berwick shirts beneath their coats sit down, the dad venting his bewilderment at his eldest in a broad Scots burr.

'Why these seats, why now?' his eldest smiled into the collar of his coat. 'All season we've been sitting up there.' His dad pointing away up the other end, 'But today, all of a sudden we have to sit here. Right in front of this stanchion. So we can't see the goal properly!'

His son said nothing, his youngest sniggering quietly.

'I know why we have to,' the dad offered in response to the stifled silence, 'Because you are a right pain in the arse!' he said as he playfully punched the offending son in the arm.

A few seats further down a gaggle of men chat away so quickly in a heavy Northumberland tone that most of it becomes incoherent to outsiders like me. Elsewhere, Scot and Englishman greet each other warmly and talk about their team's prospects, the weather, anything, just as fans up and down the country do; the ends of scarves about their necks flapping and twisting in the wind, routinely exposing the Saltire on one side, the St Georges cross on the other. With Berwick so close to the border, and so far from any other senior club, as many of their supporters travel the short distance down from Scotland's southernmost outposts to see them play as walk across the bridge from Berwick's old town. No matter that the team and the town is in England; Berwick Rangers is their club, is anyone's club, so long as they can release the sporting stereotype of animosity between these two proud old nations.

As with so many situations around the world, the closer you get to the stereotype, the more you interact with the people you are supposed to dislike, the more you see that these prejudices are meaningless and unfounded. The people in and around Berwick live together, work together, watch their football team together; they have transcended the traditional sporting divide between England and Scotland and created an identity all of their own. It may be an identity that some find inconceivable, and doubtless there surely are some dissenters that object to a team from England playing in the Scottish Football League, but today, among the 150 or so hardy Clyde supporters that had travelled down from Glasgow, none were present, before, during or after the game.

Maybe season upon season of coming down has helped them realise that Berwick are just another team wanting to play the game. More likely still, that the fans of Clyde, and all the other lower league teams that routinely travel south of the border are not bigots, and understand the pride Berwick's fans have for their club, as it is exactly how they feel about their team.

Skewed identity aside, the rest is all the same, and who is anyone to deny them that right to play football, other than the North Northumberland Football League!

Scottish League Division Two is a leveller, there is no place for prima-donnas or egos. Players, club and fans are all part of one community, they need to be in order to survive let alone flourish. Players and management are almost exclusively part time, and need a day job to supplement their income, which is why anyone arriving at the ground a good two hours before kick-off would have seen one of the Berwick backroom staff stood in their boxer shorts at the boot of their car, changing out of work clothes and into a Berwick tracksuit. When needs must!

Volunteers, passion, love keeps clubs like Berwick competitive, as witnessed by a young woman decked out in a Berwick jacket wandering the stand just before kick-off. A few minutes before half time she hurried off down the player's tunnel, suggesting that maybe she was the one to brew up the half time tea for players, referee and linesmen, but before kick-off she paced nervously.

'Shit this football is making me ill,' she said to another club official, 'Just one more win boys, that's all we need. Just one more.'

One more win would make Rangers safe from coming last and a dreaded relegation play-off match against the winners of either the Highland or Lowland Leagues. She bit at her fingernails before breaking off to smile at a couple of injured Berwick players as they ambled past,

'Have you had anything to eat?' She said, and when they shook their heads she added, 'Well I've got some packed lunches for you out the back, come on.' The two lads tried to keep up with her nervous energy.

The Clyde fans amassing behind their team's dugout were also doing their best to mask any nerves. As Clyde's manager and former Scotland International and Rangers star Barry Ferguson watched his team warm up, one of the Bully Wee called out his name.

'Barry. Barry. BARRY!' As the manager turned around he held out his tray of fish and chips. 'Would you like some fish?!'

Ferguson smiled and shook his head.

'I don't like fish,' he said, waved, and turned back to his team.

'Barry. Barry. BARRY!' He turned around again, 'Would you like a chip?!'

Warms ups complete, a final team talk over, the players ran out on to the pitch and the nervous young tea lady sank into her seat, hiding beneath the collar of her jacket.

As the league table hinted, Clyde started off the better, playing with a confidence that second spot brings. However, Berwick remained resilient, and looked dangerous on the break, and started to push Clyde back until a well taken header by leading goal-scorer Blair Henderson put the hosts ahead.

Tea lady, Scottish fans, English fans all erupted in delight while Barry Ferguson, arms folded looked accusingly at his defence. Things took a turn for the worse when shortly after the Bully Wee's midfield general, Jon Paul McGovern, limped off injured and with it Clyde started to look like a team that had run out of ideas.

In the second half they passed and passed and passed without really threatening, but it was the endeavour and invention of the team trying to stay in the league that had the team that was trying to get out of it on the back foot. When Blair Henderson made the most of a defensive mix-up on a Berwick counter attack to put the hosts two up heads noticeably dropped among the visitors. Berwick's delight, and league safety was secured a few moments later when a great passing move was finished off by Rangers' centre back Jordan McGregor to make it 3-0; Clyde's misery compounded by news at the final whistle of their title rivals East Fife beating the team they could only draw three all with last week, Montrose, 3-0.

A seven-point gap with three games to play, the next of which at home to East Fife, suggested that the Bully Wee had blown their title chances for another season; but as Alec, stick in one hand, the other holding the back of his low, uncomfortable plastic seat, shakily got to his feet to join the rest of the white mini-bus gang, at least this defeat had been less traumatic than last week. There had been no need to die a thousand deaths here, the game had been dead with 20 minutes left to play; enough time to check the table and the remaining fixtures to steel yourself for the lottery of the play-offs and maybe, just maybe, glory at a Hampden Park play-off final. Either way, Alec would be there, as he would next season, come rain or shine, through victory and defeat. And if that meant yet another trip down to England to see his team play in Europe, well so be it.

As for Berwick's band of multi-national supporters, many piled in to the supporters' club to drink Scottish beer served by an English barmaid, and toast another successful season of survival.

For an isolated team that is neither here nor there, that transcends borders and the traditional understanding of sporting identity, maybe success for them isn't necessarily a by-product of what happens out on the pitch. The very fact that it exists, in the way that it does is quite possibly a far greater victory than any three points on offer; and for that, long may they keep winning.

CHAPTER 5

Cyril Smith and the Unofficial Footballers

IN EVERY HISTORY of every professional football team there is a gap in its forensic detail; books and websites that hold appearance information for every player to have ever played a first team game, match reports from long gone fixtures, team photos more than 100 years old suddenly become vague, sketchy, when you reach the period of the Second World War.

From vast swathes of information from every game ever played before and after, the matches played during World War Two, and the players that played in them are often reduced to the odd paragraph in an appendix, maybe a list of results and names that remain an unknown to even the most ardent fan.

It is understandable perhaps that during the horrors of endless bombing runs by the Luftwaffe, the near disaster of Dunkirk, and an enemy pressing ever closer to the English Channel with invasion on its mind, the collating of football statistics didn't seem to be as important as it once had been.

However, the tone of countless football club histories when reaching the period of the Second World War seem to suggest another reason for the lack of detail during this time.

When war was declared after only three fixtures of the 1939–40 season, professional footballers, just like any other able bodied young man, were conscripted for the war effort. However, with the fear of an imminent and terrible war against an aggressor that had been taking all before it on main-land Europe, the Government and football authorities decided that football must continue. It had been a vital social outlet before the war, and it would need to continue to be, to be an escape from the harsh realities of war that the country faced.

However, as most of the players that played professionally were now otherwise engaged, clubs would have to find youngsters not yet at draft age, and amateurs that were helping the war effort by working in factories or for the home guard, or in another way that didn't mean fighting overseas to help make up these war-time teams. With only the odd pre-war professional, who had found a role in the factories or Home Guard in each team, the football history books deemed this 'lesser standard' of war-time football unworthy of the detail afforded the teams that went before and after. The matches played out during World War Two remain excluded from the 'official' statistics; players who had played before, or would play after the war would have separate records detailing 'official' matches played and war-time matches.

There can be no doubt that the standard of football played in those three ill-fated matches of the official 1939–40 season would have been greater than the seven seasons of war-time football. However, given the vital role it played in trying to keep a semblance of normality, of providing an escape from the horrors that were unfolding around it, given the bravery these players displayed in playing in extremely dangerous circumstances for the benefit of others, surely they deserve a little more credit than being labelled by default 'Unofficial players'? Players such as Cyril Smith.

When I first met him when I was a young boy, Cyril Smith was just my Grandad's friend and ex-work colleague, a man in his early 60s with a warm smile who took the gate money from a small shack at the entrance to Victoria Park, the home of Salisbury FC. He was just the nice man who sold us our programmes and asked how I was getting on playing for my boys' team.

It wasn't until a few months later, after Grandad had casually mentioned to Cyril how much I liked football programmes, that he handed to me a plastic wallet with some photocopies in from Cyril that made him something else entirely.

'Cyril thought you might find them interesting,' Grandad had said, knowing that I would love them.

Inside were black and white photocopies of seven football programmes from the war. Three were programmes featuring Southampton from October 1940, four featured Arsenal; one from the end of the 1943–44 season, three from November 1944, and all seven had the name of Cyril Smith, playing at outside left, on the team sheet. For a young boy that loved football programmes so much they were something else, they were gold dust, despite only being copies. Who else would have these in their collection?

Even at such a young age I knew they were special for another reason too; they were relics from the Second World War, containing notices on what to do if there was an air raid warning, a plea to help the Mayor's Spitfire fund in a Southampton programme:

> You will be sorry if you had no share in your own town's plane (the Spitfire was manufactured at the Supermarine factory in the Woolston area of the city), especially if it brings down a few opponents in a fair tackle.

One of the Arsenal programmes listed the names Sidney Pugh, Cyril Tooze, Hugh Glass, and Bobby Daniel: 'Four of our boys who have made the great sacrifice.'

They truly were treasures to a young boy, and continued to be, being kept safe for 30 years while others things became lost or were thrown out, until finally they resurfaced a few years after Cyril had passed away.

Flicking through them again they made me want to learn more about this kindly old man that I once knew – a self-depreciating soul too modest to mention to a football mad young boy that he once played for Southampton and Arsenal, as well as for many years at Salisbury. And as I did delve deeper, spending hours peering at faded microfilm in the bowels of my local library, the incredible story of Cyril Smith and his football colleagues came to life – a microcosm of the horrors of living through the Blitz and World War Two.

As the stories of bravery and selflessness in the face of unimaginable terror flickered across the screen of that microfilm machine, it became clear that the footballers that played on during World War Two deserved far more recognition than they had received; they deserved far better than a footnote in football's history, that their efforts, it could be argued, were among some of the most important in the history of the game. At the very least they didn't deserve to be considered unofficial footballers in the history books. For Cyril's story, like so many others from that time, is a remarkable one.

A month before Operation Dunkirk, a desperate mission whereby a rag tag flotilla of any sea worthy ship set sail to try and save Britain's troops, cut off and facing certain death after being over-run in the Battle of France, a 17-year-old Cyril Smith played his first match for Southampton. On 17 April 1940 Southampton Reserves played out an end of season Hampshire League match at The Dell, beating Air Service Training (Hamble) 5-2. It was a match in which the reserves scored their 100th goal of the season and the local paper, *The Daily Echo* wrote in the following day's edition that:

The Saints had three new young players in the game – Charles, a young goalkeeper from Woolston Boys FC, Everett, and Cyril Smith, a 17-year-old inside left, formerly a Mount Pleasant schoolboy, now playing for Pirelli-General in the JOC league and cup.

It had been a tough season adjusting to war-time life as Hampshire League Secretary Mr GJ Eden explained to the paper in June:

We got through a difficult time very much better than we anticipated. When we restarted after the war we were not very optimistic and wondered if it would be possible to complete our war-time competition, but, except for two Hampshire League matches – war reasons made these impossible and they did not affect the championship – all the fixtures were carried through.

Despite the positive outlook and the evasive explanation for the missing fixtures not being completed (it would become the norm when reading Southampton match reports from 1940 that the paper tried to keep them light in tone, the reasons for abandoned matches described as 'war reasons' or 'circumstances beyond control' rather than the actual reason: air raids – the readership well aware of the reality the paper was swerving, with German troops massing on the Normandy coast after Britain's defeat in the battle of France, and the horrors of the blitz looming over them), Cyril's first full season with the Saints would be one of the most harrowing for the club and the town. For Cyril, and, for Southampton, far worse than had already been experienced was to come.

By August 1940 and pre-season air raid warnings were the norm. More than 1,500 warnings would be sounded during the Blitz, each and every one potentially bringing with it another terrible bombing raid. Beneath it all the footballers of Southampton were trying to prepare for what, they didn't know. Travel restrictions meant matches against London sides were impossible. Fuel shortages threatened any kind of travel entirely. The Football Association had bunched together sides they thought would be able to reach one another in small 'War Leagues', adding the caveat that:

If air raid warnings cause delays during football league games, every attempt will be made to finish the 90 minutes after the 'all clear'.

It was also decreed that the score of any match that had started, but was abandoned due to 'war reasons' would stand as the final result; the idea of replaying the matches impossible given fuel shortages and the frequency in which raids abandoned games.

Southampton's one and only warm up match before the season on 23 August 1940 would be good practice for what was to come, with *The Daily Echo* once again trying not to mention the bombing campaign from above in a piece about football, as it was meant to be an escape from all that – preferring instead to simply report that:

> Circumstances cause the Saints' practice match at The Dell on Saturday to start a little late, but the people who were present saw a good, keen, interesting game.

Better still they went on to report that:

> Two youngsters, Cyril Smith and Ness, who have already indicated talent showed that they are likely to make considerable development this season.

However, a later notice would detail just how hard it would be for Cyril to develop in such difficult times:

> One of the difficulties in bringing a young side along these days when opportunities for training and practice – particularly practice – are very limited is that team work cannot be developed properly.
>
> In fact, the only chances the players have of getting together on the field are the actual matches. In normal times there would be practice matches and instruction as part of the regular weekly training.

But as the Blitz intensified, Cyril would soon find himself in a time when matches, let alone the opportunity for training were at real threat. Cyril's first match for Southampton came on the opening day of the war league season against Brighton & Hove Albion on 31 August, with *The Daily Echo* trying to put an interesting spin on troubling circumstances by writing that

> When the Saints step on the field at the Dell tomorrow evening to play their first match of the season, they will be about the youngest first team ever to play for the Saints. The average age of the 11 is only 20, with the 'veteran' of the side just 23 years of age, and the youngest, Cyril Smith, 17 years of age.

Cyril's three matches against Brighton in the colours of Southampton between August and October of 1940 would symbolise the hardship and struggles of the time perfectly. The upbeat and stoic local paper tried to help morale by painting as positive a story as it could, but the previews, reports, and match programmes couldn't hide the exceptional circumstances that faced everyone.

The bravery of the players and supporters in continuing with football during the terrible onslaught that rained down from the skies is unsurpassed, though played down in the papers of the time, who reported on Cyril's debut:

> The Saints won their first match in the second war-time league season, beating Brighton & Hove at The Dell by three goals to one on Saturday.
>
> There were 1,232 people who paid to see the game, and I am sure they enjoyed it, even though they had to go to shelter for half an hour because of an air raid warning. By the way I must explain that it is an instruction to the clubs that play must cease during a raid warning. Many of the Spectators called out 'play on', and they certainly, were willing to remain at the ground. In fact very few people left. They took shelter under the stands or in the passages. Fortunately, the match was able to be restarted, and then finished, without further interruption.

Next to the match report was a small notice on Leonard Stansbridge, the Saints' goalkeeper before war broke out, who: 'was reported missing after the Dunkirk engagement. Now, I am very pleased to say, his parents have received notification that he is a prisoner of war in Germany'. Despite the upbeat tone, there was no hiding from the realities of war.

The photocopied match programmes, a single sheet folded in two due to paper rationing, gave up most of their editorial content to air raid notices rather than match reports or club news; far more important information, especially given the circumstances of Cyril's two other matches against Brighton.

The first of two away fixtures in Brighton on 21 September ended after only five minutes due to the length and severity of the air raid above. The second, on 12 October saw the teams play, according to *The Echo's* reporter, '55 minutes, almost equally divided by the interval. The side played well... had the game run the full 90 minutes the Saints would have won'. These 'interruptions to play' as they were described, were, it must be remembered, devastating bombing raids which makes the bravery of those on the field of play and those watching more brave with only the vaguely reassuring words of the air raid notices in their programmes for comfort. At least in Southampton's programme came the mildly comforting words that:

> The terraces under the East and West Stands are deemed reasonably safe from flying splinters, etc. The passages under the West Stand, which spectators may use, are deemed of equal safety to that of an Air Raid Shelter.

For the poor supporters of Brighton and Cyril's visiting Saints team, their notice was far less heartening:

> The exit gates will be opened for those persons who wish to leave the ground, and those who remain are advised to spread out round the terraces.

It is hard, given the bullish nature of the newspaper, to fully appreciate the anxiety and fear that must have existed in the City, in the country, with deadly attacks from above always only a moment away. The upbeat sports notices and defiant attitude of the supporters, turning up to games despite such vague air raid precautions, mirrored the obtuse headlines on the front of the paper. However, Britain was in a bad way. And despite the upbeat stories of the City's football team, the photographs of Southampton taken from the time capture the destruction and devastation that was its fate.

Looking out now on the Rivers Test and Itchen that bisect the City, looking at the docks that line their banks, and where the Spitfire factory once stood, it is hard to imagine what it must have been like, felt like, to have experienced such a catastrophic bombing campaign that was designed to put both out of action. It is hard to comprehend having to try to live through it, and equally hard to know how the football team, and its fans, kept on in the face of it all.

Memories of supporter and player alike sheltering on the banks of the Itchen in the dusk, unable to take the floating bridge across to Woolston and home, whose crossings had been suspended because of the bombing raids targeting the Supermarine works building Spitfires next to its mooring, were commonplace. Both player and supporter having to cower beneath the deafening bombardment that shook the ground, and lit up the night sky a hellish red, often waiting until the early hours of the morning before being able to safely cross and reach home. And yet amongst the ever-growing troubles Cyril Smith and his team-mates tried to play football.

Through the worn reels of microfilm in Southampton Central's basement library, Cyril's Southampton career played out to the backdrop of bombing raids and abandoned matches. In a match at Aldershot that lasted a little over 60 minutes, an unnamed *Echo* reporter believed 'the left-wing pair of Smith and Laney, were well up to standard'. Against Watford at the Dell, despite losing 5-2 they started well: 'when Roper headed a grand goal. It was 17-year-old Cyril Smith who planned this goal and his move was carried on by Hassell, whose centre Roper headed into the net'. Possibly Cyril's finest moment in a Southampton shirt came against Bournemouth when:

> Spectators at the Dell on Saturday had to wait nearly two hours
> for the kick-off, but they were shouting in the first minute of the
> game when Laney scored the first of six goals which the Saints
> netted against Bournemouth and Boscombe. Cyril Smith (2), Messom, Hassell, and Roper netted the other goals for the winners.

The idea of sheltering beneath the West stand at the Dell for two hours; air raid sirens wailing, potentially waiting for a terrible bombing run to begin, all in the name of trying to watch a bit of football, or play a bit of football, is bravery beyond my ken. It is hard to fathom players, Cyril, decked out in his kit, huddled beneath the beams of the stand, stood alongside the hardy supporters, waiting for the all clear, or for the worst. To then step out onto the field in the failing light of an October evening and play, and score twice – well the paper's report could never do that justice.

Because so many matches couldn't start, or were abandoned, so as some teams had played many more games than others, the Football League created a league table that was based on goals scored rather than points gained – far from perfect, but a little more representative of where any given team would probably be, though league position was far from everyone's minds given the precarious situation. Football reports with upbeat editorials ran alongside more ominous articles, such as on 7 October when the football scores ran alongside a headline: 'AMERICANS IN ENGLAND – No More Repatriation Ships'.

As the bombing campaign intensified, football suffered even further. In Cyril's last first team match for Southampton on November 9th the paper reported only 420 spectators in attendance, and their opponents Cardiff arrived with only ten players. To make matters worse the referee also failed to make it, so members of the crowd filled in both positions.

Cyril's final two matches for Southampton came for the reserves in the Hampshire League on the 23rd and 30th November 1940, two dates that will forever be a scar on Southampton. Between November 23rd and December 1st the city would be subjected to massive bombing raids that destroyed vast tracts of it. The St Petersburg Times wrote that on the 23rd alone:

> 250 planes, dropped some 300 tons of high explosive and 12,000 incendiary bombs on the British south coast port of Southampton.
> The trans-Atlantic port was left a smoking ruin, the Nazis claimed.

Being a large port and the home of Spitfire manufacture singled the city out for special attention.

Yet despite it all the football continued, determined to keep some semblance of normal life intact. After the 23rd the football club regrouped, as the city did, and raised two sides for the following Saturday, and Cyril duly turned out for the reserves at the Dell against Cunliffe-Owen, a works team from a local factory containing goalkeeper Sam Warhurst, who had played for Nelson and Bradford City, and had been Saints' keeper before the outbreak of war. Little did Cyril, Sam, or any of the others present realise that this would be the last match played at the Dell for quite some time.

On the evening of the 30th a Nazi bombing raid even greater than the one from a week before pummelled the city. The Dell received a direct hit and would remain out of action for a little under a year. Even the comfort of football couldn't save the people of Southampton from its fate, *The Daily Echo* was unable to find any positive spin on events this time. The devastation was so great there was no water to fight the fires, and there were reports that the glow of Southampton burning could be seen from as far away as Cherbourg on the French coast.

The Daily Echo headline after two days of bombing read 'A Carnival of Hate':

> Simultaneously with the sirens at dusk on the evening of Saturday, November 30, the first of the raiders showered down their flares until the town was almost as bright as if it were daylight.

Incendiaries soon began to fall in hundreds, and with them death-dealing bombs.

No one who was there will ever forget the terrifying noises of that night, the dismal, almost ceaseless, drone of the raiders as they came and went; the screech of the bombs as they fell, and the reverberating roar as they burst, the deep woof of the biggest anti-aircraft guns and the sharper crack of the lighter ones; the swish of the showering fire bombs; the crackling of the fire that flared up all over the town; the urgent clang of the fire crew bells.

When dawn ended the night of horror, Sotonians saw a heart-breaking sight. Much of the town they loved had been devastated.

A brick in the pavement along the lower end of Southampton's rebuilt High Street commemorates the awful sight witnessed by the 'mass observation reporter' in the aftermath of the attacks: 'As far as we were concerned Southampton had ended... that was the finish of it'.

The night of Cyril's last game for Southampton, the final score of which lost among the chaos, his family's house was destroyed. Among the rubble of the days that followed Cyril and his parents had no choice but to leave, moving to Salisbury where there were houses available.

But, like the rest of Southampton's inhabitants, who the paper described as: 'Shaken physically and mentally. But, it must be recorded too, that the Luftwaffe's viciousness had not broken the spirit of the people'.

For Cyril, sadly, the distance between Salisbury and Southampton, combined with the severe rationing of fuel and transport, and his work as an engineer meant that it was impossible for him to travel; his Saints career was over after ten first team matches and four for the reserves. However, the Saints would struggle on, albeit homeless.

The Daily Echo reported on December 13th that:

The Southampton Football Club, grappling great difficulties, are keeping their flag flying. Mr Tom Parker, the Saints' manager, told me today that he expects that the club will carry on after Christmas: 'We shall, I hope compete in the football league in the second half of the season. Of course we shall have to obtain permission to play all our matches away from home if we are able to complete the whole season.'

The Saints, however, will not be able to continue in the Hampshire League. In other words it will not be possible to run two teams now. But if Saints can still run a first team, in all the circumstances, I think it is a very plucky thing to do.

Plucky is a very modest word for the bravery shown by Cyril Smith and the rest of the Southampton team that played on during the Blitz. Unofficial the games may be – but surely there are none more important in the 120 plus year history of the club? For the morale of the city and its people, for the continuation of some semblance of normality in such abnormal times, these matches deserve to be afforded the respect they deserve, and brought out from the fringes of history. So too must the bravery of the players and the supporters, who played and stood on the terraces defiantly in the face of such danger, trying desperately to keep 'the home fires burning'; players like Cyril, the quiet, unassuming old man with a warm smile that would greet me at Victoria Park in the '80s. Though for Cyril, the blitz of Southampton wouldn't be the end of his adventures in football during the war.

From the plastic folder of old photocopies Cyril's programmes jump from November 1940 to the last day of the 1943–44 season and an Arsenal match against Aldershot in early May, Cyril's name in its familiar position of Inside Left. Two and a half years on, and a month away from the D-Day landings that would signal the beginning of the end of the war, Cyril began his war-time career with Arsenal.

Though it wasn't the Blitz of 1940, a large Air Raid Notice was still needed beneath the team sheet; and the camaraderie of spirit that had been instilled by the terrors of war extended far beyond any potential football rivalry. During the war, Highbury, the home of Arsenal, had been converted into an Air Raid Precaution Centre, so all their 'home' games, such as Cyril's debut, would be played at near neighbours Tottenham Hotspur. What is now a bitter rivalry was once a warm friendship given the reality and perspective of war – so much so that in the editorial on the back of the match programme for Cyril's debut, Arsenal felt the need to:

> Again extend to our good Tottenham friends our cordial congratulations upon their success in winning the championship of the Football League South, a distinction we enjoyed last season, so that we may still feel that the cup remains in the family circle.

With D-Day yet to get underway, and the successes allied troops would achieve in driving German forces back still unknown, the otherwise jovial editorial on the back of the team sheet had a tinge of trepidation when it declared:

> Let us take this opportunity of saying thank you very much indeed to all of you who have supported us throughout the past season and to express the hope that circumstances will be such that we can carry on the good work when the next campaign dawns.

The fragility of war-time life made it foolish to look too far in to the future.

However, the following season did duly arrive, and with it Cyril played a further four matches for Arsenal, including a home match against Watford in which the club announced the names of four of its players known to have made 'the great sacrifice'.

The programme from a match Cyril played in at Stamford Bridge against Chelsea on 25 November 1944 detailed the remarkable feat of Chelsea centre forward Joe Payne who had scored 27 goals in 13 games, as well as the repair work being done to Stamford Bridge:

> The new stand is open today on one of its fleeting commissions to mark the importance of the occasion. This building, situated as it is, provides a glorious uninterrupted view of the playing area and will in course of time be most popular. The roof is once more (touch wood) weather proof, following a Hitler effort to render the Pensioners homeless.

Another notice reads:

> Jack Sherborne tells me that he is progressing favourably, though slowly, from his wounds, and although still without the full use of his arms, he is confident that he will be ready to show his paces in a blue jersey when normal conditions arrive.

Jack Sherborne made his Chelsea debut in 1937 at the age of 21, having moved down from Chorley the previous season. A crowd of more than 30,000 saw him and Chelsea lose to Wolverhampton Wanderers. He also featured in a match against Arsenal at Highbury in front of a crowd just shy of 50,000. He played a total of five first team matches before the outbreak of war, and the one small snippet of information still available about his career simply states that he retired in 1945 at the end of his Chelsea contract; the hopes from that programme the year before falling short. Jack's career, like so many other careers of players from that time, were cut short; though at least he escaped the war with his life, unlike the four Arsenal players.

Another player whose career would always be saddled with the 'what could have been' tag was Cyril Smith. Despite VE Day greeting the end of the 1944–45 season, there was still much to be done to rebuild the country, and Cyril was drafted into the RAF. A pity, as Arsenal had been sufficiently impressed with his five appearances to have offered him a contract. Like countless others, the war and its aftermath claimed the best years of Cyril's footballing career, and any chance of becoming a professional. However, considering the inconceivable suffering and loss of life that had gone before VE Day, no-one ever heard Cyril complain about it. Upon his discharge he returned to Salisbury and became a founding player in the new Salisbury FC, serving the club as player, coach, manager, committee member, gate man, and programme seller for more than 50 years.

His story is a remarkable one. It is just one story in a sea of suffering and tragedy, yet it helps to illuminate the unbelievable resilience of a people facing unprecedented times. The football that he took part in during the war may not have come up to the standard of what went before, and also came after, but few can argue that these matches, excluded from official records, are not some of the most important matches ever played in Britain. Because of what they stood for and what they were trying to achieve – trying to keep a semblance of normality, and providing an escape from the seemingly inescapable – these war-time matches that were played up and down the country in perilous conditions deserve more than a passing mention in the record books. They are too important to be hidden away among the fringes of football club histories, that is for sure.

Over the years, using patience and perseverance, I have managed to find four of the actual team sheet Arsenal programmes that Cyril featured in. To actually hold these thin, worn sheets of paper that are more than 70 years old, the faded salmon pink of the Arsenal home programmes, the grubby white of Chelsea's all having been folded in four, sometimes eight and tucked inside someone's pocket, is a quite surreal experience. It is touching history.

Unsurprisingly I have never seen a Southampton programme from that fateful 1940–41 season. If vast tracts of the city were destroyed, what hope is there of a few sheets of cheap, flimsy paper surviving? That makes that old plastic wallet that Cyril gave to me even more important and precious; a rare reminder of a defining moment in the history of Southampton, and the country. A moment that that softly spoken old man on the gate at Victoria Park, Salisbury, who would hand me my ticket stub and programme, was a part of.

May it never be forgotten.

CHAPTER 6

The Forbidden Team from a Forbidden County – Tibetan Women's Football

'IN MY OPINION, if we go on with the same spirit, training and the main aim in our heart, we will achieve a great success later on. Being a member of this team, I want this team to "believe in yourself" and win every match and tournament that comes in our way and gradually walk in the big stadiums at the World Cup. I wish nothing but the best for my team-mates, in every step of their lives.'

Sixteen-year-old Sonam Dolma's words could be those of any football mad child across the world, dreaming of playing for their country in the World Cup one day, of scoring the winning goal in the final. For so many those dreams will come to nothing, and be replaced by dreams of witnessing those chosen few that did make it to their national teams living out their ambitions for them.

For Sonam one hurdle has been overcome, sitting as she is at her national football team's training camp in a refugee settlement in Dehra Dun, India, writing her answers to questions sent from far away in her best handwriting, and her best English.

However, for Sonam and her team-mates, there are so many more hurdles that stand in their way; many, many more than most of the children with the same dreams around the world will have to face in order to realise them – because Sonam, just like all of her team-mates, is Tibetan.

Sonam's story is the story of Tibet, the story of her people. In the cold light of day, it is a very sad story of a small, peaceful Buddhist nation being let down by the rest of the world when its neighbour China invaded in 1950. The global community stood by, and continues to do so, as China began a systematic purge to deconstruct centuries of Buddhist existence high up on the Himalayan plateau; using torture, fear, and compulsory 're-education' programmes to try and discredit the Dalai Lama and his teachings.

When its people resisted, even greater force was inflicted on Tibet: monasteries and other religious sites were destroyed, people were sent to jail for possessing images of their spiritual leader, an untold number perishing under a brutal regime of forced labour. Those that wouldn't turn their backs on their religion were 'disappeared', tortured, imprisoned, and executed.

Nearly seven decades later, the operation is still in effect. The Chinese state is unable to unshackle the Tibetan people from their beliefs; a people for whom the only means of protest that garners any kind of interest from the outside world these days being self-immolation. Instances of monks, nuns, and lay-Tibetans setting themselves on fire on the streets of Lhasa and elsewhere as a protest at their plight have escalated dramatically in the last three years; in a world where all other rights have been taken away, the freedom to determine your own death is something even the Chinese Government cannot take away. It is a brutal, terrifying existence, which is why parents dream of something better for their children in the relative tranquillity of a life of exile in refugee settlements in Nepal and India.

That parents consider sending their children on a 27-mile trek across the Himalaya mountain range at the height of winter, the only time of realistically avoiding a, by then, scaled back Chinese security force that guards potential escape routes – guards that routinely shoot to kill any escapees of any age, says an awful lot about the life left behind in Lhasa and beyond. The risk of being shot, or succumbing to the elements on such a journey are very real.

It is not a journey undertaken lightly.

It is the preserve of those who have no other option.

It is a journey that children like Sonam, like the other girls in the team, have taken to find some kind of freedom.

Sonam's story is the story of her team-mates and of her people, a refugee nation fleeing persecution to be closer to the Dalai Lama who has spent most of his life exiled in Dharamsala, India, and to experience a basic freedom prohibited in their homeland.

Sonam lives in a small settlement in Nepal close to the Tibetan border, a good six days walk to the nearest road that takes her to her boarding school in Kathmandu. Tibetan Children's Villages, an organisation that looks after refugee children effectively orphaned by this gulf in freedoms across the Himalayas, attempts to bridge that gap by providing, as best they can, the life their parents dreamt of for them. By providing a home, education and the freedom of religious expression, they offer simple luxuries that those left behind can only dream of.

Such as the freedom to play the game they love. Though, even that, for Tibetans, can only be achieved through great struggle.

Football and Tibet first met in the early 20th Century when European delegations first introduced the sport on visits to the capital Lhasa. However, it wasn't until after invasion and exile that football's true potential began to grow among the Tibetan community. The only equipment needed being something resembling a ball, football quickly became a popular and accessible means of exercise as well as a much-needed source of identity within the refugee settlements of India and Nepal. Local tournaments developed into the 'national' tournament that can be seen today, where once a year teams from all over the Tibetan exile diaspora meet up to compete for the Gyalo Chenmo Memorial Gold Cup, named after the Dalai Lama's mother.

From the passion and love that was generated from these tournaments came the idea for a 'National Team', a team to galvanise Tibet's love for football, but more importantly, to represent the identity and culture of this exiled people, to highlight the plight of a nation forgotten by the world.

So, in 2001, with the help of Dane, Michael Nybrandt, the first modern day Tibetan National Team was formed. Aptly nicknamed 'The Forbidden Team', which would become the title of a documentary based on this historic side's first ever international match against the national team of Greenland, the emergence of a Tibetan team caused outrage in Beijing, who threatened trade sanctions on both Greenland and Denmark, where the match was held. Undeterred the Danes let the game go ahead, resulting in a surge of support and media interest in Tibet and their struggles, despite Greenland winning 4-1.

With that match, Tibetan football became a means to celebrate the game they loved, their country and identity, but it also became a means of respectful protest, of defiance, a voice in the world in spite of a totalitarian state trying to silence them

Unable to compete against FIFA sanctioned teams, the Tibetan National Team spent the next seven years playing exhibition matches and tournaments that were organised outside of FIFA's jurisdiction, representing their lost nation and its exiled peoples in 'rogue state' North Cyprus, as well as in a competition organised by 'rogue club' St Pauli in Hamburg, Germany. Lower key competitions in India and the small sub-Himalayan state of

Sikkim kept the team alive and vibrant, sporting the Tibetan flag on the sleeves of their smart shirts designed by sports manufacturers Hummel, and singing the Tibetan National anthem with a vigour that could bring a stadium, be it full or near empty, close to tears.

A love for football, and a love for the country they had been forced to flee had created a team that could both play the game that brought them joy, but also make a point about the plight of their people. It was a compelling, moving entity that caused embarrassment to China, and offered hope and solidarity to the Tibetan community.

But in a world where apparently 'sport and politics don't mix', the Tibetan National Football Team's journey was put on indefinite hold by the politics of sport and the world-wide economic crash of 2008.

To be eligible for entry to FIFA any potential nation must be recognised by the United Nations as a sovereign state. Without that recognition, no country can participate in competitions run by World football's governing body. In May 2016 both Gibraltar and Kosovo were accepted into the FIFA fold, despite objections from Spain and Serbia respectively, who do not recognise them as sovereign, but the UN do.

Despite being made an independent country as recently as 1950, Tibet is not considered anything other than a part of the country that invaded and still occupy the newly titled 'Tibetan Autonomous Region'. That the UN, or any of its member states did nothing to assist Tibet then only compounds their impotency to do anything for them today, given the economic might of China.

The UN's military intervention in Kosovo and the former Yugoslavia during the '90s when multiple bloody civil wars broke out as it fell apart, is a testament to how it can genuinely help those in need; the acceptance of an independent Kosovo as part of FIFA the icing on the cake. The plight of Tibet, however, only serves to remind the international community of its terrible failings.

Left to its own devices, and based in Dharamsala in the high mountains of northern India, the Tibetan National Sports Association became more and more helpless once the global financial meltdown of 2008 stripped them of the few meagre charitable donations to their cause. When they had those donations, they were at least able keep the team active, despite the seemingly impossible obstacles they had to overcome in order to find them opponents to play against. But with no financial aid, all that could be done was to keep the GCM Gold Cup alive, to at least enable some regular football, even if it meant the Tibetan football community having to turn in on itself and slip from what limited opportunities they had had in the international scene.

For young girls like Sonam Dolma, in such a climate the chances of getting to play football seemed, at best, remote. But then, she hadn't counted on Cassie Childers.

Childers, from New Jersey in America, felt compelled to get involved after her travels took her to Dharamsala, where she became enchanted with Tibetan Buddhism. A former football player herself, she came up with the notion of a Tibetan Women's team while at an exhibition celebrating Tibetan football. As inspirational as the story was that played out across the exhibitions walls, there appeared to be something missing: Women.

In the conservative and male dominated world of the Tibetan refugee settlements, Cassie could find no teams for any sport that were aimed at Women, and she saw an opportunity to help a community that had captivated her. And so was born Tibet's first Women's National Football Team.

Initially affiliated to the Tibetan National Sports Association, this new team quickly captured the imaginations of Tibetan girls, who flocked to training sessions. Maybe unprepared for the drive and resourcefulness of Childers, whose fundraising efforts provided equipment, training camps, and matches for this fledgling national team, tensions began to surface between her and the TNSA, and a society maybe not quite prepared for a new role for women; tensions that ultimately forced Cassie and the team to sever ties with the TNSA, and go it alone, forming the Tibetan Women's Football Programme.

Unlike their counterparts in the dormant men's team, Tibet's women's team have one extra hurdle to overcome within their community before they can even think about the near insurmountable odds stacked against them, and the world outside that is trying to stop them from playing the game they love.

'Since our country, Nepal, is a patriarchal society,' Sonam said 'It is said that girls are to be doing household things or only studying. They didn't let them do extra activities or what they are interested in. Those things which include soccer, basketball or any other sports they are only for boys not for girls "who think weak".'

Sonam's team-mate, 14-year-old Sonam Sangmo, added:

'I haven't faced any obstacles in participating with the Tibetan National Team, but one of my friends, Sonam Chokgi, who studies in a government school, has. She loves to play sport, but she couldn't do so because every one of the school boys said that "you are fat, you can't run fast, and you can't chase others" and the school boys laughed when she came to play soccer. Most of the time', she went on, 'she cries because of everyone insult her, in her game and body. But she has never given up. I always tell her "play more and show them that fat girl can also do anything that you can do". Now she is being good in soccer and she is improving her games.'

Eighteen-year-old Tenzin Dekyong's English is not quite as good as her two younger team-mates, but her words speak volumes for the struggles that Tibetan girls face in breaking away from the more traditional roles expected of them.

'I got problems from my parents. They didn't support [me] because they have no idea of games. And in society some use to tell us that girls can't play soccer better than them. I am sad of my parents who support my brother and sister, but find it hard to support me, and let me to play.'

In a world of sacrifice, the girls and Women of the Tibetan National Football Team sometimes have to sacrifice that little bit more in order to play the game they love. But play it they do, in the hope that it will open up new perceptions, and new opportunities for them and the exiled communities they come from – opportunities such as this training camp, followed by a trip to Goa in southern India to take part in the Goa Women's Football Festival.

'Being a player of this team I feel really fortunate,' says Sonam Dolma, 'Because we have got this wonderful opportunity among many other who are interested. It is very rare to get this kind of opportunity.'

Indeed, travel on a refugee passport, such as the ones Tibetans living in India and Nepal have, is very hard, even if the money needed to undertake such a venture is found. Without the relentless fundraising of Cassie back in the USA, none of this could be possible – as the stasis of the men's team has shown.

'Again and again it feels like we've got a big responsibility to inspire other people, especially women, who feel they are weak,' Sonam went on, 'To represent ourselves, the identity of our own country, playing with the feeling of nationality deep in our hearts, it makes us as a team feel really good.'

For Tenzin Dekyong there is also a more personal achievement in playing for Tibet that hopefully indicates a brighter future for her people, socially at least:

'I feel great that I am doing something for our nation. I feel women can do the same things like a man. I may not be much good but I am proud to be in this team. I feel so proud also to get respect. Many people know and be friendly towards us as we are in the team. I feel so happy because I am getting respect from my own brother and sister.'

Her parents may be some way off, but her siblings are a start.

The Goa Women's festival is a small tournament held over three days at the Duler Stadium in Goa. It is one of a number of initiatives that the Goa FA has introduced in order to help Women's football in the state, and precedes the first ever Women's senior and junior Leagues that will start later in the year.

Taking part in the tournament alongside Tibet are the Goa state team, local side Viva North, and Yuwa – a club based in Ranchi, the capital of Jharkhand State, that uses sport to help educate on issues such as child marriage and human trafficking. The trip for many of the Tibetan team will be one of many firsts: the first time seeing the ocean, the first time travelling outside of their settlements, the first time pulling on the shirt of the Tibetan National Football Team. For many it will also be the first meaningful act of defiance against both their domestic and international adversaries.

Fourteen-year-old Sonam Sangmo pulls back from naming the Chinese Government, and the out-dated conservatism that has held women back within the Tibetan community, but her measured words are powerful none the less. They point to a child far older than her years; that has had to witness and endure hardships that most of us, thankfully, will never have to experience.

'I am playing soccer for Tibet. I have a big responsibility on it. The most important thing is that we are here for our nation, Tibet, and we have to fight against the worst heart and worst mind.

'When we are playing the game we have to show them that any kind of girls, fat or thin, can do these things without and fear or hopelessness,' She wrote, 'We have to show them that we can do it. If anybody asks you that can you do this, we must say "yes, I *can* do this". So we have to say yes full of spirit in our heart, and full of bravery. We should show that we should not give up in any way of our life.'

Goa, with its hot sandy beaches and palm trees, with back packers and high end tourists splashing in the warm waters of the Arabian Sea, is probably as far removed from life in the Himalayas as you can get. It is yet another step on an adventure that many of the Tibetan Women's team never thought possible.

Tenzin Dekyong recalls how she came to learn of this team, how chance, and the vision of Cassie Childers has led her to such adventure.

'I only knew about this team when I was in school. Cassie came to our school and the TNSA told us about her, and from then I dreamt and wished that I will be select and play my best for my own nation. Finally, Cassie and TNSA contacted us, and we are here now, doing our best.'

And their best is most definitely good enough in their first match against Viva North, where goals by skipper Jamyang Chotso (two), Ngawang Otsoe and Dhondup Lhamo resulted in an emphatic 4-0 win described by Cassie as 'a beautifully played game by both teams. This was our most challenging match yet, but despite the heat our gals came out on top again. Oetso had one of the best goals I've seen, off a flick on an indirect free-kick.'

A match in a small tournament held over three days in Goa was never going to be covered by the world's sporting media, but the local press that did managed to capture an image that maybe speaks louder than any words could.

Caught in a moment in time, a Tibetan player, with the ball at her feet, looks to run toward goal. With the Tibetan Flag emblazoned on her shirt, the look on her face is that of someone in the midst of truly expressing herself, her determined look is one of joyous concentration; the innocent pleasures of playing a game you love. Behind her spectators sat on the grass pitch-side as well as in the cool looking whitewashed stands, looking on intently as a Viva North player tries to catch her opponent up. With a smile spread across the Viva players face in a way that I don't think I have ever seen in such an action shot, we will never know how this little passage of play unfolded. Whether she caught up to her Tibetan opponent or not, that image capturing the joy that the freedom of expression can offer hints at a reward far greater than a last-ditch tackle, or a goal.

It is the essence of why so many people fall in love with such a simple game.

One wordless photograph, and the emotion captured within justifies all the hardship and heartache that it took for Tenzin and her team-mates to get there, and quite possibly their opponents too; the joy of human expression priceless in what it symbolises.

Just as Cassie Childers made the Tibetan Women's team a reality, so too does she celebrate their achievements, win, lose, or draw. With a humility and grace, she enjoys every match for what it is: a victory for the girls that get to play the game they love, in the name of the country they love. So, it is no surprise that a 6-0 defeat to a strong Goa state team in the final two days later is met with a stoic pride.

'You can't win them all. How boring would sports be if you did! The opponents were so strong, and though we fought, we just couldn't seem to get the ball in the net. Well played by all. We are proud to have taken second place in the Goa Women's Football Festival. The girls weren't sad for long! By the end they were teaching Tibetan dances to the Goans!'

As with the men's team, this Tibetan side doesn't measure success by victories and goals scored. Instead it is opportunity, having a voice out on the pitch, being able to sing your national anthem, and the freedom of expressing yourself that signify a far more profound victory. This may all come at a relatively anonymous tournament in southern India, but for a people denied even the most basic freedoms in their homeland, and struggle for true gender equality in their exiled communities, the Goa Women's Football Festival *is* the World Cup, given the opportunities it has provided them.

From a position way, way out on the fringes of world football and politics; maybe as far removed from the bright lights of mainstream football as it is possible to get, the Tibetan Women's National Football Team shines. For what it has instilled in its players, and the positive message it provides, it has become one of the most important teams (albeit a 'forbidden one') in world football.

'I always think that every time, every day this team are doing their hardest work and their best on the game,' young Sonam Sangmo writes slowly, in her neatest handwriting. 'I want this team to be in the magazines and on the front covers. I always want this team as the most successful team in the world, and they get the fame in the world, fame that is full of respect.

'Never give up – in every way of your life. No matter how many problems come in your life, never say "I can't". You just need courage to face that problem. Never listen to what others say about you. Just listen to your soul and heart 100 per cent.'

'We have a big responsibility.' Tenzin Dekyong added, 'To show girls that we can do whatever, and don't ever think that I can't do this. Just try it and give your best then you may get a new life. Never give up. My message for girls is not to listen to the people who always try to stop your dreams. Just believe yourself.' She went on, 'For me I believe myself, I can do sport and be a player of international or state level. Don't give your freedom to others to control your life. Follow your dream.'

It is clear, by the way in which this group of exiled and orphaned Tibetan refugee children have taken this opportunity in Goa that they all want to follow their dreams. Dreams that they refuse to have shackled, by China or anyone else. Whether the route to the Women's World Cup and their ultimate dreams will ever become a reality for this group of girls remains to be seen. Given the politics of sport it seems unlikely.

But who would bet against this group somehow finding a way to play against the greats of the women's game, that one day they will grace the stadiums that have featured in World Cups gone by?

With passion, heart, determination and joy they have already achieved so much.

'I am playing for the Tibetan team and for Tibet, and I've many people who follow me and support me,' Sonam Dolma concluded. 'I've got big responsibilities, like to inspire other women that "we can do it as well". We can do anything if we do it from deep heart.'

Even from the furthest reaches of the world game, from a position of exile, refugee status and economic and political impotency, the positivity and drive that the Tibetan National Women's Football Team possess would make you a fool to bet against them. For this group of players, when it comes to their dreams, no matter the obstacle, nothing is impossible. Given all they have already had to face and overcome in their short lives, they just might be right.

Postscript:

In May 2016, the TNSA announced the formation of a national women's team. Recognised by the Central Tibetan Administration, or the exiled Tibetan Government, it was stated that this new TNSA run side is the only 'official' national team for Tibetan women.

In an article published by Lobsang Tenchoe of *Tibet Express,* the TNSA and Cassie put their sides of the story forward; Cassie complaining that a year or so after its formation, her and her team had to go it alone because funds raised to help provide a sporting outlet for women were being diverted to the men's team, that the TNSA had had no interest or appetite for a women's team. Kalsang Dhondup of the TNSA denied that he ever said that, or attempted to move money away from the women's team. Among a community that has lost so much already, it is another tragedy that differences, whether personal or societal, split those trying to do good in the name of the Tibetan people.

Whether this new TNSA women's team has arisen, some five years since Cassie's first started changing perceptions of what Tibetan Women could be, due to the amazing publicity and opportunity it has generated, we will never know. Whether this new TNSA funded side, whose stated aim is to 'celebrate women's participation in sports and to empower' can flourish in the way Cassie's has will also remain to be seen. There is still the issue of little to no funding that has blighted the men's side and which could threaten this fledgling team before it has even started.

Without Cassie and her girls of the Tibetan Women's Football Programme leading the way however, would this new team, with or without funding, even exist? Without their trailblazing and questioning of traditional gender roles within the Tibetan community, would the TNSA have made the jump to start a women's team with the aim to 'show your skills, fulfil your dream'? All questions that will remain unanswered.

Whatever the outcome of this new team, whether it can provide more opportunity for more girls and women to express themselves in the way that Cassie's Tibetan Women's Football Programme has done, or whether it will struggle like the Tibetan Men's team, this labelling of it as the 'official' National team only serves to highlight the struggles every Tibetan has to face, and even more so now the girls of Cassie's team.

In a world in which the 'official' TNSA backed Tibetan football teams are not recognised by FIFA and their country isn't recognised by the United Nations, the exiled Tibetan footballer's path to his or her dreams are littered with seemingly insurmountable obstacles. For the girls and women of Cassie Childers's Tibetan Women's Football Programme, being told that your team that is not only unrecognised by the world's political and sporting bodies is now also not recognised by your own exiled government may well be as frustrating as it is upsetting.

This team that has achieved so much. It has broken through so many boundaries, socially, politically and sportingly, and is now an unofficial and unrecognised national team of a refugee community with a new national team that isn't seen as official or recognised by any 'official' sporting body on the planet! It is just another obstacle for Sonam Sangmo, Tenzin Dekyong, Sonam Dolma, and the rest of their team-mates to try to overcome. In their lives they are used to doing this; it is just a part of what they have to do, every day in order to survive, to thrive. And despite everything, and with the help of Cassie Childers, you just know – officially unofficial or not, that this football team will do just that.

CHAPTER 7

A Club on the Edge – Port Talbot Town

FIVE MEN SLOWLY gathered at the far end of the bar, welcoming one another as each arrived and bought their pint before joining the solemnity of the group. Three generations of Port Talbot supporters were present; the youngest, in his 20s, whose green army surplus issue cap sported a number of Port Talbot badges was the last to arrive and listened in to the conversation that had already started.

One of the three men in their 70s, who leant against the clubhouse wall beneath the shadow of faded pennants celebrating long ago league and cup victories, took a sip of his pint and shook his head.

'Never in all my years have I ever seen anything like this.' He looked washed out as they spoke about their club, the pain and sadness writ large across his face.

'It really is unbelievable. I can't believe it all, not after everything else,' The fifth member of the table, a man in his early 40s, said, and for a moment they all fell quiet.

All across the clubhouse similar conversations were being had around small wooden tables scattered about the L-shaped floor, the bustle increasing as kick-off drew on and old friends met up, as they had been doing for decades, to watch their team. Though this time their warm greetings, the odd outburst of laughter that momentarily drowned out the TV showing the lunch-time kick-off, had a feeling of gallows humour about it, a desperation for anything, a bad joke, anything to lighten the mood.

Like a punch-drunk heavyweight boxer rolling back on their heels, trying to clear their spinning heads before the next potentially devastating thrown glove, the assembled crowd were hurting from what must have felt like a series of soul crushing knock-out blows over the past couple of months.

For the home fans assembling for this meaningless end of season Welsh Premier League fixture against Bangor City, Port Talbot being safe from relegation, but cut adrift from the mediocrity of mid-table, they knew that their club, just like their town, were on the edge.

Port Talbot lies between Cardiff and Swansea on Wales' south coast. It has been known for one thing and one thing alone for as long as anyone cares to remember: Steel. The huge steelworks that dominates the skyline as the M4 curves round, revealing the shimmering sea, distant hulls of great oil tankers, and Port Talbot, is the life-blood of the town, and has been the largest artery of the British Steel industry since the industry began, providing one third of the country's annual production. The great industrial tangle of vast, dark weather beaten pipes, cooling towers, vats, and blast furnaces that loom over and dominate all points of Port Talbot are as spiritually tangled and interwoven among the narrow streets and back alleys that house the town's population, who rely almost solely on the plant for their living, as they are physically prominent.

The town's fortunes are married to the steelworks, and since the industry's hey-day in the '60s and '70s, when the plant employed some 20,000 steelworkers along with countless other jobs that serviced the plant, Port Talbot's fortunes have dwindled. Now only 4,000 remain, and the steelworks' owners, TATA, announced in January 2016 that, due to China flooding the market with cheap steel that has had the industry making huge losses for some time, some 750 jobs would be lost by the summer.

Worse was yet to come when in March the company announced the real prospect of the plant being closed completely. This final, devastating blow would, the town's inhabitants explained in interview after interview with the countries major media outlets that flooded into it, could be the end of Port Talbot.

Former and current steelworkers, along with those running businesses that relied on the steel plant, spoke of people already leaving the area, with there being no prospects for their children, let alone for themselves. Families that could claim generation upon generation of steelworker were being forced to abandon their town, heart broken at having to give up on their home, on Port Talbot.

It was suggested that if the steelworks went then they may as well seal off the motorway exit to Port Talbot, as it would be as good as dead; a modern-day ghost town.

No final decision has been made by TATA, who are looking for a buyer, but the plug could be pulled, at any moment, before such a lengthy process could be completed. If indeed there is a buyer out there.

The town, whose industrial roots date back to the 12th century and the Cistercian monks at Margam Abbey who forged iron axes, tools and swords only a few hundred yards from the modern-day plant, is living day to day on the edge of oblivion.

Port Talbot Town FC is not immune from the seemingly terminal decline of this proud Welsh town. The Steelmen's home, The Genquip Stadium, is nestled behind narrow terraced streets lined with tired looking houses. The turnstiles to the ground look out on a small back alley just big enough for a car to squeeze along past graffiti daubed garage doors and rickety wooden gates. Behind one end of the ground a small footpath strewn with a broken vacuum cleaner and other fly-tipped material leads off into another warren of streets and houses. Picturesque the home of Port Talbot Town may not be, but the love and passion that its supporters have poured into it is clear to see.

The Genquip Stadium (named after the club's main sponsor, a firm providing mobile and static storage units, toilets and offices, most likely the steelworks being one of its principal clients) is as tired as the surroundings that have built up around it. It is old and ramshackle in places, with unwanted hoardings and other rubbish piled behind a broken set of goalposts to the side of one small stand. An old and boarded up toilet block stands alongside a couple of newer small pre-fabricated huts that look to house a programme shop when manned and a storage room.

It looks like a great many non-league grounds that endure through the love of their supporters, volunteers, and a make do and mend survivalist attitude that can circumvent an abject lack of money; with the realities of its environment and the town's history, this club more than any other must surely have had to rely on the community they serve to remain in some kind of business.

No matter how tired this old stadium may seem, the love that it instils in its supporters is plain to see. Above the menacing looking exterior wall as you walk along the cramped back alleys to the turnstiles a mural in the blue and white of Port Talbot Town tries to brighten the mood and the drab back wall of the clubhouse. Inside those same exterior walls are painted once again in the blue and white of Port Talbot. Brighter than the harder to reach mural outside, it is easy to imagine the band of faithful volunteers that come each off-season to give it a fresh coat.

Another intricate mural of the club badge behind the discarded hoardings and goalposts looks a little more faded, those volunteers probably too scared to tackle such a delicate operation for fear of ruining such a precious symbol. A hand painted banner hanging limply at the back of the relatively modern main stand suggested the favoured location for the vociferous Port Talbot ultras that are well known across the Welsh Premier League. Famed for their noisy and colourful support involving flags, drums, and a seemingly never ending repertoire of songs and chants, the Port Talbot ultras are yet another symbol of how important this little ground in south Wales is to those that populate it. Support that a good hour before kick-off have congregated in their clubhouse, and are trying to make sense of what has happened to their town, to their football team.

As if the plight of the town and steelworks isn't hard enough, their club in recent weeks had been thrown into turmoil as well, leaving the band of five at the far end of the bar, along with all but those who have made the four-hour trip down from Bangor, in a daze.

A football club is meant to represent the community it stems from, and far from the money and bright lights of the top end of the sport, this remains the case; a club being for the fans, by the fans, a focal point for the local area, a source of identity and pride. However, those clubs lower down the food chain that do reflect their environs, that are a by-product of where they are based, that don't have the benefit of a wealthy benefactor to smooth over any financial difficulties, like the supporters that populate their terraces these clubs thrive and struggle depending on the fate of their town. And like the town, Port Talbot Town FC is in real trouble.

As the Steelworks began its decades long decline, contracting from that high-water mark of 20,000 workers to at best 3,250 by the summer, so too did the town, and the club. Employment became harder to come by, poverty came easier. Businesses that relied on the steelworks began to fail and close as the steelworks contracted, adding to the town's woes. In a one industry town, other opportunities for an unemployed population trained and experts in one thing, steel, have been virtually non-existent. Port Talbot has been left to die a slow and painful death.

Without local businesses to support their local team, the costs of running a semi-professional football club can quickly appear daunting. As businesses dwindle so too does the pool of potential advertisers and sponsors. A local club is the perfect tool to reach a local audience for small and mid-range local businesses, but if they fail and none replace them, as witnessed by the ever-growing heap of unwanted advertising hoardings behind the broken goal, the local football team suffers.

As the local population becomes poorer, the turnstiles begin to chatter less and less on match day; often not through apathy, but through the simple economics that the paltry £6 needed to gain entry could help put food in your children's mouths, or clothes on their backs. Port Talbot's average attendances hovers around the 200 mark, one of the worst in the Welsh Premier League, but not unsurprising to the committee tasked with, season upon season, keeping the Steelmen viable. Volunteers try to step in to perform tasks that no longer can be paid for, but it is papering over the cracks of a far bigger problem; a problem with no answer, a problem that is here to stay and could indeed get a lot worse for the football team and the town.

Playing in the Welsh Premier League, the highest tier in Welsh football, is a source of pride for all its teams. With the potential to represent your nation on a European adventure through the qualifying rounds of the Champions and Europa leagues after a successful season on the pitch, maintaining your status at your countries top table is paramount. For Port Talbot Town and all its troubles this must count double, survival among the best within the Welsh football pyramid, given everything they have to contend with is a tremendous achievement. However, it is an achievement that may be taken from them regardless of their endeavour, as the first of the crushing blows to hit the supporters in the club house was announced the week before.

Every club that plays in the Welsh Premier League needs a licence to operate within it, which is normally a formality if all ground grading and financial compliances are in order. So, the news that Port Talbot had been denied a licence for the following season sent shockwaves around its supporters.

Rumours that the club had been unable to pay its players for a number of months, that financially it was at breaking point came as a body blow to the faithful few who were still able to maintain their love for their club by passing through the turnstiles each week. A season that had seen the Steelmen successfully stave off relegation could be undone by the seemingly terminal decline of the town and the club; the desperation and helplessness that these supporters had hoped to leave outside the Genquip stadium's gates, for a couple of hours at least, had found their way in.

The expense of travelling the length and breadth of the country to compete in the Welsh Premier League on average crowds of 200 had seemingly left Port Talbot forever in the red, with the players wages the breaking point for the administrators of the league.

Demotion to the Welsh League, which is predominantly based along the countries south coast, would ease those financial demands. However, relegation by any other means than a lack of endeavour out on the pitch would be a severe body blow to an already punch-drunk club and set of fans, which is why the club immediately appealed the decision. But even then, with this result pending, worse was yet to come.

Three days before the Steelmen's penultimate league match against Bangor City came the news that an investigation was under way regarding betting irregularities concerning their match from the week before, a 5-0 away defeat at already relegated Rhyl. The allegations swirling around that some of the Port Talbot squad had bet on their own team being beaten by five, a fortnight after they had beaten the same team by four clear goals, rumbled around the clubhouse from table to table in stunned disbelief. No matter that it was a meaningless match that had no effect on league position, the notion that some of the Port Talbot players had possibly thrown a match, or contrived to do so, and that it had been picked up by the bet monitoring services that detect a spike in bets on certain results for certain games, was a betrayal of everything that these already world weary supporters stood for.

The least any supporter deserves for their £6 is an honest match between two teams doing the best that they can; it is the foundation block of what makes football such a beloved sport the world over. And to those supporters that had made the arduous four-hour trip up to Rhyl to see their team play that potential betrayal of this fundamental trust must smart even more.

I had witnessed these Port Talbot die hards after an equally long trip up to Bangor a couple of months earlier; four of them, who had crammed flags, banners and a large drum into a car all in the name of Port Talbot Town, their team, and who sang, drummed, and danced from minute one to minute 90 in honour of their heroes in black (their away colours).

To have made yet another long trip up to the north coast of Wales only to see your team lose 5-0 is dispiriting enough, though it is a given that that can happen and supporters face it with the same gallows humour that those in the clubhouse were attempting in the face of these latest body blows. But to know that you had spent an eight-hour round trip to see a match the result of which had already been predestined? That the players of your team had possibly decided that your journey would be a wasted one before you had even set off? Having, hopefully, never been in that position I can only begin to wonder how that must feel. And after everything else: the licence failure, the potentially game ending final nail in the coffin of the steelworks that could finish their town once and for and that loomed over them, over everything, and that could fall at any moment, a club on the edge doesn't really do Port Talbot full justice.

The five men spanning three generations at the end of the bar tried to rationalise it all in the hope that talking things out may help make some sense of what was going on. From the constant sighs and shakes of the head it was clear that it wasn't working, this final betrayal possibly one too many to take.

'The players know the rules,' one of the elder statesmen said. 'They know that they can't bet on any football in Wales. Full stop.'

'And if they wanted to bet so bad then why not get a mate to put it on for you. It can't come back to you then can it?' Another said, 'Though that isn't the real point here is it?' He trailed away to ponder the notion of their own players conspiring to lose by five.

'I read somewhere that roughly half a million pounds is bet on the Welsh Premier League every weekend, mainly in the Asian markets.' The youngest said, 'It is crazy, just on our little league.'

An injured player, that had been out of action for some time so had not been on the coach to Rhyl, or around the dressing room on match days for a while, stood between a rock and a hard place as he came over to say hello.

'Do you know what is going on?' one of them asked him desperately, but the player, maybe out of innocence, maybe out of a loyalty to his fellow team-mates who were only under investigation and hadn't been charged didn't say much.

'I really don't know. I've not been around the lads too much of late. I've been mainly in the gym doing physio.' He stood quietly and listened as one of the five said he'd heard rumours it had been as many as eight players involved, shaking his head at the thought of it.

Despite the troubles at the steelworks and with the licence for next season looming large over them, the club's ultras would no doubt have filled their section of the stand and sung, drummed and chanted their team on as always throughout this meaningless match at the end of a long hard season. But the apparent betrayal of some of their beloved team appeared to be the final straw. The ultra's, the young man at the bar with the badges on his cap included, had decided to make a stand by holding a silent protest.

So as not to deprive their ailing club of their desperately needed entrance fee, the vocal support had decided to pay, but remain in the clubhouse for the afternoon; their silence the only meaningful voice they had. Flags remained unfurled, drums hidden from view, their spot in the stand empty save for their limp banner on the back wall, leaving those of the 160 crowd that had ventured pitch side to watch in virtual silence as the teams came out from the tunnel. As the music faded away from the PA system a deafening hush descended, only a few bouts of applause from some of the old-timers in the stand and the smattering of away support broke the protest. Shouts of encouragement from both sets of players echoed about the floodlight stanchions as this most extra-ordinary of games got underway.

Playing semi-professional football for Port Talbot, like at most clubs in the Welsh Premier League, is not a lucrative proposition. For ten months a year you have to make great sacrifices to your partners and family: mid-week training sessions after work, long away trips taking up entire Saturdays, mid-week fixtures demanding time off from work. It is a labour of love that far outstrips the money earned.

However, to young couples and families it is money, no matter how meagre, that helps supplement incomes and keeps heads above the water line. Losing that income, if the club cannot find the money to pay you, but still having to maintain your levels of dedication must be hard. Clubs the country over that run into financial difficulties almost always see a downturn in form on the pitch; the subconscious feeling that your work isn't being respected when a club fails to pay its players can only lead to an inevitable dip in morale and performance. It is human nature, and would affect any of us in any profession if we had to endure the same. But to the Steelmen's credit, despite appearing to not have been paid, they have successfully fought off relegation and with games to spare. And that is no mean feat, which probably makes this alleged betrayal of the fans by the players so much harder to take.

Despite not being paid, trying to make money by betting on your own team is a dangerous game. In the Welsh Premier League rules, any player found guilty of doing so or attempting to fix the result of a match can face a lifetime ban from football. They can expect their registration to be held by the league, meaning that they couldn't play in England, or anywhere else instead. It would be a life sentence on their sporting ambitions.

At the same time, if your family are really struggling, and you haven't been paid, if the rent or mortgage is in arrears, then the temptation must be considerable. It in no way condones it, but if you are, like your club and town, on the edge, and it appears on paper to be a quick and easy way to make some money, how many of us would lose our morals for an hour or two? It is a question I guess none of us can truly answer unless we have found ourselves in the same position, no matter how we would like to believe that our sporting integrity, and our respect to that small hardy band of supporters would make us make the right decision.

Whether it is a matter of desperation that has led to this mess, or, if proven to be true, a case of simple greed, only time will tell. Until that time however, it is hard not to want to consider the former over the latter, because the latter is so overwhelmingly unpalatable.

Despite the silent hostility from the empty terraces, Port Talbot's players play with a fierce determination that suggested they had a point to prove. As they first repelled a spell of Bangor pressure, who needed the win to keep their play-off chances for a spot in next season's Europa league alive, Port Talbot began to look dangerous. Thundering in to tackles, sending probing passes down the wings, the Steelmen seemed determined to put in a good performance, and deservedly took the lead through a well worked Jamie Latham goal. The old-timers dotted about the stands, and those stood on top the grass bank behind the goal nearest the clubhouse applauded and cheered, momentarily forgetting their conflicting emotions. Behind the clubhouse windows it was unclear whether the goal had been met with any emotion from the protesting ultras.

At half time Port Talbot still had their lead, and as the smattering of support that had ventured outside headed back to the clubhouse for a cup of tea or something stronger to combat the chill in the spring air, the steelworks in the distance continued to plume smoke and steam that drifted toward the hills inland. It was a scene that had always been, had been repeated for decades of Saturdays long since forgotten to time, save for the odd goal and victory, or championship win as commemorated on the clubhouse walls.

How many more Saturdays there might be to come was a question with a far more uncertain answer.

Never mind how few there were, the importance of this club to the lives of the men and women, young and old, who queued for their half time tea and chips, was palpable. It may be a run-down club in a town all but written off by the rest of the country, but to them it was everything; as ingrained in their identity and DNA as their family tree, and Saturdays would not be Saturdays without it.

Second half and Bangor City threw everything at Port Talbot; midfielders were replaced with attacking wingers and auxiliary strikers in search of the win that would keep them in pole position for a crack at Europe. The Steelmen buckled, but didn't break, holding Bangor back, then advancing on counter attacks in the space left by their visitors attacking formation. The game began to swing from end to end; Port Talbot nearly scoring again before the almost inevitable Bangor equaliser, Sion Edwards scoring from outside the box after more good work from half time substitute Christian Langos.

It was captivating stuff, and the endeavour on show seemed to anesthetise the ultras protest a little. As Port Talbot looked to get back in front, the instinctive pull of their team began to drag some of the protesters outside, and the stand they usually congregated in began to fill out a little, lured by their passion for their team and the unfolding drama out on the pitch. By the end there were even a few chants, though the drum and flags remained absent, as they attempted to help Port Talbot over the line.

But it wasn't to be, and the game ended a draw, which wasn't good enough for Bangor, who would now have to rely on others in order to make the last play-off spot. For the fans of Port Talbot, a draw was neither here nor there, a point being irrelevant in their position. More important was the display of their team, which contained passion and determination in equal measure, which helped, if only for a short time, to help them forget everything else that loomed large over them all. As some shook hands and headed home for their tea through the narrow-terraced streets beyond, others headed back to the clubhouse for a drink to help steel themselves for whatever was to come.

While the future of the steelworks still remains in the balance, and the impending storm that could hit regarding the betting irregularities has yet to manifest itself, at least one of the hammer blows on the town of Port Talbot has been confirmed.

A few days after the Bangor City match, the Welsh Premier League upheld their decision to withdraw Port Talbot Town's licence, ensuring they would be forced to move down into the Welsh League. Their hard earned and hard fought status in the top flight of Welsh football will be no more once their final home match of season is complete. The irony that it will be Rhyl, the team that had already been condemned to relegation, and had been beaten out of sight one week, before winning 5-0 the next, that will receive a stay of execution is no doubt not lost on anyone. For the faithful supporters, this is a big blow, and leaves their club, after such a long, hard season, on its knees and in need of regrouping.

Hopefully for those five supporters spanning three generations, trying to make sense of it all back at their table in the clubhouse, for all the other souls populating the stands and grass banks of the Genquip Stadium, hopefully for their club and their town, relegation is the last blow that will befall Port Talbot. But sadly, you can't help but fear that that may well just be wishful thinking.

CHAPTER 8

The Club That Wouldn't Die – Accrington Stanley

ON A SIMILARLY sunny day to the one spent in Port Talbot a few weeks earlier, the atmosphere outside Wycombe Wanderer's ground couldn't have been further from the one that had blighted The Steelmen's small band of supporters. It felt more like a wedding reception than the prelude to a football match, standing in this temporarily erected marquee on a bright Saturday afternoon on the last day of April.

As the beer tent quickly filled with a fair chunk of the 500 or so Accrington Stanley fans that had made the long journey down to this industrial estate in Buckinghamshire, the floor began to bow and bounce to the rhythm of laughter, a never-ending repertoire of songs celebrating their heroes: the Stanley players, and the infectious outbreak of dancing come '70s punk style pogo-ing. Behind the temporary bar a couple of staff worked manically against this tide of euphoria to keep the beer flowing; security guards appeared carrying more crates every few minutes suggesting that they had grossly underestimated the severity of the party Accrington Stanley were bringing.

It looked and felt like the vast wedding party scene in *The Deer Hunter*: the unbridled love between a group of lifelong friends manifested in a wordless play of drink, song and dance – all ecstatic on their friend's good fortune to find love and get married.

Only in this marquee in Wycombe there weren't a handful of buddies that felt their friend's happiness as if it were their own, there were hundreds; hundreds of best men and bridesmaids to their football club that felt compelled to celebrate their lifelong friend's good fortune until they were physically incapable of doing so anymore. It may not have been all playing out to the back drop of a loud, billowing Pennsylvania Steel works as in the film, but at the end of an industrial estate, where Wycombe Wanderers' home is located felt close enough to marry the two groups of friends from towns mostly forgotten to the outside world together.

Outside, with the singing of yet another round of adulation for striker Billy Kee in full swing, people stood around to take a breath, to take it all in, because to the supporters of Accrington Stanley, this kind of thing doesn't happen every day. In fact, it has never happened before, stood as they are with only two games to go, on the brink of their first ever promotion from the Football League's fourth and lowest tier.

As another emergency beer run is carried through by burly security guards one fan utters, to no one in particular as he watched the party unfold before his eyes:

'I never thought I would see the chance of another promotion, at least not without getting relegated back into the non-league first!'

As the revelries continue it is hard to believe that it is only 1.30pm, and the first of the two matches that will define the supporters' and the club's season hasn't even started yet, indeed it is still 90 minutes away.

Despite those that are suffering badly from a bout of nerves at being so close yet still so far – like Adam, a softly spoken school teacher from Preston, and one of the die-hards that can be found on the terraces home and away, season after season, who looks pale and shakes his head: 'I've not slept for days. I'm a wreck!' he said before continuing to pace nervously about – the majority of the Stanley fans are going to celebrate no matter what. Lose the two remaining games, and Accrington will still be in the play-offs; win them and they are promoted automatically as runners-up to Northampton.

It has been a remarkable achievement, and, as they change their song to revere 'the ginger Cafu' in lone defender Brad Halliday, it is one that the fans in the marquee want to celebrate no matter what. Because for clubs like Accrington Stanley, scenes like these hardly ever happen, and if football results reflect the resources that every club has at its disposal, then they should never happen.

But for Accrington Stanley, the club that wouldn't die, they are used to defying the odds.

In the ten seasons since they returned to the football league, and based solely on the resources that every club has at its disposal, Stanley have been made favourites by bookmakers to finish last and return back to the non-league every season, even this season where they have achieved such a lofty position in the table with only two games remaining.

And every season, despite having the lowest playing budget and smallest fan base by some way in the entire Football League, they have proven the bookmakers and the rest of the footballing community wrong, with the end of season celebrations in the Crown Pub that overlooks their tiny Wham Stadium home usually toasting another narrow escape from the trap door out of the football league.

But this season, this one is different, and has gone beyond even the wildest pre-season expectations of the most defiant lifelong Stanley fan.

All of the factors that have made this club unique in keeping it in the football league, that help make up for only having a tiny fraction of the resources of every other club in the league, have turned it into one of the greatest small-time sporting achievements in lower league history. It is a story that most who follow the game at the top levels will never hear about, or will dismiss in the shadow of Leicester City winning the Premier League title; another tale of a David slaying far greater goliaths. But despite being lost out on the fringes of the football community, the story of Accrington Stanley and their remarkable rise is one that deserves just as many plaudits, maybe even more given the scale of their task.

Just outside the changing rooms at the Wham Stadium is a sign that greets the players just before they step out onto the pitch. It reads: 'This is Stanley – The Club That Wouldn't Die.' It helps to warn visiting teams that, win, lose, or draw, they will need to fight for anything that they get.

The spirit encapsulated in this sign is the mantra that knits this small team from Lancashire together. It helps detail their past, as well as how they survive in the present. It is a simple mission statement on how Accrington Stanley do the things they do. To those that know the club's past, those words are all that are needed; to those that don't, a little bit of explanation is required.

Accrington is a small town in the heart of Lancashire that has always lived in the shadow of its much larger near neighbours Burnley and Blackburn. Only 13 miles from Preston and 20 from Manchester, this small town of 40,000 people was once at the forefront of the cotton and textile industries during the industrial revolution. It was also famous for 'The Accrington NORI' brick, purported to be the strongest in the world and was used in the construction of the Empire State Building in New York.

As the industrial boom gradually ground down to a near halt and works contracted, Accrington, like many small towns in the north of England, did its best to adapt and survive. It was to this backdrop that the resurrected Accrington Stanley Football Club was reformed in 1968 – hoping against hope for better fortune than its predecessor that folded mid-way through the 1961–62 season.

Like the town itself, Accrington Stanley knows it will always be in the shadow of its far more illustrious football neighbours. Burnley and Blackburn, six and four miles away respectively have both played in the Premier League in recent times. Indeed, Blackburn won it in 1995, and as the Stanley fans descended on Wycombe, Burnley had just reclaimed their place at English football's top table. Regardless of the leagues they have found themselves in, these two fiercest of rivals have always been the main draw for the regions football fans.

In addition, with Manchester just a short train journey away offering the global giants of Manchester's United and City, as well as numerous clubs from satellite towns in Greater Manchester, the more glamorous sporting options on offer have meant Accrington Stanley have always had to operate on a very small fan base, and with next to no money.

The club's early history was one of battling to survive in the football league as well as on the balance sheet on small but passionate crowds, with one fatal decision to buy a new stand for their then Peel Park ground the killer blow in tipping that balance into the red. When bills remained unpaid during the 1961–62 season the receivers were called in and the gates locked on Peel Park. To the small band of Stanley supporters, who had been there through thin and thin, being withdrawn from the football league and having their club dissolved was heartbreaking.

It was also something that couldn't be allowed to stand; they wanted their club back, and so began a long, painstaking journey to resurrect the club that finally resulted in the new Accrington Stanley, playing on a pitch behind the Crown Pub, joining the Lancashire Combination League for the 1970 season. From there the club slowly grew, and gradually rose through the non-league ranks until 2006 when, inspired by former player turned manager John Coleman, they won the Football Conference title and their place back in the Football League.

So began ten years of competing and surviving in the fourth tier of the Football League, against clubs with resources that far outstretched those of Stanley. Where Accrington could rely on crowds of 1,200, they had to compete against the likes of Bradford, and more recently Portsmouth, who could easily command attendances ten times as big. Indeed, Portsmouth attracted attendances pushing 18,000 on a regular basis during Stanley's latest season of defying the odds. Even the more modest sides in the lowest level of the Football League could expect to operate on at least double or triple the gate receipts and income of Accrington.

On paper Stanley shouldn't have ever stood a chance; they should have gone straight back down that first season back in the Football League, and then every season since. But football isn't played on paper, and the clubs with far greater resources can't draw on the backs to the wall spirit that has been instilled in the small band of supporters, committee members, management team and players that fuel Accrington; a spirit highlighted in the sign by the players dressing rooms.

It is a spirit that begins with the supporters, who make up for their paucity of numbers with their dedication to the cause; taking cars and trains when there aren't the numbers to pay for and fill a coach to far flung places like Plymouth and Gillingham, singing and cheering as if they were in far greater numbers, no matter how outnumbered.

It is the spirit of the Supporters club – a band of volunteers who run a shop in the local market hall and work tirelessly to raise funds that have helped plug gaps in Stanley's finances. It is a spirit that manifests itself among the board members and management team, that strive to preserve this little institution, never outstretching their meagre resources on players they can't afford, or non-essential maintenance works (when the groundsman, Buzzer, switches on the sprinklers on the pitch it is said all the taps in the toilets run dry, due to some mysterious and unaffordable plumbing anomaly!) It is a spirit understood and embraced by the players, many of whom have arrived at the Wham Stadium over the years as free transfers having been released by clubs higher up the food chain; buying into this potentially final opportunity that they have been given to resurrect their career at Accrington.

Like the club itself, that no-one ever gives a hope in hell to, so to these players have been discarded. But John Coleman and his assistant Jimmy Bell seem to have the knack of seeing which have been thrown back unjustly, or at least have something about them that suggests they can do a job for Stanley. And through that determination to take this second chance, Coleman and Bell mould these players into a team, but also into better players and individuals, as witnessed by the rise of Josh Windass and Matt Crooks.

Windass arrived from non-league Harrogate Railway, Crooks after being released by Huddersfield. After a good 18 months at Stanley both had signed pre-contract agreements to move to Scottish giants Rangers in the summer.

A second chance in the Football League is one thing, but at Accrington Stanley you need to buy into the entire ethos, that we are all in it together: from the striker given another chance to prove himself, to the supporter's club and the rest of the fans on the Clayton End, to Keil Clitheroe, who runs the club shop, the ticket office, and can be seen helping Buzzer the groundsman, or Naz the kit man if needed. At this club, more than any other in the professional leagues, it truly is an institution far greater than the sum of its parts.

The rundown, but ramshackle charm of the Wham Stadium, the unwavering dedication of its small band of supporters and board members, the manager who instils the pride and respect his players need to represent the fans, the club, indeed themselves; they all know that on paper, in the cold light of day this just shouldn't work – that a little club, from a small town, followed by 1,200 or so, that play in a small ground behind a pub that can't even be seen from the road, should be rubbing shoulders with, let alone beating teams like Portsmouth is insanity.

And yet that is what Accrington Stanley do. Every year. For more than ten years, making up for resources with spirit, togetherness, and an endeavour to prove themselves right and everyone else who has written this small town from Lancashire off as wrong. And it has led them all the way to an industrial estate in Wycombe on a bright sunny Saturday afternoon in late April...

You could hear them long before you could see them, before they invaded the ill-prepared marquee. The distant chanting growing louder as the contents of the seven supporters' coaches that had made it down from Accrington spilled out onto the car park behind some bland industrial unit a short distance from the entrance to Adams Park, home of Wycombe Wanderers. A wall of noise, they marched and sang straight in to the beer tent and made good with their promise to have a great time.

For a team that usually took no more than 70 or 80 fans to away games, this crowd close to 600 was more than impressive, especially given the circumstances in which this army of partygoers was assembled.

Ash Seed, one of the die-hard Stanley Ultras that you could spot on any given Saturday afternoon or Tuesday night on any terrace where Stanley were playing had managed to find businesses that were prepared to sponsor a coach each. This sponsorship meant that the club could offer subsidised travel for anyone that wanted to be at this potentially historic match. Ash, more than anyone else, knew how expensive it was to travel to see your team. After all he did it every game, wherever it was.

Subsidised travel could be the difference between 200 fans turning up rather than 600 fans, as in a town and region where traditional industries had been decimated, money was always an issue, and was a deciding factor in going to see Stanley play, be it at home or away.

As the team coach pulled up, ghosting slowly past the marquee and the singing that spilled out of it, and unbeknownst to Ash who was in the thick of it, the faces of the players that looked out on such support appeared to grow more determined. Sitting up in their seats to take in the view, it was as if they had all grown in stature on seeing this sea of support, all for them, helping to steel them for the battle ahead. The dedication of the travelling few always saw the players turn in their very best, week in week out; always taking the time to applaud their small band of followers. But 600? It was unheard of. For Ash, though he didn't see it, all his hard work had just paid off, long before a ball had even been kicked. Yet again the ingenuity and dedication of the Stanley family had just exceeded the sum of their parts.

Standing in the sun drinking a beer, taking it all in was Stanley's Chairman Peter Marsden.

'After ten years being involved with this club, after everything that I have seen, I really should write a book about it all,' He said, 'Though I doubt many would believe it!'

For a group of board members trying to keep a club afloat on a wing and a prayer at the lower end of the football pyramid, their insights and experiences put down on paper may very well find itself accidentally placed on the shelves of the fiction section, so unbelievable they must appear to those that follow football at the money drenched top end of the game.

Only 18 months before this momentous day in Buckinghamshire, the club was the victim of a break-in. A door and a window had been prised open, so as on the morning of an away match at Shrewsbury, the players arrived to discover that all their boots had been stolen. With time running out before they had to board the coach, and on the worst wages in the football league, most of the squad couldn't simply afford to go out and buy another pair. Nor did the club have enough ready cash to sort the players out. After a bout of frantic calls and texts to mates who they thought might be roughly the same size as them, the players managed to cobble together enough borrowed boots to make the game, which they promptly lost 4-0 in their ill fitted footwear.

Such can be the life of a footballer playing for the team with the smallest playing budget, the smallest fan base, and the worst resources in the Football League's basement.

Indeed, every pre-season, as John Coleman attempts to assemble his squad for the coming year, there are stories of players that Stanley attempted to sign who turned them down to sign for teams in the non-league who were able to offer more money. In a way, that has helped the club's cause; with the players that come to the Wham Stadium really wanting to be here, to prove themselves. Though if promotion were to be secured, there would be a lot more players clamouring to pull on the red shirt of Accrington Stanley during the next pre-season.

'We've got where we are,' Peter Marsden explained, 'Through a real togetherness, the fans, the players, everyone. It is a real community club. It is for them.' He points at the marquee and the fans fanning out from it. 'Whatever happens today, or next week, this is what it is all about,' He says as he looks out at a family spanning three generations of Stanley fans enjoying the moment, celebrating their club, their town, the pride of belonging to Accrington Stanley all too apparent.

As the clock ticks on toward kick-off, kids jump up and down and sing with the young men in the marquee, more middle-aged folk that braved the party to get their beer circle the edges, not quite able to let go like the young ones.

Further out, the old-timers that have seen it all, their club folding, coming back, sit on the few chairs on offer and survey the scene with a quiet, dignified pride. It is small time. It will largely go unnoticed. It is amazing.

Inside the ground there is a short calm before the storm, while the stands basking in spring sunshine remain largely unoccupied. Dotted about the away end a few people needing a few moments of quiet contemplation after the dizzying party outside sit and ponder their fate.

Mother and son partnership Julie and Adam, who are also a regular feature on the terraces at Stanley away games wear conflicting emotions on their faces. Adam has special needs, Julie explains, and Stanley is his life, the excitement of another imminent match writ large across his face. As with the tradition of dressing up to the last away match of the season, Adam is dressed up as the tin man from *The Wizard of Oz*! Julie is clearly not doing so well, the nerves of what just might be getting to her.

'It's unbearable! So close, yet...'

She dare not say anything more, and we ascend the steps up to our seats, and wait, and wonder on all the possible permutations that the mathematics of a 46-game season drawing to a close could throw at us.

The scenario before kick-off on this sunny, April afternoon was a standard end of season affair compromising a myriad of potential outcomes: if Stanley win and Bristol Rovers fail to win, or Oxford United lose, then little Accrington Stanley are promoted. If Stanley lose and their two nearest rivals win then they will drop to fourth, and go into the final day of the season a week later outside of the automatic promotion places, and facing the prospect of the play-offs and a potential play-off final at Wembley. If all three teams win then we go, as we were, into the final day, where the whole nerve shredding experience will start all over again!

As the players came out to start their warm-up, the away end began to fill. The songs that had been sung on a never-ending loop in the marquee began to grow louder as the party left the beer tent and filed through the turnstiles, filling the back of the stand to capacity and sending a wall of noise down onto the pitch.

It was a joyous sight, and it was hard not to remember back to the last away game of the season before, where 60 or so Stanley fans had made it down to a meaningless mid-table match against Dagenham & Redbridge, one of the only teams with a comparable budget and fan-base to Stanley.

On a day in which Stanley were soundly beaten 4-0, the only memories of note were the moving minute's silence on the anniversary of the Bradford City Stadium fire that claimed as many fans as were stood in the away end in Dagenham that day. Beyond that, the only other event to stand out that made the long trip worthwhile was and a spontaneous moment of hilarity that still lingers!

As with today's end of season away day, the sun had been shining, and Ash Seed, his near identical brother Harry, Julie and Adam, and the rest of the small band of Stanley support were in high spirits – singing as if their lives depended on it!

During another rendition of one of their songs (songs that had also got some of the Dagenham fans on their feet and dancing along!) a wayward shot from a Stanley player sent the ball high up into the away end. Mid song and arms raised Ash, or possibly Harry, saw the ball fly toward them. Instinctively, as if he were out on a pitch in his mind's eye, he dived at it, launching himself over the rows of empty seats in front of him, connecting forehead to ball and sending it back out where it came from before disappearing from view in a heap. One second, two, then he re-appeared, arms outstretched, and without missing a beat, carried on with the song he had been singing! It was another small-time moment of legendry that both sets of supporters applauded him for.

As the players warmed up for this far more important match in the present, that match from a year ago also helped to serve a cautionary tale. Dagenham, Stanley's opponents then, and their southern cousins in relative sporting poverty, had been relegated a few weeks earlier and were dropping out of the Football League all together. After promotion into the third tier of English football, then relegation back into the fourth, and a number of seasons punching well above their weight in pushing for the play-off spots, one bad year and they were gone, into the even greater obscurity, in the mainstream media's eyes, of the non-league. It was the knife-edge that they and Stanley had no choice but to exist on; another reason to enjoy the highs when they come along.

And enjoy them the Stanley ultras were.

Somehow managing to overcome their nerves, no doubt through more than a little Dutch courage that they had been consuming for hours, the ultras at the back of the stand kept the party and the singing going into the match, despite it being a tense and even affair that was only interrupted for the quieter, older, and far more nervous contingent in the seats nearer the front by a couple of drunk, and very late Stanley fans dressed as Batman and Superman weaving their way to their seats, waving at everyone and no one!

True to their profession the Wycombe players gave their all, despite it being a meaningless match to them. They owed it to their supporters, and they owed it to themselves in playing for their futures. There is no such thing as a long-term contract in League Two; clubs simply cannot afford to offer them. The best a player can hope for is a two-year deal, meaning every other summer they are hoping and playing for a new deal, somewhere, anywhere, to keep their professional career alive.

Even at clubs with greater resources than Stanley, the average League Two player will not be on vast sums of money in comparison to the fan on the terraces. And in such a precarious short term situation, one bad injury lay-off could be the difference between getting a new deal and being able to pay the mortgage, or not. No, if the Wycombe players were going to end their home campaign on the losing side, then Accrington would really need to work for it.

And work for it they were.

News quickly began to filter through that both Bristol Rovers and Oxford were winning comfortably, and though Stanley were playing quite well, a draw would see them drop to fourth.

At half time (even then the ultras didn't stop singing) with the score still goalless, Stanley had it all to do.

In a game that was so important, to one of the sides at least, it was never going to be a classic. Stanley had played with more freedom during the season, and as the clock ticked down, despite all that was riding on the result, they kept trying to do what had got them to this position, by playing neat passing football.

The tension that had seen them struggle a little in the first half gave way to a fearsome desire that Wycombe just couldn't match. And slowly Stanley pushed them back, further and further toward the goal and the travelling support, until, with a little more than ten minutes remaining, they forced a free kick just outside the penalty area. Rangers and Scottish Premier League bound Josh Windass placed the ball, then curled it brilliantly round the wall, only for an equally brilliant save by debutant Wycombe keeper Benjamin Siegrist, who tipped it onto the post. The next few seconds seemed to take an eternity, as the ball bounced back off the post and back into play. Even the ultras paused to hold their breath as a Stanley player, more desperate to reach it than the Wycombe defence prodded it goal bound, where it weakly crossed the line despite a last-ditch attempt to hook it clear. Delirium! One nil!

That it was the most unlikely of scorers in centre back Mark Hughes, who hadn't scored all season seemed a perfect allegory for the entire Stanley journey. Hughes, who had been released by fellow League Two side and at the time relegation threatened Stevenage in January, was given another chance in the professional leagues by John Coleman in February, and had gone on to prove himself a vital member of the Accrington defence. That it was another Stanley redemption story that had put them ahead in this most important of matches, well it just had to be.

At the final whistle the scenes of jubilation were only slightly tempered by the news that Oxford and Bristol had also won, and that it would go down to the last day of the season.

As the players saluted the travelling support and vice versa, there was plenty to feel jubilant about.

To those that had been at Dagenham at the end of the season before, or at any of the away matches in the ten years Stanley had been in the Football League, being a part of a 600 strong away support, watching a Stanley team as good as this one, finding themselves second in the league with one game to go, rather than just above the drop zone; there were plenty of reasons to celebrate.

As the fans began to drift away to the coaches, apart for the ultras at the back of the stand who stayed to carry on singing for a good 15 minutes after the final whistle, it was a case of 'same time next Saturday.' For this small band of passionate support, you knew that, top of the league or not, when it came to Stanley that would always be the case.

The Wham stadium is buzzing, and it is still a good two hours before kick-off.

People are milling about expectantly, waiting for the ticket collection booths to open so as they can finally get hold of their much sought after ticket. This final day of the season has captured the imagination of the town like no other, and Stanley's little ground could have been sold out twice over, such was the demand to get in on this success story.

The newly erected fan-zone marquee in the car park behind The Clayton End stand, as provided by the supporters' club, is doing a brisk business in pre-match beer; a 50-50 split of supporters trying to calm their nerves a bit or have a massive party to celebrate what their team has already achieved.

Face painting for the children is momentarily interrupted by a request from a drunk lad in his 20s for two large red and white love hearts on his cheeks, along with the name of Tariqe Fosu emblazoned across his fore-head. Fosu, a young lad on loan from Reading had been a sensation since he arrived, making him an instant cult hero, and it is all his friends can do to catch their breath from laughing so hard at the scene of their mate, pint in one hand, a lolly in the other, sat on a child's seat while the giggling face painter finishes off Fosu's name. Job done and he returns to his mates, before spotting Winstanley the club mascot, demanding he have his picture taken with him; his mates laughing and slipping from view among the growing crowd as they trail in his newly painted wake.

With Accrington's ground, it truly is a case of blink and you might miss it. Nestled in a dell behind the Crown Pub on Livingstone Road, it is quite possible to miss the tops of the stands between the trees that line the back of the pub's small car park. The only other indicator of a Football League ground being close by is a small brown sign with the club name on it, pointing down an unlikely looking narrow residential cul-de-sac that ends in more trees and a small community tended garden.

Nick, the Supporters Club chairman looks exhausted as he stands outside the club shop cum ticket office. Not only has the fan-zone had to be arranged, but the small shop that the supporters' club runs in the market hall in the town centre has been selling tickets for the match from dawn till dusk since the Wycombe result the previous Saturday.

Nick is an inspiration and a walking example of the Accrington Stanley spirit. With his small band of volunteers Nick has raised through fundraising nights, auctions, programme and badge stalls, collection buckets an God knows what else close to £30,000 that initially was going to be spent on upgrading the changing rooms – changing rooms that England manager Roy Hodgson famously turned his nose up at while manager at Fulham, instructing his players getting ready for a third round FA Cup tie in January 2010 to get back on the coach and change into their kit back at their hotel. With the arrival of majority shareholder Andy Holt, who fell in love with the club and felt a need to invest in the infrastructure of what is commonly known as 'the biggest little club in the world', the changing rooms were no longer in need of the supporters' clubs help.

But, Holt had offered, how about using that money to create a fan-zone, for the supporters to have some place to meet up before and after matches?

That excited kids, and even more excited older kids, could get their faces painted and meet the mascot, hang out with old friends and make new ones, is all down to Nick and his band of colleagues. Asked if he has ever seen anything like this before he shakes his head,

'No, never, this has never happened before, this level of excitement. It's like the town has finally woken up to what it has right on its doorstep. It is great to see. I don't think I have ever known a match sell out before, let alone have a demand so great we could have sold it out twice over!'

In typical self-depreciating Stanley style Nick had posted a tongue in cheek message on Twitter claiming that the £15 tickets for this sold-out match were now swapping hands on the black market for upwards of £15.20!

The buzz around the place, to anyone that had been to see Stanley play on any given Saturday in the past ten years was truly worthy of bewilderment. For a club and fan base regularly expecting crowds of no more than 1,500 for a home match, where a leisurely stroll from the pub a few minutes before kick-off is sufficient time to pick up a programme, pay at the turnstile, and find a favourite spot on the terrace, this clamour is truly something else!

Keil, the ticket office and club shop manager, who has doubled up as pretty much every other conceivable job that a football club could need doing, looks just as tired as Nick. Clutching a walkie-talkie in one hand and a fist full of tickets in the other he explains how it has been a non-stop operation since the Wycombe game to get this final match organised.

'With all the demand, we've just not stopped, working late into the night all week to get everything done. It has been crazy; brilliant, but crazy!'

As with every other visit paid to the club shop to say hi to Keil, you just know that it is a labour of love. This is his club, from way back when he first saw the team play as a boy, back in the non-league, to now, working for his club, every hour spent over and above the average line of duty is an hour spent doing something he truly loves and believes in. From stories of being the kit-man away at Southport in the Conference days, cowering in the corner of the changing rooms at half time as John Coleman laid into his underperforming side, to getting the rollers out on the pitch during torrential downpours to help the grounds-man get a game on, Stanley are in Keil's DNA. People like Keil, like Nick, well they *are* Accrington Stanley's DNA.

They see past the ramshackle and the rundown that makes up a significant portion of the Accrington Stanley experience. Yes, the toilets have seen better days, and struggle when the sprinklers are on. Yes, the changing rooms aren't fit for Premier League Prima Dona's, but the love and affection that goes in to maintaining as best they can the club shop, the function suite, the offices, the changing rooms, the stands and terraces – that is what the true soul and spirit of football looks like.

As match day grinds into life, old friends meet up and lean against the barriers on the Clayton End stand, as they had done through thick and thin, year on year, the Wham stadium having long since captured their hearts. Looking out, daring to dream, the sun-drenched hills of East Lancashire beyond rising up to meet blue sky; the tips of wheeling arms from a hazy wind farm whirr silently in the distance. At the far end, Stevenage fans shield their eyes on the exposed away terrace, chatting to one another. Others craning over the back of the terrace watch an amateur match on a public pitch beyond; another unique idiosyncrasy of the Accrington experience.

As with the love that has been poured into every brick of the Wham Stadium, it is hard not to fall for the place and the club when meeting those that give the club its heartbeat. People like Adam, the softly spoken schoolteacher from Preston, who at Wycombe was nervous, but here, standing in the sun by the fan-zone, just 90 minutes from the unthinkable and League One, well he is rendered virtually incoherent with nerves.

'I, I, I don't know,' He stutters, 'This is unbearable! I've not slept. I've just stayed up thinking about all the possible permutations. It's a nightmare! And I just want it to be over I want this so bad! To see Stanley in League One,' He trailed off and shook his head, shifted nervously from foot to foot, then, 'Oh look, its Piero's Dad!' He ushers us over to a familiar face in the father of Stanley winger Piero Mingoia.

Piero's Dad, no first name needed when you are the father of a Stanley legend, can be found at every Stanley game, home and away, always the first to shout his son's name in frustration if a pass goes astray, but also the first to celebrate when his boy scores. It is another case of unconditional love for Stanley, the club that gave his boy a second chance when Watford released him. He shakes everyone's hand, ruffles the hair of my 12-year-old nephew, who has also fallen for Stanley despite living five hours away on the outskirts of Southampton, and whose favourite player is Piero.

With the clamour for tickets Adam pulls out his and shows it to Piero's Dad.

'Are you in your normal seat? I couldn't get mine so I am a bit further down'. Piero's Dad scrambled about his pockets until he found his envelope and pulled out his tickets.

'Oh my God,' He said in his broad Italian accent that hadn't dimmed from decades of living in the UK. 'I hope so! After four years of sitting in the same seats, to not on today of all days...' He leaves the obvious terrible ramifications of superstition hanging in the air as he searches for the seat numbers, then sighs when he sees familiar ones, holding his hand to his heart.

It is clear that everyone is feeling it; from Piero's Dad dreaming of his son and the club that has looked after him so well reaching League One, to Adam, Keil, Nick who had been there in the non-league days, and who never imagined in their wildest dreams that Stanley might be on the verge of finishing second, runners-up in the league that they had mostly battled to survive in. To Ash and Harry Seed and the Stanley Ultras that made up for in numbers with a pride and passion that surely couldn't be surpassed anywhere else within the football pyramid.

A passion hidden by trees, houses, and the pub; just a brief flash of red stanchion in-between as cars and buses drift past unaware of the nervous excitement beyond.

Now, now the time for dreaming was almost over. With kick-off approaching it was time for the fan-zone to empty out, and for the ultras to orchestrate a magnificent sea of flags and banners to greet the Stanley team.

As the team came out, four huge red and white standards were unfurled behind one goal and waved, their tips almost higher than the roof of the stand behind them. Smaller red and white foil flags crinkled and snapped as they were boisterously waved about by children and adults alike. Matt Crooks, injured in a match against Plymouth in March, meaning he would never play for Stanley again before his move to Rangers in the summer, came out on to the pitch on crutches, his ankle in a cast.

The emotion of the moment, in wanting so badly to see the club that resurrected his career, that gave him the opportunity to move on to a bigger club gain promotion saw him make his way toward the Clayton End and the ultras, a steely look of determination on his face, before tottering on one good leg and raising his sticks above his head, waving them so wildly it looked like he might fall in his attempts to gee up the fans.

The fans responded, roaring Crooks and the team.

All was set for a fairy tale ending to a fairy tale season, and the remarkable story of the smallest team in the Football League finishing, for one season at least, on an unbelievable high.

But sometimes life, and sport, can be cruel, and fairy tales, no matter how deserved, can wither and fade right at the last...

Accrington Stanley, up until this final day of the season, had been the only team in all three divisions of the Football League to have scored in every home game they played. But this final match against Stevenage, a team

like Wycombe the Saturday before, who only had pride and one last opportunity to earn a new contract to play for, it seemed like the football Gods
had turned their backs on Stanley.

After a forgettable first half in which Accrington failed to convert two
chances when clear through on the Stevenage goal, the second began to
unfold with a creeping sense of Greek tragedy; with a feeling that it had been
predestined that Stanley would draw a blank.

But even so, despite news filtering through that Oxford were comfortably beating Wycombe and were as good as up, Accrington drawing
would still have been enough as Bristol Rovers were being held by long
relegated Dagenham. But everybody: the manager, the players, the fans
knew that relying on others to do them a favour was a dangerous game,
and so with time running out John Coleman brought on Shay McCartan;
a lucky charm who always seemed to come off the bench and find a goal
when it was needed.

One decent first touch later, then a vicious half volley on the edge of the
penalty area with his second McCartan smacked the ball against the cross-
bar, it cannoning back out to safety for Stevenage. *

Everyone rooting for Stanley seemed to stand still for a second, head
in hands, unable to fathom how such a sweet strike hadn't nestled in the
back of the net. It would not be the last time they would do that, as not too
much later defender Matty Pearson's header came back off the bar, then as
the clock began to wind down a bullet header by McCartan, that for all the
world looked certain to fly in hit the bar yet again. It just seemed fate that,
no matter how hard they tried, Stanley would not score on this day of all
days.

Worse was still to come, as news quickly filtered down that Bristol Rovers had scored a last-minute winner against Dagenham, and had overtaken
Stanley into the final promotion spot on goal difference.

Management, all the substitutes on the bench were on their feet, some
with heads in hands, others shouting to goalkeeper Ross Etheridge to
abandon his goal, and race up the other end of the field, where the Stanley
onslaught of the Stevenage net was still on going; where players, keeper
included launched themselves desperately at every lost cause and half chance.

Headers flashed wide, panicked shots were saved by the Stevenage keeper, who tried to soak up as much time as possible to help his

punch-drunk team-mates who were buckling, but not breaking under the Accrington assault.

The five minutes of added time seemed to go by in a flash, and as the referee blew the final whistle the Stanley players sank to the floor, exhausted, devastated, heartbroken at not quite being able to get that one goal that they needed.

On the terraces the Stanley Ultras paused for a moment at the final whistle, then started a round of applause for their fallen heroes on the pitch. That they had not quite made the automatic promotion spots was not for a lack of trying, and they deserved to be celebrated for an amazing season exceeding all expectations. And with the never say die spirit of the sign above the player's entrance, the ultras began a rendition of 'Que sera sera, whatever will be will be, we're going to Wembley, que sera sera', in reference to the play-offs that the club now needed to steel itself for.

A home and away leg against Wimbledon awaited, win them and a Wembley final against either Plymouth or Portsmouth would be the prize. Win that and Accrington Stanley would find themselves in League One.

It wasn't the script that anyone had hoped for at the start of the day, but Stanley's season was still alive, and as one fan outside the fan-zone tried to cheer other crestfallen Accrington supporters up as they filtered home by explaining, 'We are Stanley, we never get to do things the easy way. Come on, we've just finished fourth! With 85 points! What a season! And we may yet be going to Wembley!'

In the immediate aftermath of being so close to promotion and just missing out, it is understandable how players and fans alike were left teary eyed and lost for words. But the very fact that this small group of players that had been deemed surplus to requirements at other clubs, that this small band of supporters who kept the club going with their love and enthusiasm had found themselves in fourth spot, despite the supposedly insurmountable odds of having to compete with much bigger clubs on much larger budgets, many of whom had found themselves a long way behind Stanley in the final placings, well it was simply remarkable.

It was Accrington Stanley, the club that wouldn't die, the club that is forever greater than the sum of its parts. Whatever lay in store for Stanley, the hard way is the only way for this small club in the shadow of so many bigger ones. Whether in League One or League Two, the bookmakers will make them favourites for relegation, just like each of the last ten seasons.

And just like each of the last ten seasons, you can't help but root for Stanley to prove them wrong.

Postscript:

It wasn't to be. Despite two valiant efforts over home and away legs against Wimbledon, Stanley were once again victims of a cruel fate when, yet again, a seemingly goal-bound Shay McCartan header in injury time somehow stayed out.

A wonder save from the Wimbledon keeper denied Shay and Accrington what would have been a deserved equaliser in the first leg; leaving players and fans alike to stare up into the dark, London night, and hope that things could turn around in the return fixture the following Wednesday.

And a Josh Windass penalty and then a fantastic strike from all of 30 yards by Piero Mingoia, which no doubt had his dad beaming with pride and jumping around in his lucky seat, looked set to steer Stanley Wembley way.

However, a bullet header from evergreen striker Adebayo Akinfenwa sent the match into extra time, and a second Wimbledon goal swung the tie in their favour. A 3-2 aggregate win sent their 1000-strong travelling fans into raptures, and their team to a playoff final against Plymouth.

For Stanley, their amazing season fell just short right at the very last. What would have been ten days looking forward to a first ever Wembley final for the club was instead replaced with emotional farewells.

Loan players such as Brad Halliday and Tarique Fosu, who had played such an important role in Accrington's year now had to leave and return to their parent clubs, their first taste of first team football over for the time being.

Defeat for Josh Windass and Matt Crooks, whose careers had looked like being over before they had even started, before their chance at Stanley, meant they would be packing their bags for a new life north of the border a little earlier than they had hoped. A career with Glasgow Rangers and Old Firm derbies against Celtic beckoned, as did the very real chance of League titles and Cup victories, even European football. Leaving as better players on the pitch, and more grounded people off it than when they first arrived, their Accrington schooling will hold them in good stead for whatever the future brings for them.

Piero Mingoia, discarded by Watford, and unwanted by all but Stanley three years ago, found himself very much back on the wanted list after more than 150 appearances for Accrington.

A move much closer to the family home to play for Cambridge United was an offer he couldn't turn down; the Wham Stadium faithful having to wave goodbye to a hero on the pitch in Piero, and a good friend and familiar face in Piero's dad in the stands.

While the future seems bright for Matt, Josh and Piero, this play-off loss means it will be a tense time for those Stanley players whose contracts expire in the summer, as the nervous wait to see if they have done enough to be offered a new deal begins. From the possibility of promotion to League One through a Wembley final one Saturday, to finding yourself unemployed the next; the realities of life as a player in League Two can be very cruel indeed. The prospect of an uncertain summer scrabbling for a new contract somewhere else, in a market place where there are far more players looking for professional contracts than there are squad places available, is not an enviable position to be in. For some, play-off disappointment may only be the start of their troubles.

As for Nick, Adam, Keil, Ash and Harry, Julie and Adam, and the rest of the Stanley faithful, disappointment will quickly turn to pride at such a great season, then hope for the next. Because for those that love Stanley this was just one chapter. Come August there will be a new one unfolding with untold potential and possibility, and maybe some new heroes to worship and sing about during another year of defying the odds and exceeding expectations. After a few weeks kicking their heels next seasons fixtures will be announced, and they will be able to start planning for away trips to Grimsby, Cheltenham and Crewe.

And with them, the magic can start all over again.

Kick-off in Dudelange.

Palestinian Under 15 team – 2003

Back row, Left to right: Imad Zaatari, Najib Abu Nahla, Khaled Kwik, Maan El-Qutub

Middle row: Moataz Ghazi Buhaisi, Mahmoud Alsiqala, Alam Shabbir, Hamada Rikhawi, Mohammed Hinnawi, Ahmed Al-Haddad, Hamada Ayedi, Mahmoud Sarsak

Front row: Mohammed Zash, Khaled Madhi, Yasser Batneeji, Mohammed Borais, Abdullah Abu Suleiman, Omar Fares Abu Shawish

Jamal's picture (photo: Jamal Zaquot).

Palestinian team football under 15

The under-15 Palestinian Football Team (photo: Jamal Zaquot).

If football shirt could talk (photo: Jamal Zaquot)

Mahmoud Sarsak, West India Quay, London (photo: Victoria Sarsak).

Stebonheath Stadium, Llanelli.

'We must be mad' – Alec and his fellow mini-bus companions in Berwick.

'Barry, do you want a chip?'

The Genquip Stadium, Port Talbot.

The Stanley Ultras in full song at Wycombe.

Promotion fever at Accrington Stanley.

Selfoss and the storm-battered trees.

The stunning home of Víkingur Olafsvik.

A storm brewing over the Racecourse Ground, Wrexham.

Gary and his sprinklers at Macclesfield.

CHAPTER 9

At the Edge of the World – UMF Víkingur Olafsvik, Iceland

IT IS ASSUMED that life on the fringes of football, for whatever reason, equals a life of obscurity. Be it through politics, finance, status or geography, those existing on the periphery of the beautiful game are expected to remain there; an eternal and forgotten footnote to the giants of the sport.

No-one, however, seems to have told Iceland this, a flag bearer for the small, isolated underdog nations of the world, whose qualification for the 2016 European Championships and subsequent heroics in France flew in the face of all perceived logic that major tournaments are the sole preserve of the traditional big guns.

Knocking out Holland, one of the world's most Iconic footballing nations and 'the best team to have never won the World Cup', and finishing above Turkey, who finished third in the 2002 edition of football's premier competition, Iceland exceeded all expectations in reaching France for Euro 2016.

Traditionally Iceland had always been a team that propped up whatever World Cup or European qualifying group they happened to be in; no surprise given their position as one of the smallest and most isolated countries in Europe.

This island of fire and ice, with its vast glaciers and towering active volcanoes, cut adrift from mainland Europe, its isolation complete among the distant and treacherous oceans of the North Atlantic, has a population of little more than 300,000. By reaching Euro 2016 it became the smallest ever country to qualify for a European Championship or a World Cup, and lined up against Cristiano Ronaldo's Portugal, Hungary, and Austria in the group stages.

It seems inconceivable that a nation whose population is only slightly greater than the population of Southampton made its way onto such a big stage. Even with Southampton FC's famed youth academy churning out top players at an alarming rate, the idea of one town producing enough home-grown players of a standard to defeat world giants such as the Netherlands, is quite staggering in its apparent impossibility. But for a nation that deals in the extremities of all that nature can throw at it; of long and vicious winters in almost total darkness, that cut off isolated communities for weeks at a time, huge storms that pound the coastline and its nation's fishermen. The threat of volcanic eruptions such as the Eldfell eruption of 1973 that flooded half the town of Heimaey with lava, or the 2010 Eyjafjallajökull event that grounded all flights either side of the Atlantic, their perceived image by mainland Europe of being a footballing insignificance seems a trivial obstacle to overcome in comparison.

By travelling through Iceland's stunning terrain and meeting its remarkable people, it becomes apparent that their perceived weaknesses as understood by the ill-informed on mainland Europe turns out to be the essence of what makes Iceland, both on and off the football pitch, so strong. The reality of living on the fringes of the world has instilled an identity and belief, a rugged determination, a perseverance and togetherness that is now translating into success at the game they love more than any other. The very act of journeying to this land of fire and ice, for someone that has never been before, gives a first tangible hint that its population, by necessity, are hardy and resourceful enough to make anything happen.

After three hours of flying the week before the 2016 European championships were due to start, the first signs of Iceland began to manifest as the plane descended beneath the clouds, and a lone rocky outcropping appeared rising up out of a fog bank that hugged the ocean. Like a breaching whale frozen in time, it's isolation in the vast expanse of sea was a precursor to the country that would follow; a warning that you were truly arriving in a land far, far from anywhere else. A snow covered volcanic peak looming menacingly on a distant headland only helped to accentuate the feeling that you had really come to the end of the line. Beyond Iceland lay the inhospitable wastes of the arctic; and a life unimaginable in the face of such rugged menace.

Leaving the airport, you couldn't help but be reminded of those early pictures sent back from the first Mars rover missions; the road from the terminal surrounded by undulating plains of black volcanic rock. Inland, snow covered mountains forged by, in geological terms at least, recent devastating volcanic eruptions loomed.

A sign outside the airport warned new drivers to the island that most road accidents in Iceland occur by people staring at the awesome views they are confronted with rather than watching the road, and to use the frequent stopping points to take it all in; easier said than done in an alien landscape of such breathtaking beauty.

While it is a place of great, rugged wonder, Iceland is also one of the most geologically unstable. With 30 active volcanic systems that have, over the past 500 years, generated one third of the global lava output; the events at Heimaey in the '70s, and the more recent eruption at Eyjafjallajökull pale in comparison to the 1783 event that led to one quarter of the population perishing, either from the initial volcano, or the devastating effects it produced. The fall-out generated a vast rancid blanket of smog that blocked out the sun, causing crops to fail, and livestock and their owners to die. Volcanologists believe a large eruption from Volcano Katla, beneath the Mýrdalsjökull icecap only 100 kilometres from the capital is imminent; though imminent on a geological scale could mean one, ten, 100 years, maybe more.

Indeed, as if to highlight that its nation's capital can be just as susceptible to the effects of the countries geological make up as anywhere else, that nowhere is safe from the realities of living on such an active island, the smell of sulphur permeates the water in shower cubicles, and the local pool is heated by subterranean hot springs; vapours drifting on the surface.

Reykjavik, the world's most northerly capital basked in a June equinox sun that remained high in the sky for more than 20 hours every day. Only for a few early morning hours did it dip just beneath the horizon to cast the city in a dusky half-light, before rising again.

And after a long, dark winter its population was making the most of every moment. Young children played in their gardens and in the parks until their eyes couldn't stay open any longer; their laughter and shouting drifting on the crisp, clear air long after ten in the evening.

Older kids played football in an old ground once used by local side Thróttur Reykjavik, their shouts echoing about a bank of crumbling terracing beneath the shadow of the National Stadium.

Many of the adult population took walks on the sea path that looked out at a bay dotted with trawlers and whale watching boats coming and going. Groups of ambling locals and tourists wandered slowly to the bustling city centre and the old town with its colourful patchwork of Scandinavian styled houses, overlooked by mountains and glaciers that cast long shadows, to search for a bar to take in a drink or two.

Beyond the bars, and on the final quay of a sprawling harbour a great trawler that worked the wild oceans off Reykjanes Ridge and the Grand Banks to the south of neighbouring Greenland, where some of the most violent and treacherous seas ever recorded by man reside, stood propped on huge wooden stilts while repairs were undertaken to its hull. Showers of sparks rained down onto the dry dock carpeted in clumps of seaweed as men dangled precariously with their welding tools.

Beyond the Whales of Iceland museum, that feature life-size models of the 20 different species of whale that could be found around the islands waters, stood as further testament, if it were needed, to Iceland's credentials as a far-flung country on the very edge of mankind's reach; the haunting whale-song drifting from the exhibitions entrance a fitting soundtrack to the nations isolation.

Reykjavik is by far the largest settlement in Iceland, and is also the traditional hub of football in the country. Nine of the 12 clubs in the Icelandic top flight are based in and around the capital, and a fair number of the clubs in the three national leagues beneath the Pepsi Deildin are too. Regional teams, with a far smaller pool of players to choose from, struggle to compete, however there are notable exceptions.

IBV Vestmannaeyjaer, from the small island of the same name and based in the town half destroyed by lava in the '70s, has been a mainstay in the top flight for a number of years. IA Akranes, some 60 kilometres from the capital are also a regular at the top table.

It is a quirk of fate that the lower down the leagues you go in Iceland, the further the distances needed to travel to matches become. Lower league teams from the capital regularly have to make the 800 kilometre round trip to Akureyri Iceland's second largest town, using winding coastal roads with severe speed restrictions that snake between lava fields, sheer cliffs, and looming mountains. Worse still for the players of second division Huginn who are based in Seydisfjordur, a small town on the far eastern coast, and as far away as you can get from the capital, who often have to contend with 1,300 kilometre, 16-hour round trips to away games. With crowds in the Pepsi Deildin averaging around the 1,000 mark, the players of Huginn know their efforts in the second division will be witnessed by a fraction of that number.

But in Iceland, where far flung towns are really no more than a couple of thousand strong in population, a crowd of a couple of hundred registers as a significant percentage of the community's support. In fact Iceland come top of the European league table for the percentage of the population regularly attending football matches, with some 7.5 per cent of the nation supporting their local teams. Compared to 3.2 per cent in England and 1.7 per cent in Germany, Iceland is more than two times ahead of the next highest nation. With the league season running from May to early October, and preceding a long, dark and bitter winter, you sense players and supporters alike do not begrudge the vast distances needed to travel; making the most of the freedom that daylight and calm weather offers them to enjoy the outdoors and a football match.

Morning in Reykjavik and a thick fog bank looms beyond the harbour mouth, ominously consuming a lone trawler as it slips out to sea. It is a reminder that even in the benign and soothing perpetual sun of early summer the weather can still threaten in such a remote spot in the North Atlantic.

As if that fact needed highlighting, a sombre display on a quay of the harbour detailing all the ships lost in the waters around Iceland did just that. That there were too many for one map of the Island, and that a display board for each decade of the last century was needed to mark the spots where each ship sank only helped to remind of the perils of life among such extremes that vast North Atlantic storms can bring.

The initial plan for a football double header over one weekend had been to watch FRAM, one of the larger and oldest Reykjavik clubs that had fallen on hard times and were playing in the second division of Icelandic football.

However, due to the National team preparing for one final Euro 2016 warm up match against Liechtenstein a day or two later, the national stadium, and FRAM's usual home was unavailable.

With the twitter feed detailing where their match was to be played sailing way above my extremely limited comprehension of Icelandic, it was back to the map and the fixtures list for a new destination – Selfoss.

Some 50 kilometres east of Reykjavik, the journey to Selfoss is one of mind boggling alien beauty. Leaving the coast and a large set of barriers that close the road should it become impassable during the winter storms behind, the road to Selfoss climbs up onto a vast, desolate plateau of volcanic mountains dotted with snow and ice drifts dug in to sheltered crevices and ravines. Between them, lava fields frozen in jagged outcroppings stretch out across vast rubbled flats like images from the first moon landings, or the sepia images Heinrich Harrer took in the 1940s of the Tibetan plateau before the Chinese invasion.

Finally, after kilometre upon kilometre of wind whipped desolate beauty among bleak, towering peaks, the plateau began to give way to a steep and winding road that snaked back down to sea level and a more verdant scene of green fields with grazing sheep and horses. Passing through another set of open barriers that marked the far end of the mountain pass, you couldn't help but feel that the inconvenience of being cut off from the capital if a heavy storm hit would be met with a measured perspective from the locals. Even with the snow chains that all car tyres in Iceland need during the winter, there is clearly an appreciation that the police don't close roads lightly, and that being stuck out on such a treacherous road in a bad storm would never be worth any meeting or social event.

The journey to Selfoss beyond the mountain pass rarely strays far from the coast. Always in the shadow of sheer ravines that mark the beginning of the countries desolate interior, nature had found a way; lush farmland thriving on this narrow sliver of land between sea and bleak mountain, even populating the lower slopes with hardy heathers and moss, the odd alpine flower seeded here by a millennia of trade winds.

Selfoss, population 6,000 sits among this small lush corridor, straddling the river Olfusa that churns on a fast current down from the glaciers, breaking over a rock-strewn river bed to create dangerous looking rapids and white-water. Feeding the fields around it, Olfusa makes Selfoss feel a million miles from Reykjavik with its greenery, sheep, and farm land. Tractors and other machinery trundle along the main drag, from which the town fans out.

Beyond Selfoss, the road heads out toward the great volcanos of Katla and Eyjafjallajökull and on a very long and winding road towards the little populated eastern coast. One lucky guess, and a right turn down a quiet street off the main drag, and the welcoming sight of the Icelandic Football Association's flag fluttering on a flag pole suggested that I had stumbled on the right place and UMF Selfoss.

Founded in 1936, UMF Selfoss would be very easy to miss. Comprising of a club house and one roofless stand that ran half the length of the pitch and left its occupants open to the elements, the club was hidden from the road by a tall stretch of trees. Those that faced pitch side and toward the sea a mile or so further on, stood bent and bleached by decades of winter storms.

As if the elements had managed to creep in to the clubhouse itself at some point, a cabinet of trophies, pennants and photographs contained one old black and white team picture as bleached as the exposed bark of the petrified trees outside. What looked like water damage had stripped most detail from it, leaving just the faintest of outlines of players, some more defined than others, lining up to pose for a team photograph. All signs of a year, their names, most of their features lost. However, it had been kept in the cabinet all the same, meaning something to someone, even now.

Outside, the oversized mini-bus of Selfoss' opponents pulled up outside, and the players of Thor Akureyri got off and attempted to stretch out the 400 kilometre plus trip from Northern Iceland along similarly winding and spectacular roads as I had taken. No easy feat, but one they seemed to achieve with ease, as before the assembled 300 spectators, Thor proceeded to control the game right from the kick-off.

Sigurdur Marino Kristjansson bossed the match in the middle of the pitch for Thor, suggesting that he had a future brighter than Iceland's second division. With the ball seemingly stuck to his feet he dribbled and passed his team into dangerous positions time and time again.

However, despite Kristjannson dominating, there was plenty more to take from the game.

Both sets of players played neat passing football, although Selfoss did so mainly on counter attacks after absorbing more Thor pressure; Selfoss looking threatening at times, but with Thor remaining in control. It was a captivating and skilful match between two sets of players who were comfortable with the ball at their feet. But despite the intrigue and ebb and flow on the pitch there was something distracting me: The Selfoss centre back, who among a sea of shouts and calls in Icelandic between the players, and songs and exclamations from the stand and from those on the grass bank on the far side of the pitch, seemed to be shouting out in what very much sounded to me like an accent from somewhere in northern England.

'Attack the ball. Pressure. Play it out wide. Come on Selfoss.'

Without a programme or a team sheet available (only the larger teams from Reykjavik bother with them) it was hard to know whether it wasn't my mind playing tricks on me – so institutionalised to hearing generic shouts from countless matches up and down the UK.

At half time and with the score at 1-0 to the visitors after a well worked free-kick just before the break, my intrigue got the better of me and I couldn't help but knock on the door to the little press box at the back of the stand to see if they could shed some light.

Selfoss defender Andrew James Pew, 36, they told me, did indeed hail from the north of England. Beginning his career in the North-West Counties League with Poulton Victoria and then Cammell Laird, the fifth tier of the non-league pyramid in England, Pew first tried his hand at a career in Iceland with Selfoss back in 2006, before coming back to play for Colwyn Bay in the Unibond League Division One North in 2008. He returned to Iceland to play for third division Arborg in 2011, before switching to fellow third tier side Hamar in 2012. In 2013 he returned to Selfoss and the second division in Iceland where he has remained ever since, becoming a virtual ever present in the team and notching up close to 90 appearances and 5 goals in the process.

He wasn't the only foreign player in the Selfoss line-up it turned out: Giordano Pantano hailed from Italy, and Jose Teodoro Tirado Garcia and Ivan Martinez Gutierrez both came from Spain, and the number 16, James Mack, had arrived from the USA.

Before I could fully wonder on and digest the fact that these players had somehow found themselves here in the second division of Icelandic football, playing in front of 288 people on a thin sliver of land sandwiched between the north Atlantic and a volatile volcanic wilderness, the second half began beneath worsening skies.

Before the break clear blue skies that had followed me across the mountain pass from Reykjavik had made the first half a warm, benign experience. But then, and as is always the possibility in Iceland, the weather changed suddenly, and clouds tumbled in from the sea, bringing with it a cold onshore wind that whipped the line of flags across the top of the stand. Given the bowed trees behind the far goal you got the sense that the wind only ever blew from one direction – the sea. It was only ever a matter of how hard.

Selfoss nearly equalised with a shot from James Mack that cannoned back off the post after a solo run, then Andrew Pew nearly added to his five goals with a powerful header that fizzed narrowly wide. The 20 or so Thor fans that had made the long trip to support their team did their best to encourage them, while one old-timer from the Selfoss contingent cracked a joke in Icelandic at the expense of a nearby visiting player that had the rest of the stand chuckling.

From the press box the muffled sounds of a commentator chattered excitedly into his microphone, his voice becoming louder and shrill whenever the hosts threatened. An old woman in the front row shouted the name of the hosts every minute or so, clapping encouragement, doing her best to will the ball in the back of the net. But despite her best efforts, and despite a Thor side that still seemed in control of the match, but had become a little leggy in the final minutes – maybe their long trip finally catching up with them – the visitors held out despite a last minute Selfoss onslaught for a deserved victory.

Channelling their inner Viking spirit, the Thor players roared at the final whistle before jogging to their small huddle of supporters to join in their celebrations, and show their appreciation at their dedication; all in that small band happy that their long trip had been rewarded with another three points that added to an already promising start to the season. Sitting in fourth place after five games, and only two points off top spot, maybe they would be able to go one better than last season, and reach the promised land of the Pepsi Deildin?

For Selfoss, defeat meant slipping to fourth bottom, and possibly a dawning realisation for some of their foreign contingent, that life in Iceland's second division could well be much tougher than they thought.

Both teams had given their all, and played some very attractive football that was a pleasure to watch. For Selfoss and Andrew Pew, sadly Thor were just that little bit better.

As the Thor players and supporters celebrated, applauding one another before waving, then steeling themselves for their five-hour drive home, the Selfoss crowd drained away, leaving their team to a huddled post-match debrief on the pitch before a deflated warm down in a strengthening wind.

As the clouds grew more menacing, the skies becoming more leaden, the journey back to Reykjavik hinted at the realities of life at the edge of the world. Climbing the steep winding road back up onto the volcanic plateau, the absence of warm sunshine made the snow speckled black mountains and the sea of jagged lava fields seem even more alien, and more than a little bit menacing beneath building ashen skies.

It was easy to imagine the perils you could face if you found yourself up here during a storm or blizzard; a steep treacherous descent the only way out, and no real respite or shelter among such awe inspiring, desolate beauty.

Stopping at a small one pump service station that consisted of little more than the pump and a small outbuilding where you could pick up a welcome coffee, there was plenty to take in and consider of the surroundings, as well as the match just witnessed, as a chill wind began to whip and howl, buffeting the huddled station and its few inhabitants.

Something had been nagging at me since Andrew's very first shout of encouragement in his broad northern counties accent. Why, and how, of all the places on earth does an Englishman find himself here, in the shadow of great volcanoes on the edge of Europe, playing Icelandic second division football? Thankfully, they were questions that managed to find answers.

'Because the football is of a very good standard, technically and tactically wise. You get a better opportunity here than you do back in England, and I'm part of a club and town where everyone is so warm and welcoming to you.'

Daniel James Hatfield, 22, from South Normanton, Derbyshire is a goalkeeper for Selfoss, and was on the bench for their match against Thor. He epitomises the spirit of adventure, and desire to make it as a footballer, that finds players from different parts of the world plying their trade in the most unlikely of places.

'I first came to Iceland in 2014 when I signed for an ambitious fourth division side called UMF Skallagrímur Borgarnes. Before then I had been playing for a few non-league teams back home like Sutton Town and Matlock Town reserves, and I'd had a few trials with some professional clubs in England, but nothing materialised.

'I then went up to Scotland in 2013,' he added 'to play for Selkirk of the Lowland League, but left after three months for a fair few reasons. After leaving Scotland I wanted a better opportunity than what I was being given in England, so I decided to look elsewhere. I knew someone who had played in Iceland a few years before and he tried to get my name known. I sent my CV out, and eventually Skallagrímur offered me a trial, and then a deal to sign for them.

'They signed me', he went on 'and another three foreign lads to really push on and get promotion, but unfortunately after a decent summer we just missed out on the play-offs, and I left the club after a really enjoyable summer spent with some great people. Wherever I've been in Iceland I've found the warmth and welcome from the fans and locals. It is a great environment to play your football.

'In February 2015, after receiving an offer from Gibraltan side FC Britannia after a successful trial there, I chose instead to go back to Iceland and a trial at Reynir Sandgerdi, who had just been relegated from the second division. They offered me a contract, but I chose to go back to Skallagrímur, as I had had such a good time there before, and I thought it might be a better stepping stone for my career.

'We started the 2015 season brightly,' he said, 'and I was playing well, but arrangements behind the scenes that had been promised weren't being delivered, which coincided with someone from an academy in Spain offering me the chance to join them for training, with the promise of some trials with clubs over there, so I took the plunge and left Iceland.

'I joined up with the academy in August, but the trials with the Spanish clubs that were meant to be already in place never materialised,' he said. 'Then I had a possible move to a club in Malaysia fall through, so I was extremely relieved when UMF Selfoss offered me a trial in December of last year!

'I went on a two-week trial, after which they offered me a one-year contract for the 2016 season, which is how I find myself here,' he went on, 'I am part of a very good set up that is aiming for promotion up into the Pepsi Deildin. I am with a group of quality and ambitious players and staff here, and am thoroughly enjoying my third summer here in Iceland.

'The football here is of a really good standard, both technically from the players, and tactically from the coaching teams. I am part of a team and a town that makes you one of them – like all my experiences around Iceland, the locals are so warm and make you feel so welcome.

'Apart from really moving levels up in my football I have also found some great friends from my travels playing abroad, and for me that is truly a blessing. Playing overseas is definitely something I'm happy to have been able to, and I feel very fortunate to have done so.'

With the season only just starting, Dan had already played a couple of games for his new club. And at only 22, time is most definitely on his side. He epitomises the universal bond that football has created, even in the most remote spots on earth; where players and supporters alike travel to the most unlikely of places for new adventures and experiences; the universal language of football transcending traditional barriers of communication, culture and religion, to create new friendships and the most unlikely of allegiances.

Even in a small, remote town in Iceland, the old-timer cracking jokes at a player's expense, the cheers and passion of the supporters, the animated gesturing from the coaches in the dug-outs; it really could be everywhere and anywhere, so universal the shared experience. Even on the edge of a volcanic plateau on an island just shy of the Arctic Circle and isolated among the wild seas of the North Atlantic, for the 90 minutes of the match, Selfoss feels like home. And to Dan, Andrew, Giordano Pantano and the other band of international brothers trying to make a living out of football, for the summer months at least, the little town of Selfoss *is* home.

However, Selfoss, despite being surrounded by spectacular scenery, and being home to just 6,000, is far from the most isolated place to live and play football, at least in Icelandic terms, as the journey to Olafsvik the following day would prove.

Situated at the end of the Snaefells peninsula a good three-hour drive from Reykjavik, and sandwiched between the wild sea and the imposing Snaefellsjokull volcano, Olafsvik, population 1,100, is the epitome of Icelandic isolation.

The westernmost settlement of its size in Europe, this little fishing village's football team won the Icelandic first division in 2015, earning them the right to play in the Pepsi Deildin for only the second time in their history. The first time, in 2013, Víkingur Olafsvik only managed three wins all season and were promptly relegated back into the lower leagues. Having already equalled that tally after only six games this time around, and sitting near the top of the table, there is real belief that a similar fate won't befall them this season. Indeed, a good 2016 and this small fishing village could even qualify for Europe; surely becoming one of, if not *the* smallest club ever to achieve such a feat.

To experience top flight football at its most remote in Iceland you have two options: IBV Vestmannaeyjar on the small island of the same name, which compromises a 35-minute ferry ride from the mainland after a 120-kilometre drive from the capital, or UMF Víkingur Olafsvik, a three hour plus drive along 190 kilometres of remote roads onto a peninsula known only for the Snaefellsjokull volcano made famous by Jules Verne in his novel *Journey to the Centre of the Earth*.

Ferry timings and the football calendar decreed that a trip to see IBV would mean it would be impossible to catch two matches over one long weekend, so Olafsvik, by default, became my destination. Once on the long journey north, you quickly begin to question why there had been any debate, so beautiful the countryside that confronts you is.

The scenery around Reykjavik and on the trip to Selfoss had been stunning, but the coastal road north quickly became a thing of breathtaking wonder. Lava formations protrude from coastal shallows like the shattered ribs of long since floundered shipwrecks, while the road snakes between the ocean with its treacherous shoreline on one side and looming mountains that are sometimes pushed further inland by ragged plains of frozen lava on the other. Plumes of vapour drift from hidden fissures; a constant reminder of the volatile geology beneath your feet. Lone wooden churches sit isolated on cliff-tops, looking out to sea; seemingly servicing no one. Small clusters of houses and cabins in the middle of nowhere huddle beneath the shadow of great, ominous peaks shrouded in cloud.

The closer to the Snæfellsnes peninsula you get, the more the scenery ramps up even more, with vast fractures appearing in the mountainside, created by millennia of spectacular waterfalls cascading down from the glaciers beyond. Now home to thousands of nesting gulls, these great chasms have become big enough for hardy adventurers to explore.

Even man-made structures try to compete with nature. The Gufuskálar radio mast near the settlement of Hellissandur is the tallest structure in western Europe. Standing at 412 metres high it rises up on a cliff top, the thick supporting cables keeping it in place against savage winter storms fan out from it like an enormous industrial maypole, some crossing the road before being anchored into the rock beyond.

All of it however is simply a prelude to the menacing Snaeffelsjokull and the mountains preceding it at the end of the peninsula. Their peaks lost in the cloud, it is easy to see how this place captivated Jules Verne enough to make it the beginning for his epic adventure, as it towers over everything. Standing in the tiny settlement of Arnarstapi, a cluster of houses and fishing boats huddled in a sheltered harbour at the foot of the volcano, the majesty and awe of it looming over you, its true size lost to the cloud, Snaefellsjokull and the mountains around it feel like a gigantic cresting wave waiting to swallow you up.

It seemed a serendipity that my travels through football had brought me to this place, as *Journey to the Centre of the Earth,* along with my grandfather's *National Geographic* maps and the tall tales he would make up for me had played a major factor in stoking my passion for mystery, adventure and travel. I had listened to the audio book of Jules Verne's classic over and over again on my little tape player in my bedroom as a child. Listening under the covers in the dark to the story of young Axel, his Uncle, professor Otto Lidenbrock, and Hans their guide as they travelled to this very spot and beyond, I would dream of adventures out there that I might one day undertake.

It seemed a happy quirk of fate that chance and timing had brought me here to this majestic, desolate spot, as the connection between the location of Víkingur Olafsvik and the story only became apparent long after flights and schedules had been arranged. No matter the circumstances, it was an awe-inspiring view, looking out at as my fictional predecessors had done.

Olafsvik lies on the northern edge of Snaefellsjokull, and can be reached from Arnarstapi by a road that creeps up and past the volcano's peak, or by a coastal road that skirts around it and is roughly 30 kilometres longer in distance.

No matter how much I wanted to try the mountain road, sitting in my small hire car and looking up at a single lane gravel track that rose steeply up and was quickly lost among the cloud, it was clear that it wouldn't be up to the gruelling task, so the coastal road through rugged lava plains it had to be.

Beautiful though it is, even by Icelandic standards Olafsvik is in the middle of nowhere. Right at the far tip of the Snaefells peninsula, there are no trains, planes, and there is only a limited bus service to Olafsvik and the shadow of Snaefellsjokull. The only way to this little fishing village is by car, or a supporters' coach from the visiting team on a match day. As the coast road that hugs a sheer rock face for dear life banks round one final time to reveal the village beyond, it is easy to imagine it regularly being cut off during the dark winter months. Indeed, the mountain pass road from Arnarstapi is regularly closed even during the summer due to the weather.

Olafsvik, even in a country of little settlements, is small. And as the treacherous road rounds one final bend it finally reveals itself – a small harbour, three trawlers idling dockside the first signs of civilisation. Old fishing nets heaped in front of a few small warehouses and workshops sit alongside the small police station by the harbour. Across the road, the village rises up steeply. A bar and a few small roadside shops give way to a bank of colourful houses beyond that nestle on a grassy shelf that looks back out at the trawlers and the grey sea lulling beyond thick harbour walls. In the distance, another peninsula of equally stunning beauty drifts in and out of view behind banks of low lying cloud.

Olafsviksvollur, the home of Víkingur Olafsvik, is perched behind the main road, next to a small indoor swimming pool, and sits in the shadow of a glacial waterfall that tumbles down the steep cliffs overlooking it, no doubt originating from the snow strewn mountains and volcano beyond. A modern church with a sharp Nordic steeple rises up from a sheer grass bank by the corner flag, and is, like the rest of the village on first inspection, deserted.

Finally, a young boy on a bicycle weaves lazily down a side street before cutting in front of the bar cum restaurant where a few of the tables inside look to be occupied. The bell of a small craft shop and museum rings as a couple of travellers exit and begin to wander towards the harbour. In an isolated country with the most northerly capital in the world, the three-plus hour drive to get to Olafsvik leaves you in no doubt that this little village is remote, and then some; its quiet streets only serving to reinforce that.

It and its football club are truly out on the fringes even of Iceland and Icelandic football, let alone anywhere else. How the football club survives, let alone thrives, with such a tiny population to support it is pretty much unfathomable to an outsider. This is after all, the club that beat Selfoss, Thor Akureyri and large Reykjavik clubs like FRAM to the first division title last season. And now it is breaking the capital's monopoly of the higher reaches of the Pepsi Deildin as well.

'How?' is a question you find yourself asking a lot in Iceland: how can those few fishing boats in the harbour face some of the most treacherous seas in the northern hemisphere? How do these tiny communities survive in such devastatingly beautiful isolation? How does a football team from a tiny fishing community at the tip of a remote peninsula take the country's top flight by storm?

Anton Jonas Illugason, a young man in his 20s and club manager of Víkingur Olafsvik talks in impeccable English as he scales a fence behind one goal to change the flags on a line of poles; handing them down so as he can connect the newer flags to the line, before hoisting them up into the brisk onshore winds.

'Even for the small time here in Iceland, we are smaller again!' He says, partly bursting with pride in his team and community, but also simply stating the realities of life here in Olfasvik. 'We have spent most of our lives in the bottom division of Icelandic football, so we are enjoying mixing it with the big boys in the Pepsi Deildin. We did it before in 2013, but we went straight back down, only winning three games all season – we aim to do better this time! Either way, we are loving every minute of it.'

So how is it possible, I asked, that a village team from a tiny community (Anton corrects me when I wrongly suggest that Olafsvik's population is around the 6,000 mark – 'No, no – 1,100, that is all') can break into the top flight of one of Europe's up and coming footballing countries?

'The same as the national team really,' Anton explains, 'Through togetherness, stability, hard work and belief. With good coaching, players improve over time, even if we only have a small number of players to choose from.

'I am the only person on the payroll here at Víkingur, other than the players.' He continues, 'Though I am here full-time there is no way I can do everything by myself. Thankfully we have 23 volunteers that do all sorts of jobs, both on match days and during the week. The players help out too in their spare time. The board consists of three people, and they don't get paid either. The town loves its team and we all work, the whole community, to make it as good as it can be.

'Two of the board work out on the fishing boats,' He points to the harbour as we walk across the pitch once flag changing is complete, 'But as soon as they are back on land they are up here working for the club.'

In the benign calm of a Sunday afternoon in June, being a resident of Olafsvik seems an idyllic life set among staggering beauty. It is hard to fathom the extremities in weather and climate that they must face year-round; the fishing boats that the club's board members crew, though peaceful now, having to battle ungodly seas way out among the North Atlantic. Those same fierce storms that would threaten the trawlers also rolling in and battering the coastline and Olafsvik, that has to cower in the darkness of winter behind the harbour walls, the roads in and out impassable. To the uninitiated, it is unimaginable. To Anton and the community of this fishing village, it is life. However as we walk across the lush grass of the Víkingur pitch that Anton lovingly tends (one of his countless jobs as the club's sole employee) he hints at the unimaginable when I comment on the wonderful state of his pitch.

'It is very hard, to keep it this nice. Two winters ago, we had a very bad winter; there was nearly a foot of ice covering the pitch, nearly the whole winter. When that happens I have to get out and try and break it up to allow a little oxygen to get to the grass so as it doesn't die. We have a roller with large spikes on it which we use, and when we broke the ice up the smell of rotting vegetation was awful. The pitch was in a very bad way, we had to put a lot of work in to bring it back.'

When I mention having been to their North Atlantic neighbours, The Faroe Islands, where nearly every pitch now has artificial grass, Anton nods.

'We are looking at artificial grass – but it is very expensive. It would make life easier but,' he shrugs, 'Until then I will have to keep praying for mild winters!'

By the time we walk up past the neat banks of blue seating that run, exposed to the elements, along three quarters of the length of the pitch in front of the clubhouse, the Olafsvik players have started to arrive. Milling about by the coffee urn, drifting in and out of the changing rooms, they all greet Anton with hearty hand shakes or bear hugs.

He explains that the squad is a mixture of full-time and part-time professionals, that it would be too expensive to have a completely full-time squad.

'We have seven foreign players in our team. It is easier to get them to come here to Olafsvik than Icelandic players from Reykjavik. They don't want to come all the way out here when there are so many clubs in and around the capital. Foreign players however, they are coming to Iceland for a new adventure, so they think "why not Olafsvik?" This year we have a Brazilian, a Pole, a Swede, three Bosnians and a Spaniard!'

When I ask him how the players find it, adapting to life in an isolated village in Iceland, far from anywhere, he shrugs.

'I tell them all the same thing: this town is what you want it to be. If you just sit in your home watching Netflix on your computer, then the town will always be strange to you. But if you get involved, if you get out and about, then you will get so much out of the experience. The town loves its football players after all.

'Our Spanish keeper is thinking of starting Spanish lessons here in the town, for anyone interested. Another one of our foreign players who has been here for a number of years has married an Icelandic girl and has a small child – so sometimes you can no longer distinguish between who is Icelandic and who is not, as they have become such a part of the community.'

As Anton searches the kitchen for a tea bag to make me a drink – 'We are a nation of coffee drinkers,' – and smiles as he opens and closes all the cupboards before finally finding a small box of tea, he explains why the foreign players are so important to a small team like Víkingur.

'We really do need the extra help. In the children's age groups we usually only have 12 or 13 players in each team, because our town is so small. So when you need a bigger squad for the adult teams (we have a women's team as well, in the first division – played four, won four!) we really do rely on recruiting further afield.'

Just as he says that a perfect case in hand presents itself when William Dominguez Da Silva, Víkingur's Brazilian import, wanders in looking for some sugar for his coffee, which is easier to come by than the tea. Sugar secured, he gives Anton a hand shake and heads back to the coffee urn.

William Dominguez, 28, began his career in his native Brazil in the youth teams of Ceilandia FC, before, at the age of 19, and like so many Brazilians before him, decided to try his luck and make a living abroad. In 2010 he signed for Spanish third division side Atletico Balearas, playing 15 times before moving to fellow third tier side Huracan Valencia. During his 27 matches for Huracan he came up against the reserve sides of La Liga giants Valencia and Real Zaragoza, but at the end of his one season with them he was on his travels again, this time to fourth division Alzira.

One season there was followed by two at fellow fourth division side Acero, but at the end of the 2014–15 season, with no new contract offers in Spain, and his aspirations of making it to the higher reaches of Spanish football seemingly over, William Dominguez had a big decision to make.

Should he return home after a five-year career in Spain, that would be the envy of any supporter without the talent to play professionally, but no doubt not what he had dreamt of as he boarded a flight to Europe five years earlier? Or should he leave the warmth and sunshine of Brazil and Spain behind and take up the offer of playing for some team called Víkingur Olafsvik, from the middle of nowhere in Iceland, and play in the second division of Icelandic football?

Thankfully for William and Víkingur, his aspirations and dreams of playing professional football didn't wither in the Spanish fourth tier, and he set off to the Snaefells peninsula in time to play 31 times for Víkingur, and become a key part in their 2015 championship winning season.

With a new contract secured, Dominguez' career had been given a new lease of life as he and his team-mates set off on the adventure of playing in the top flight.

'People like William, they come because the Icelandic league is a good standard of football,' Anton said, stirring his coffee. 'After years of developing good coaches, building indoor pitches so as people can train all year round, we are seeing big improvements and a strong league. If a team does well in our league they can qualify to play in Europe, and we aren't push-overs anymore, even there.

'One of our Pepsi Deildin sides, Stjarnan, almost qualified for the Europa League group stages a couple of years ago. They finally lost to Inter Milan at the San Siro in the final qualifying round. It will happen, an Icelandic team qualifying for the group stages of Europe, and soon I think.'

All of which makes Víkingur's story even more impressive, I suggest, in being up there among it all with only a tiny population. Anton smiles.

'We are very proud of our team and what we have achieved. The board backs the manager, they let him sign up the players he wants early so as they know they are really valued. Trust – continuity – belief.'

When I ask him if he thinks Olafsvik are a one off, if there is little chance of other teams far from the capital breaking their monopoly of the top flight he shakes his head.

'No, we have Akureyri in the north of Iceland. It is the second biggest town in the country and has two strong teams: Thor who you saw yesterday, and KA. Yes, it is far away, but KA have lots of funding. They are the Manchester City of Icelandic football and should get promoted into the top league. But any team can do it, if they really want it.' Just like the national team, I suggest.

'Just like the national team! We are all really looking forward to the Euros. Usually I pick a team to follow at all the big tournaments, and I keep forgetting that I don't need to this time around!' he laughed. 'We have a really good team. They all play abroad in bigger leagues, mostly in Scandinavia, but also in Germany, Italy, and England.

'But they are all home grown through good coaching and being given decent opportunities. You know that if you do well here there is the chance of moving to the big leagues, playing for your national team, that scouts are here watching Icelandic players, and the foreign players too.' He said, 'If anyone does well in our league the scouts take notice, because they respect the league. Even though we are confident of our team, and proud, it is still amazing that we, such a small nation has made it.'

As if to underline the achievement of Icelandic football, its nations Football Association released a flow chart detailing just how momentous their participation in the European championships of 2016 really was. The chart explains that of a population a little over 300,000 strong, 33,000 play football. Of those, 23,000 are actually registered to a club in Iceland, and of the 23,000 registered players 15,000 are male, of which 3,000 are adults. From those 3,000 adults there are only 100 full-time professional footballers either playing in Iceland or abroad for the national team manager to choose from. And yet despite that, despite its place way out at the fringes of the football universe, Iceland have achieved the seemingly unthinkable. Unthinkable at least, if you aren't Icelandic!

Before he rushes off to continue with his myriad match-day tasks Anton rustles about through some boxes until he comes back with a Víkingur scarf and hands it to me.

'So you know which team to support this afternoon!'

And with that, and a warm handshake, I leave him to it, spotting him a short while later scaling another flagpole at the entrance to the ground, his phone ringing in his back pocket, no doubt requesting more help elsewhere.

Víkingur's tiny Olafsvikurvollur ground is crammed with delightfully unique quirks and endless signs of the love that Anton, his band of volunteers, and the community at large (pardon the pun) have obviously poured into it. The only accessible point for the supporters is the bank of immaculate blue seats in front of the clubhouse that look out toward the harbour. Behind each goal curves a fence containing advertising hoardings that the odd unscrupulous soul unwilling to pay the £8 to get in, can park up and view the proceedings from the comfort of their own car.

The far side of the pitch houses the dug-outs for the substitutes and coaching staff, and, on closer inspection, the fence behind them looks out on a sheer drop of ten feet or so, down onto a road below; floodlight stanchions, and a viewing platform consisting of two shipping containers on top of one another edge out into the road. A couple of narrow, steep paths lead from small gates either side of the dug-outs for ball-boys and girls to scrabble down to chase wayward balls as they roll down toward the harbour.

Everything about Víkingur's home is neat, tidy, and well maintained; and in the shadow of its beautiful surroundings it is one of the most idyllic places to watch a game of football.

Idyllic, yes, peaceful no, as a pair of arctic terns squawk and flutter angrily from fence post to fence post behind the far goal as Anton and his helpers put out the goal posts, corner flags, and do a bit of last minute sprucing of the pitch markings.

As soon as Anton's team have retreated they noisily descend back into the goal mouth, still put out that they had been disturbed from their foraging for worms and grubs among the turf. For the terns worse was to come, as not long after the final touches had been completed pitch-side, the teams slowly jogged out to start their warm-ups.

Standing their ground as best they could the pair dove and circled around numerous balls pinging across the pitch from player to player, skittering forwards and back near the corner flag shrieking their displeasure, before retreating to the hoardings should a ball or player come too close.

Maybe they were angry at the intrusion on the pitch, after all it was theirs the rest of the week; maybe they were voicing their unhappiness at the choice of music that began blaring through the PA system.

After two games in Iceland it was turning out to be a trend, the music. Both here and at Selfoss the day before, uncensored hip-hop from the coarser end of the rap spectrum belted from the speakers, dropping the 'F' bomb and the 'N' bomb left right and centre. As they rapped about their 'bitches' and the like with a liberal peppering of swearing, the Olafsvik support began to assemble; small children and old-timers seemingly oblivious as they met up and chatted while profanity sounded out across the pitch, the harbour, the bay beyond.

As activity began to ramp up around the ground it was then that the community nature of this club really came to life. From the young girls selling tickets in the clubhouse entrance, a small cash tin and a block of tickets sat on a table in front of them, to the men and women in the little kiosks selling popcorn and coffee, it was a glorious testament to what had been achieved here, that this little cottage industry of volunteers was preparing to host a top-flight match. Old friends greeted each other warmly, some stood only in their Víkingur replica tops on a day when the weather had most definitely turned for the worse.

The clear blue skies of the days before had been replaced with a chill wind, the threat of rain from menacing dark clouds out to sea. But the folk of Olafsvik and Iceland are made of tough stuff, and while I huddled beneath my new scarf and my coat, barrel chested fishermen lounged and laughed in their short sleeves as they sipped at their coffee.

As kick-off approached, the bank of blue seats became lost beneath a throng of excited people. Behind them, more supporters congregated along the wall separating the seats from the walkway back to the clubhouse.

It really did feel like the entire town had turned up to support their team; the official crowd of 625, supplemented by a row of inhabited parked cars and a few heads peeking over the far fence meant that a great deal of the village were, indeed, here.

Though it was hard to remain focused on the here and now of an impending football game, the build-up around me slipping, unable as I was to stop myself drifting back to the scenery that dominated everything. To the first-time visitor it is a wonder that anybody can get anything done here, such is the rugged beauty that surrounds everything. It is virtually impossible to prevent one's attention slipping slack-jawed into the horizon across the bay, the mountains looming and drifting behind vast banks of snagged cloud, or up into the glacial peak beyond the village and the hidden wonder of Snaefellsjokull, it's hard to know how any visitor catches any of the match on offer.

Having seen football matches next to a ghost town decaying in a UN buffer zone in Northern Cyprus, and on a scrap of land normally used for archery high up in the Himalayas, watching a game beneath the shadow of a sub-glacial Stratovolcano is most definitely right up there as unique experiences go.

Víkingur's opponents are Fylkir from the capital, and as he strides past and across the pitch to take his place in his dug-out, the visiting boss looks very familiar. His name stands out among the names read out over the PA system while the teams line up to applaud the fans and shake hands – Hermann Hriedarsson.

Hriedarsson is one of Iceland's modern day football legends. Maybe not as well-known as his contemporary Eidur Gudjohnsson, who played for Chelsea and Barcelona among others, Hriedarsson had a career that would be the envy of any of the players lining up in front of him. Starting off with his home-town team IBV, Hermann went on to play for Crystal Palace, Brentford, Wimbledon, Ipswich, Charlton, and Portsmouth in England, before returning home to finish his playing days with the team where it all began.

And while he may hold an unenviable record of having been relegated from the Premier League in England five times, more than any other player, he also can boast 315 Premier League appearances, an FA Cup winner's medal with Portsmouth, that led to a season playing in Europe, and 89 caps for Iceland on international duty. You don't get to play that many games at that standard without being an exceptional player, and he is an example of how Icelandic football is moving forward so quickly.

In coming back to his homeland, first as a player with IBV, then manager, and now as boss of Fylkir, his knowledge and experience is helping a new generation to progress, as witnessed by his team straight from kick-off.

With Kanye and Jay-Z silenced, the match began to a chorus of 'Víkingur, Víkingur' from a section of fans who had propped themselves up on part of the steep grass bank that rounded the pitch to the village church.

However, it is Hermann's Fylkir who press and pass the ball about quickly, giving the home side no time on the ball, and little opportunity to get into the game. As the chants and shouts of encouragement ebb and flow, the Arctic terns relentless shriek at the gross inconvenience of it all drifts across the pitch.

Fylkir's early dominance nearly pays off as they are unlucky not to score on a number of occasions; a last-ditch tackle, a goal line clearance, the post saves Olafsvik from going behind.

The home side live off of scraps, the odd break-away and counter attack, but for the most part they have to dig in and try to hold on.

But despite being under the cosh almost constantly, Víkingur looked like a side that believed in themselves. The supporters didn't get on the players backs, who held out and stuck together on the pitch to weather the storm; home-grown and foreign player alike putting their bodies on the line for the club, their club.

As Anton had said, a lifetime among the lower leagues of Iceland had instilled a determination to enjoy the experience of being in the top flight, to make the most of every moment, every opportunity. And it was that determination that helped the team and the fans stick together and hold out; every counter attack met with roars of encouragement, the battling players applauded for their efforts.

At half time, despite not getting a real foothold in the match, they were still level. With the wind picking up a little, and the first spots of rain threatening to become more prolific, T-shirted Víkingur fans headed off for another coffee, satisfied with what they have seen.

As the second half began Fylkir began to run out of ideas, their game plan, though spot on in running the game, yielding no results. Víkingur, now wise to their tactics began to play themselves into the match a little more, especially after the introduction of substitute and football nomad William Dominguez, who began to add a little width and Brazilian flare to the proceedings.

With the ball moving about much faster Olafsvik found themselves with more space and time, and the match became a game of attack and counter attack as both sides went for the win.

Their determination to make the most of their opportunity in the top flight, and the opportunity that Víkingur had given them in a contract, to pay them back for believing in them where others hadn't, meant that the home side looked like they would go right to the very end.

As the clock ticked down and Fylkir, now out of ideas, looked to see the game out and take a point from their long away trip, Víkingur had no such plan. Deep into time added on at the end of the game Olafsvik attacked one last time, Dominguez pushing down the left wing before the ball found its way looping across the edge of the box. Bjorn Palsson, another substitute, took the ball on the half volley and buried it high into the top right hand corner of the net, and for the first time that afternoon the roar of delight from the home fans drowned out the agitated terns. It was a victory born out of the very essence of the club; the determination to survive, to thrive in an environment that, to the outsider at least, looks nigh on impossible. It is an essence that has instilled a necessity to never give up, to persevere, no matter what. And there it was, manifested in a last gasp win that took Víkingur joint top of the table, second only to FH on goal difference.

For a club from an isolated peninsula on the west coast of Iceland, from the westernmost settlement of its size in Europe, a summer of performances like that could see them qualify for the Europa League, or maybe with an unlikely league championship, possibly even the Champions League. Given what they have already achieved, it will not be determination or dedication that defeats them in these aims.

As the team applauded the fans, who hugged one another and whirled their scarves above their heads, horns blaring from the cars up on the bank behind one goal, you couldn't help but root for this tiny community, both on the pitch, and just in life in general.

On a football front they have exceeded all expectations to be where they are. And looking out at the sea beyond, the imposing scenery all around you couldn't help but think that this little community had also exceeded all expectations in surviving, in thriving among such staggering isolation.

As the ground began to empty, and the happy supporters slipped away back home, leaving the Arctic terns to their pitch, and the village as quiet as it had been on arrival, it was hard to imagine in the calm of June just how much this little community has to cope with during the long night of a north Atlantic winter.

Despite Anton hinting at it, the realities of a bitter, dark winter here feel that little bit beyond true comprehension. The idea of Anton trying to tend to his pitch under a foot of ice, of the board members out at sea among vicious winter storms and blizzards, this small cluster of low lying houses clinging to the edge of the world in a perpetual night, beneath deep snow and facing down wild, churning seas beyond the harbour walls; I think it truly must be seen to be believed.

However, the journey home hinted at the extremes this little community had to endure.

Leaving on the northern road, rather than retracing my steps back the way I had come, Olafsvik quickly slipped from view, and the sign post for the road that would ultimately lead all the way back to Reykjavik came into view. Anton had asked if I had come by that road when I had commented on the beauty and isolation of his home town.

When I had said I had gone right the way round the peninsula from the south he nodded, and smiled, said nothing. But as the road began to rise up and narrow as it climbed steeply up into the clouds I remembered the look on his face, that seemed to suggest that you had seen nothing yet, had no real idea of just how beautiful, just how isolated Olafsvik truly was until you had taken that road. As the road snaked its way up into a thick shroud of cloud, shadows began to rise up above the car; mountains looming among the gloom. Large patches of snow slipped away and up from the road side littered with lava rock, suggesting this mountain pass was rarely troubled by clear skies and sunshine, all the while the temperature gauge on the car plummeted down into single figures.

As visibility reduced down to a few metres among the clawing cloud, and the road ramped up on a seemingly ever steeper trajectory into the mountains, the urge to pull over and stop became ever stronger. Only there was nowhere to stop; the road the only haven from sheer drops, steep rock faces, unstable sheets of loose slag, and God knows what else that might lay beyond the chill fog. It was a spine-tingling, hair-raising experience, and one that surely only foolhardy tourists ever took.

However, from the volume of cars that came up behind me, then quickly pulled around and left me in their wake, this wasn't the case. The mountain pass cut a good 30 kilometres off the journey from Olafsvik to anywhere, and as such was the locals' road of choice, when open, rather than taking the long coastal road round.

Sat in the gloom of this alien landscape, gingerly creeping up to the summit, Snaefellsjokull hidden away to my right, I finally began to truly understand the totality of Olafsvik's isolation; the spine-tingling wonder of the Snaefells peninsula's terrifying, overwhelming beauty finally exposed in its entirety. From somewhere, just lost among the cloud beyond my windscreen, the shadows of young Axel, Professor Otto Lidenbrock, and their guide Hans crept gingerly on toward the volcano's summit and the beginning of their great journey.

Clutching the steering wheel so as little blood could reach my fingers, I shook my head at the thought that the Fylkir team coach would no doubt be following in my footsteps on its way back to the capital. Insanity I thought. But in reality, it was just life, living on the edge of the world.

The success story of the Icelandic national team, and the emergence of their domestic football league is a cautionary tale to all those that advocate a restructuring of international football. The chatter demanding a pre-qualifying tournament for the 'smaller' nations, so as to reduce the self-imposed fixture congestion of all the 'bigger' nations through the bloated and overblown Champions League and Europa League structure has long been suggested.

However, Iceland's success in qualifying for Euro 2016, then holding Portugal to a 1-1 draw in their first match, drawing with eventual group winners Hungary in the second, before beating pre-tournament dark horses Austria to finish the group above Ronaldo's Portugal, and then humiliating England with a routine 2-1 victory in the last 16 offers even further weight to the notion that all national teams must be treated the same.

Without the opportunity to test themselves against the best, the 'smaller' nations' opportunity for development is stunted, and the magic of the sport, a simple sport that captivates and unites so many, and is available to anyone with anything that looks like a ball, is diminished. Coming from a tiny principality, or a distant land of only 300,000 people should not limit your dreams and ambitions, and shouldn't mean that you are denied playing the bigger nations.

That fishermen from the Faroes, bin men from Liechtenstein, and bank clerks from Gibraltar can aspire to play against the champions of the world only serves to bind the universality of football, and its magical ability to enable anyone to dream, together. Without it the bond between the young child with a ball at their feet and Lionel Messi, Cristiano Ronaldo and the rest is lost. After all, through dedication, imagination, ingenuity, and perseverance anything can happen, even among these smaller nations; just ask Iceland – a team that used to prop up every qualifying group they were in. Ask Birkir Bjarnason, who thanks to those that went before him, became the first Icelandic footballer to score a goal at a major international tournament.

Despite coming up short against France in the quarter-finals of the Euro's, Iceland's success in humbling Cristiano Ronaldo, Austria, and England proves that a life on the fringes of football needn't mean a life of obscurity. Even from a sparsely populated land of fire and ice, and from a pool of just 100 male professional football players, great things can happen.

As they boarded their team bus in the perpetual sun of a late Reykjavik evening one week before the Euro's began, looking out the windows at their national stadium where they had just finished one last training session before their final warm-up match; the snow on the mountains beyond shimmering, the players of the Icelandic national football team dared to dream. As the coach pulled out and away, a row of faces lost in their own thoughts slipped from view, the low drone of the diesel engine fading away up into the crisp, clear air.

While confident in their own ability they couldn't have imagined, even in their wildest dreams, of the achievements they were about to etch into Icelandic folklore; Birkir Bjarnason, scorer of that first ever goal, and Kolbeinn Sigthorsson, whose goal knocked England out, sat among the sea of faces looking up at the majesty of their nation's rugged beauty, a nation no longer dismissed as a foot note in world football.

They may not have won the tournament, but winning can come in many guises, and for Anton and his fellow compatriots in Olafsvik, Selfoss, Akureyri Reykjavik and beyond, Bjarnason's goal, that last gasp victory over Austria, and progressing to the quarter finals by knocking out England was worth more than any medal ever could.

A little piece of magic from the edge of the world.

CHAPTER 10
Adriano Moke

FOOTBALL IS ONE of the true international languages that can circumvent most of the divisions that riddle our planet. Be it religious, cultural, political, or simply the barrier of communication (there are no less than 6,500 active languages in use around the globe today) football can side-step them all and create kinships, even friendships based on a mutual love for the game. A tattered old ball on a beach at a holiday resort can bring together children from different countries; children who cannot speak a single word to one another, and have them play happily for hours. After that common thread has been woven, those same children can find themselves playing poolside, or in a park, the ball no longer necessary to bind them.

Countless conversations, of a sort, start in taxis between one tired person recently disembarked from a long-haul flight and a taxi driver, who come together despite a crippling language barrier, over a pennant hanging from the rear-view mirror.

'Manchester United.' The taxi driver says, pointing to the iconic crest dangling as he weaves his way through the strange city skyline, giving his passenger the thumbs up, who in turn smiles and gives him the thumbs down, pointing to himself.

'Me, Southampton!'

'Ah, OK,' The taxi driver nods, 'Southampton,' Returning the thumbs up, before a staccato conversation of player's names and accompanying sound effects and facial gestures to register just how good the taxi driver thinks they are.

'Rooney!' A nod and a sharp intake of breath, then a big smile 'Champions!' The remainder of the taxi drive being spent in the warm glow of a bond being created so far from home. For a time all potential divisions disappear, overruled by a simple love of a game.

Across the planet, to varying degrees of profundity, people with no other common ground find a connection through football, even in the most unlikely of places. If you can find it among the rival armies in the trenches and killing fields of World War One on Christmas Day 1914, if you can find it among the unified teams of Hutu and Tutsi in Rwanda a little over 20 years on from one unleashing a brutal ethnic cleansing that claimed the lives of more than one million people from the other, then it is no great surprise that smaller connections proliferate every waking hour somewhere on earth. Football is a universal language, offering unlimited opportunities of connection, revelation, and understanding.

However sometimes, in some cases, this universal language can say so little, can fail elements of society by not using its true potential. Sometimes football shies away from issues that affect those that love it, and by doing so, by being such an important cultural focal point for so many, can assist in denying those people the strength they may need to go and find the help they require.

In England, there is a polarity between the very top of the men's and women's game.

In the women's set up England Internationals can talk openly, if they choose, about their sexuality. Casey Stoney, Arsenal captain and veteran of more than 100 caps for her country, can come out to universal admiration, safe in the knowledge that she won't be berated from the stands because of it.

To date, no male England player has dared to do the same. Why? Possibly because those running the men's strand of the sport haven't been as proactive in educating, supporting, and empowering players and fans alike as the women's game have.

Brighton and Hove Albion supporters are subjected to homophobic chanting at every game they attend because of their town's large and openly gay scene. The language used is shameful, however the FA have done nothing about it, citing that individuals caught using homophobic language will be prosecuted. But who will catch them? Stewards? And are they expected to single out one person in a thousand-strong crowd chanting, or should they throw them all out? The laws in place are a show and little more. The FA could hand out bans on away fans for repeat offenders, could punish clubs with hefty fines, but they don't.

The issue is largely swept under the carpet at the coal face of a match day, and homophobic chanting is unofficially accepted in the men's professional game. Any wonder then that gay players do not feel inclined to come out?

Within ten years homophobia could be reduced to isolated incidents of stupidity and ignorance by a tiny minority, such as racism on the terraces is today, met with banning orders and fines, if only the FA wanted it to be. But they haven't taken the lead, haven't used their governance of a game that is a religion in England to strike out against intolerance and the taboo.

Sexism and opportunities for women in the men's game, opportunities for ethnic minorities, freedom of expression for the gay community; football has the opportunity to eradicate the intolerance and to educate, to use the power of the game to better the sport and the society that loves it.

There is another strand of the taboo that football, like society, has been institutionalised by a lack of knowledge and fear into ignoring. It is a taboo that has me driving to a storm lashed and wintry Racecourse Ground, or the Glyndwr University Racecourse Stadium as it is now known, in Wrexham.

It seems ironic that in order to write about depression and how it is seen in the men's professional game in England I have had to leave the country, but none of these issues stop at the borders to Wales, Scotland, or Ireland. And despite very much being in a different country (as with Bangor in previous travels to Wales, Welsh is the language spoken first on all tannoy announcements at the Racecourse ground, and is prevalent among overheard snippets of conversations between stewards and fans alike as you wander around outside) Wrexham do in fact play in the English football pyramid, along with Swansea City and Cardiff City.

That Wrexham, and a Vanarama National League match against Woking in the fifth tier of English football, is my destination of choice is all down to one brave man that has stood up and spoken out among a sea of silence.

Again, unlike the women's game, where before and during the 2015 Women's World Cup there were a number of interviews with key England internationals talking openly about their battles with depression, how they began to cope with it and the problems that had caused it, the only stories about depression in the men's game usually arise after it is tragically too late for some poor unfortunate.

For all the inspiration and hope that Karen Carney and Fran Kirby gave to those struggling with such a debilitating illness by talking about it, deconstructing it, talking about how to combat it, in the men's game the only stories about depression mostly come after some tragic event, and the death of a famous footballer/ex-footballer/manager, or a very near miss such as when Clarke Carlisle tried to take his own life, but somehow survived.

As someone who has been affected by depression, both personally and through other family members, and is now on the other side of it, it seems baffling why people don't talk about it. The horror, incomprehension, trauma, grief, guilt and so much more that hit me like a tidal wave when my father took his own life in 2007, after decades of struggling with depression alone, locked away in his own head, and then a few short years where he was getting help, though it came too late, made me want to talk about it, though not straight away, but eventually.

In the aftermath of what happened to my father it was very easy to get sucked in to a survival mode, living in my head much like my father had done, compartmentalising feelings away so as you could just get through the day, holding back the inevitable emotions that kept pressing like a bursting dam to be let loose.

It was a basic form of survival.

It was also depression manifesting itself.

It was a tough journey to come back from, one that took more than three years of counselling. Three years confronting the eternal, impossibly contradictory feelings of complete empathy with a man that had fought so hard to keep his and our lives together, who had just run out of fight and options, with that of anger and sometimes hate at being abandoned, at being left in a world of horror and turmoil to pick up the pieces due to his act.

It was an eternal fight of contradictions – both feelings existing at the very same moment, both impossibly right – having experienced that, having had to try to flatten down my dead father's hair in one of Southampton General Hospital's crash rooms so as it looked more like him for his wife and daughter who were on their way that unspeakable day back in March 2007. The looks of sorrow, and ashen horror on the faces of the medics, policemen, nurses and doctors that hugged the walls of the room, the emotion in their eyes yet to transfer to mine, still stuck in shock and disbelief, their profound wish to be anywhere else but there writ large across them.

After that it seems incomprehensible why you wouldn't want to talk about it, to think about it, to try and help prevent such unspeakable horror from happening again to another person, another family. Yet after every tragedy of a famous footballer/ex footballer/manager taking his own life, the football community seems to blink incomprehensibly, grieve with gushing obituaries and anecdotes, comfort the close friends and relatives left behind who stand bewildered, haunted, a look I saw all too often in the mirror, then hunker down until the next one.

Any attempt to tackle the issue, as a sport and as a society that lives for that sport flickers for a short while then fades, the subject becoming taboo, too scary to confront once more.

But then, out of it all, stepped forward Adriano Moke.

The Racecourse ground, Wrexham, is one of the grander stages in the Vanarama National League, or the Conference as it has been known previously. It is a division where former mainstays of the football league, regular big hitters in the non-league scene, and a smattering of up and coming teams from the regional leagues below it all converge to create one of the most interesting competitions in the football pyramid.

Nowhere else could you find a league that can throw up fixtures between a team like Tranmere Rovers, who not so long ago were playing in the second tier of English professional football, who played in the league cup final at Wembley in front of 75,000 people, and teams like Eastleigh from the outskirts of Southampton, who at the same time were playing local league football against village teams in front of a handful of spectators. It is a glorious melting pot of the down at heel, the once great slowly turning around a period of disastrous fortune, the perennial giants of the non-league, and young upstarts shaking things up. Wrexham, it would be fair to say, are of the second category.

Like Tranmere, Wrexham's Racecourse ground must be high on the list of most keenly anticipated trips for most players, fans, and clubs of the National League, when the fixtures are generated in the summer. Like

Tranmere, Wrexham have known better times, their 10,000-capacity stadium a testament to previous endeavours and a towering venue by comparison to many in the National League.

Back in the glory days Wrexham reached the quarter finals of the European Cup Winners Cup, losing to eventual winners Anderlecht, two seasons later in 1978 they won the third division title. Numerous Welsh Cup victories that entitled them to European competition resulted in a famous win over Porto in 1984, beating them 1-0 at home before pulling off a thrilling away goals victory despite losing 3-4 in Portugal. They also lost 5-0 on aggregate to Manchester United, the eventual winners, in 1990. But by the time of that Manchester United tie, Wrexham had slipped into the fourth division, and indeed came 92nd out of 92 in 1991, only escaping relegation into the non-league by virtue of Aldershot folding and resigning from the league.

With the club apparently on its knees, the magic of the FA cup came to their rescue via an old club hero in Mickey Thomas, who in 1992, in the twilight of his career at the age of 37, scored an incredible free kick that remains vivid in the memories of all that saw it, enabling lowly Wrexham at the foot of the fourth division to knock out reigning English champions Arsenal. That it was a veteran of the great Wrexham team of the '70s that scored it, coming back to his first love after all those years made it seem all the sweeter, watching the highlights from afar on Match of the Day.

Walking about the Racecourse ground an hour or two before kick-off, when the place is only beginning to stir for the day, it is easy to imagine the ghosts of the past drifting around the stands and streets; three sides of the stadium remaining pretty much as they appeared through the fog of time, only the Mold Road stand having been replaced by a new one, after been deemed unsafe in the wake of the Bradford City fire disaster.

The Kop Stand behind the far goal that was once the largest all standing terrace in the football league and paid witness to those great European nights, to promotions and relegations, to that Mickey Thomas cup goal, has also been condemned as unsafe, and now looks on silently at the rest of the Racecourse, empty save for the odd steward milling about past rows of peeling crush barriers. Ivy, shrubs and trees claw at the Kop's corrugated roof, slowly consuming it, so much so that from the street behind the only signs that it is anything other than an over-run, derelict plot, are the towering floodlights in each corner. It is an unusual sight to see rows of toilets that once served the Kop standing prone among the wild undergrowth behind it; the roofs that covered them long since fallen in to leave them, row upon row, exposed to the elements and ruin.

The Kop is an open metaphor for Wrexham's fate in recent times, and so too the looming storm clouds that have bruised the winter skies of Britain for months, dragging it into a perennial state of gloom and impending menace.

After 87 years of membership to the football league, Wrexham were relegated into non-league in 2008. Bankruptcy and oblivion nearly followed, saved only by the fans who took over the club in 2011 and now run it with the care and devotion that only fans can. It has been a traumatic time for the supporters of this proud old club, and there is no magic wand to bring back those glory days, but at least it is theirs, and therefore in good hands, albeit not in the league that they want to be in.

But with no white knight or rich benefactor, promotion will have to come the hard way, the right way: through hard work, teamwork and talent.

Wandering through the busy Turf Hotel pub beneath the shadow of the Mold Road Stand, the very pub in which Wrexham AFC was formed way back in 1864, friends decked out in replica shirts talked animatedly about team selection, current form, which hasn't been great, and possible transfers to strengthen the squad.

Younger lads and lasses congregated around the pool table stand trying to conjure up ways of getting served at the bar. Outside the pubs main entrance, the rich smell of cooking onions from the burger van lingers in the air, the griddles smoking and drifting up into the bleak skies alongside steam from the tea urns.

It is both a typical and unique picture; typical in that these are and will be scenes played out around countless grounds up and down the country this week, and next week, and hopefully for as long as time; unique in that these Wrexham fans, having seen their club come so close to oblivion, have a certain sense of perspective that informs them that winning isn't necessarily everything, that yes they do want promotion back in to the promised land of the football league, but not by throwing money they don't have at it, and potentially putting their club in financial jeopardy once again.

Patience, though often not the preserve of the standard football fan, and prudence is the key.

Wrexham are a team and a club in rehabilitation, in rebuilding mode. It is a big club, with a big ground, and a big reputation, but it is also a club taking small, considered, nurturing steps back from where it found itself. In many ways it is the ideal club to take care of a player that has been doing much the same thing with his own life: Adriano Moke.

Adriano Moke was born in Portugal to a father that had played for Sporting Lisbon, so it was no great surprise when Adriano began to show signs of promise of his own, prompting Manchester United to sign him at the tender age of ten. Though it didn't quite work out in Manchester, he was offered the chance to join the academies of first Leeds United, then Nottingham Forest.

Whether being so far from home at such a young age, combined with the intense pressure and desire to become the only thing he ever wanted to be, a professional football player, contributed to the onset of what would become depression a few years later would be hard to determine.

Whether this illness that later virtually crippled him began to hinder him while playing youth football, the pressure preventing him from expressing himself fully, would again be hard to definitively answer. Either way Adriano found himself released from, first, Leeds, and then Nottingham Forest, ending up at the Glenn Hoddle Academy in Spain, an institution helping young lads like him get back on their feet having been let go by professional academies.

Playing in the fourth tier of Spanish football under the tutelage of Hoddle and his coaching staff gave his dreams of making it professionally a second chance, and when the offer of a contract at National League York City materialised he took it with both hands. Adriano became a central figure in the team that went on to win promotion back into the football league and win the FA Trophy at Wembley Stadium. Then, a move to Cambridge United didn't work out and he found himself out on loan at Tamworth, and then Halifax in what was is now the National League north.

He helped them win promotion via the play offs back in to the top flight of non-league football, but, when they didn't offer him a contract for the following season, Moke hit rock bottom; the years of pressure and stress on such young shoulders took their toll and Adriano found himself shutting down physically and mentally, unable to get out of bed, unable to do anything.

It was the Professional Footballers' Union, or PFA, who helped him realise that he was suffering from depression, and offered him help which he took with both hands. After a lot of hard work including counselling sessions where he could talk freely, he found himself well enough to earn a contract at part time Stockport County back in the National League North. It wasn't where he had hoped his career would take him, but it was another chance, and one that he took, impressing enough for full time Macclesfield Town of the league above to come calling.

Up until that point he had kept his diagnosis of suffering from depression a closely guarded secret, understandably afraid as a lot of people suffering from the condition are, afraid that it being common knowledge may prejudice or hinder their chances of working and having a career.

And for Adriano, in the cut throat world of men's professional football, a world where it has been virtually impossible to talk about anything taboo, opening up about having depression seemed a ludicrous notion.

All that was about to change, however, as the Macclesfield manager John Askey, who had learnt about Adriano's battle through the PFA, encouraged him not to be scared to share his story, to keep talking about it to help both himself and maybe others who were suffering in silence. And that is what Adriano has done, becoming one of the very first active professional footballers to speak out about depression, to talk about what can be done to combat it, that seeking help, talking, not being scared to confront it is a massive step forward on any road to recovery.

To prove the point, Moke helped inspire a team that the bookmakers had down for certain relegation to an incredible season where they were in the play-off spots right up until the final weeks, when injuries to a small squad finally caught up with them. But maybe more important than the final lofty league position was the response from his team-mates and supporters on the terraces to his openness about depression, both of whom gave nothing but support and empathy, shattering the taboo at least in one small part of Cheshire. Adriano's recovery and openness, and everyone's reaction to it have been a small, non-league success story.

It remains to be seen if any Premier league player would be so brave; if the clubs, the intense media spotlight, crowds in excess of 50-60,000 would be so kind and nurturing. One would like to think so, one can only hope so.

However, the fact that no player has come forward, just as no player has come out as gay suggests that, in their eyes at least, now is still not the right time.

The 21st century is not the world that my father grew up in, where, in the '60s and '70s, you dealt with what would later be known as depression by suppressing it all, blocking it out in whatever way you could – tough it out. Be a man. We can only wait and see.

As Adriano's recovery continued, so did his career, and after a great season at Macclesfield one of the National League's big names, Wrexham came in for him.

The Racecourse isn't quite Old Trafford, Manchester, but, for a young man who has been through so much, the 10,000 capacity (that figure not including the derelict kop) home of the Red Dragons is an impressive place to play your football and wouldn't look out of place in the Championship. It is a club, despite having to live within its means as a fan run entity that has promotion as its aim, so its recent league form of three straight defeats makes the storm clouds gathering above an apt backdrop.

Today's match against non-league top flight mainstays Woking is a must win, to get their season and their march up into the play-off spots back on track.

Beneath the Glyndwr University Stand, the wind swirls and kicks up little dust storms about the feet of those queuing for a cup of tea or the like to try and keep them warm. The sounds of music playing over the tannoy system drifting as a particularly strong gust rattles the rows of seats above our heads, as if to remind us of the ice cold welcome that awaits our steep trek up and out of the gloom of the bowels of the Racecourse ground, blinking into the stark skies above. Beyond the lifeless Kop a storm is brewing, and fans brace themselves, shuffling deeper into their coats, waiting for the game to begin.

Considering an earlier downpour that left the pitch heavy at best, odd patches of standing water at worst, and a buffeting wind, both Wrexham and Woking began to play some very attractive football, Kieran Murtagh of Woking scoring a belter in front of the empty Kop before Wrexham's Dominic Vose curling in an exquisite free-kick to level matters.

It is captivating stuff that helps to stifle that disappointment of Adriano being on the bench, and at half time, as the storm that had been threatening all afternoon finally hit, black clouds rolling menacingly over the dusky Kop trailing veils of torrential rain, I watched Moke warming up on the pitch, bobble hat pulled down to keep out the weather. To see him laughing with fellow sub and ex-Accrington Stanley hero James Gray, to see them pinging balls across the ever-deteriorating pitch to one another, was great to see, though I hoped that it wouldn't be the sum total of his efforts that afternoon.

In the second half, as the conditions worsened so did Wrexham's fortunes. A well worked move by Woking's tricky winger John Goddard enabled Joe Quigley to tap home from close range to send the 100 or so Woking fans who had made the long trip into raptures. As the rumbling of discontent began to gather in the stands, Wrexham brought on first James Gray, and then with ten minutes to go, Adriano Moke.

Wrexham pressed for an equaliser, but a bad kick out by Wrexham keeper, Rhys Taylor, gifted Bruno Andrade with the killer goal after a mazy run past two defenders. With that, a number of the cold, wet, and now thoroughly fed up Wrexham fans gave up on the day and made for the stairs back down in to the bowels of the stands and the exit, the storm among the darkening skies above getting ever stronger, rain drumming furiously on the corrugated iron roofs above.

But in those final minutes, and for the home fans the excruciating five minutes of added time after it, while everything else around him seemed to be falling apart, there was one person still encouraging and trying to drive the ball forward.

Adriano Moke, it would appear, plays football much the same way as he deals with and talks about depression: with passion, tremendous effort, and relentless energy. Like a player given a second chance at life, Moke took those mostly meaningless minutes on the pitch in a game that had already been lost, and did the very best he could with them.

Not letting heads drop around him, he retrieved long Woking clearances and drove the ball forward trying to find the pass that could lead to what would have been only a consolation goal.

It was a performance that only someone who thought they might never play again, might never be able to do anything ever again, could give. It was a performance by someone who was relishing every single second he got out on the pitch, and who was not prepared to let a single one go to waste. That it was his 25th appearance of the season, a niggling injury being the reason why he didn't start, suggests that he had played a key role in Wrexham's season. Though it would be a season that would ultimately fall short in the goal of the play-offs and promotion, it was not for a lack of trying and passion on Adriano's part.

For Adriano, it was another season reclaimed from the jaws of depression. No matter that the team didn't quite reach its goal, it was a season of opportunity and freedom to do the one thing he loved to do, as witnessed during the dying moments of a lost match one cold winter's day.

And if ever the ultimate is achieved, and a return to the promised land of the football league is secured, then you can be sure that Adriano Moke will take that opportunity with both hands as well.

It is hard to think of anyone else that would deserve it more.

CHAPTER 11

Sarah Wiltshire and the Women's Super League

SARAH WILTSHIRE IS the sort of player that first made you fall in love with football as a child. Her flair and imagination out on the pitch; the thrill of the ball seemingly stuck to her feet, weaving past players before finding a defence splitting pass or the corner of the goal, is reminiscent of that player, or players that first captivated you, and helped get football under your skin for life. The skill and vision that these players with natural flair and ability possess often elevates a simple sport into art, and makes the act of passing, dribbling, shooting sing.

The first time I ever heard of Sarah was during a Women's World Cup Qualifier at the Cardiff City Stadium on a rainy night in 2014. Playing for Wales against an England side one win away from qualifying for the finals in Canada and a summer of thrills, heartache and a third-place finish that would cement them as the second most successful England side of all time, it was Sarah that stood out in a relatively one-sided match. Despite Wales being outgunned, and succumbing to a 4-0 defeat, it was Sarah's display that lingered long into the night and beyond.

Picking the ball up in a seemingly impossibly crowded midfield, she found herself space with some neat footwork, then drove at the English defence, finding neat passes to colleagues to set up attacks, tackling back to retrieve the ball before starting all over again. In a side under the cosh from a dominant England team, her vision and determination offered a welcome respite to Wales' defence, and a little hope where there appeared to be precious little.

It was spellbinding stuff and had me on the edge of my seat. It reminded me of watching Kevin Keegan and Mick Channon, young Steve Moran and Danny Wallace in the Southampton teams of the '80s, whose displays in the English First division would light up the terraces of The Dell, and send children like me home to try and repeat their feats in the back garden in replica kits. Sarah, like those memories from The Dell, lifted the soul and inspired my inner child to pick up a ball and to dream.

Only a few thousand spectators sat watching Sarah's creativity in the Cardiff City Stadium beneath a deluge from the heavens that night. It didn't matter one bit. And that is the point.

This elemental magic that inspires and lifts the soul never has been, and never will be the sole preserve of what is generally perceived to be the games' elite. If it was then it could not have flourished into the most popular sport on earth; in deed it would have withered and died long ago.

For every Messi and Ronaldo being beamed into millions of televisions across the world, there are countless others at every level of the game captivating supporters, no matter how few, no matter the absence of mainstream media; losing themselves in a simple expression of love and passion for the sport, players like Sarah. In a world that is constantly changing it is the fundamental mainstay in a game that now spans three centuries.

As a child, for every trip to The Dell there were as many visits to Victoria Park with my grandfather, the then home of Southern League Salisbury. There, semi-professional players like Kevin Dawtry would enthral with wicked free-kicks and incisive passes, often resulting in a goal that would herald the hooting of car horns from those spectators sat in their cars beneath a row of trees beyond one set of goalposts. The only difference between Southampton and Salisbury that I could see as a young boy was status and the size of the crowd and ground.

No matter that First Division Southampton played in front of crowds of 20,000, and Southern League Salisbury turned out to 200; the drama out on the pitch was just as enthralling, and the experience of getting caught up with the crowd, no matter the size, as intoxicating. Yes, the standard was different, but the endeavour was not, with two teams playing out the most important game of the weekend, to them at least, with full blooded dedication. To a young boy that loved football, there was no fundamental difference between the experience of First Division and Southern League football.

The way in which both levels captured the imagination and focus for a full 90 minutes meant that both Kevins, Keegan and Dawtry were held with the same level of awe and reverence to me; both programmes from Salisbury and Southampton collected and kept safe with the same care and attention due to the information on both clubs that were contained within. It did not matter that Dawtry, a former Southampton apprentice who made only one league cup substitute appearance for the first team before a short spell at Crystal Palace, followed by a run in Bournemouth's first team in Division Four before going semi-pro, was not a full-time First Division player. All that mattered was those 90 minutes on a Saturday, when if at Victoria Park it was Kevin Dawtry that I wanted to grow up to be, just as much as I did Kevin Keegan if I had been at The Dell; playing out their moves in the local park or my grandparents back garden with equal passion.

It is definitely a fan thing, that maybe even players don't quite understand, who probably hold their careers up in a more critical light.

Which is perhaps why a look of confusion and a little amusement crept across Kevin Dawtry's face when, during one hot, humid, mosquito ridden evening at a long lost '80s pre-season training session that he was running for a local side, I arrived on my bike to ask for an autograph in one of my Salisbury programmes.

I still have it. It still means something all these years later because of the enjoyment I gained from watching him play.

It is why I still have four page programmes from my local village team, Blackfield & Langley, who played in the Hampshire League on a roped off park pitch. The names of George Kerr and Colin Burdle may not have travelled far beyond The Waterside; a stretch of land near Southampton in the industrial shadow of a vast oil refinery, but their creative displays for Blackfield warranted me to highlight their names in those primitive programmes, so as to make permanent their hero status. It was no matter that they worked at the oil refinery, or in a factory or warehouse on a nearby industrial estate; on a Saturday, on a roped off pitch they could become something else with their trickery and guile, with a well taken goal.

In more recent times *Sky Sports'* flagship show, *Soccer* AM, used to celebrate the seemingly endless array of tricks and wonder goals that a fourth division player called Lee Trundle used to score for Swansea.

Season after season he would be celebrated without any comment as to why he was still playing in the fourth division. Indeed, when a move to third division Bristol City arrived, it didn't quite work out for him and he returned to Swansea to see out the remainder of his professional career, ironically just before their meteoric rise up into the Premier League, where his goals and skill would have been broadcast worldwide.

Just because it isn't shown on television doesn't mean it didn't happen. For a generation of Swansea fans, Lee Trundle's exploits rank as highly as their rise to the top of the game, a League Cup win, and European football the following season.

Ironically, after a few years out of the game (officially retiring after a short spell with now defunct Neath in the Welsh premier League) Trundle recently returned to the pitch for Welsh League Division Two Llanelli, and in true magical Lee Trundle style scored an injury time hat-trick only moments after coming on for his debut!

For me memories of goals by George Kerr and Kevin Dawtry, and sitting with Grandad in Salisbury's ramshackle Victoria Park, linger alongside some of the sports' biggest moments. Status is nothing, expression is everything, because it is the true soul of football, fuelling everything that is great about it.

However, there is that chip on every lower league or non-league fans shoulder, that their hero deserves more credit than they get, that their teams attractive style of play deserves more people watching them.

Players and teams like Sarah Wiltshire and her Yeovil Town ladies side.

Sarah and Yeovil Town Ladies are hardly on the extreme fringes of football, sitting top of Women's Super League Two by the time Sarah and I arrange a date to meet up in July 2016. At the half way mark in the season they are three points clear and starting to dream of promotion to the very top of the Women's game in England, where they would play match after match against those same England players from that World Cup Qualifier.

However, given the exposure that the Women's game is afforded by mainstream media outlets, it can feel to its supporters that Sarah's talents and the talents of countless other players in the Women's game are being given short shrift.

It is great that the BBC have a show, albeit broadcast late at night, on the WSL and Women's football. They also show England home internationals and the FA Cup final. BT Sport offer WSL matches live, which is a massive step forwards. However, SKY, ITV, and nearly every mainstream broadsheet and tabloid newspaper gives only a passing mention to the WSL and the national team; the exception being when England finished third in the 2015 World Cup.

To the supporters of the WSL and Women's football in general it is both a small bone of contention, and a unifying bond that makes the WSL a very special league. Being cut off from the exposure that the men's game receives has been as much a blessing as it has a hindrance. It has enabled the league to forge its own identity, its own standards for it is predominantly, but by no means exclusively, female dominated followers.

The bond between club, player, and supporter means that the young boys and girls on the side lines have direct access to their heroines on the pitch, who always stop after a match to sign as many autographs as is needed, and pose for as many pictures as required, chatting to the next generation of players with a care and interest that guarantees both respect and devotion. Even after their Continental Cup final defeat in 2014, an Arsenal Ladies side, full of internationals and featuring one of the best players the Women's game has ever produced in Kelly Smith, put their disappointment to one side to thank their supporters and spend as long as it took to sign the programme, shirt, flag, of every fan that wanted them signed.

Standards are different on the pitch as well as off it, where the histrionics that can sometimes blight the men's game remain largely absent; allowing the neat passing style that most WSL teams use to flourish.

It is a league of skill, technical proficiency, flair, and excitement that has, year on year more supporters buying in to its spirit of fair play on and off the pitch. In fact, since the Lionesses success in Canada at the 2015 World Cup WSL 1 attendances have rocketed by an average of 40 per cent, and in WSL 2 Sarah's Yeovil Town have been averaging crowds at Huish Park around the 700 mark.

However, for the Continental Cup match where Sarah and I arrange to meet, Yeovil are playing at nearby Sherborne Town's picturesque Jones Stadium ground, as the Huish Park pitch is being re-laid. It is a home from home for Yeovil Town ladies, as it is where they used to play their WSL matches before this season.

On a warm and sunny Sunday afternoon in July, the meandering back roads through Dorset and Somerset that lead to Sherborne weave through quaint villages and sprawling farmland that ride the rolling hillside. Ornate gateways to stately homes and thatched cottages make for a welcome change to the usual motorway drudgery of football trips; as refreshing as the WSL that I am about to watch.

The Jones Stadium, home of Tool Station Western League side Sherborne Town, sits quietly among a patchwork sea of fields and tree topped rolling hillside. The faint and oddly rich scent of manure fertilising some unseen, distant field of crops immediately made the place seem familiar, welcoming, as that smell had been the backdrop to countless summers at my Grandparents house in a remote village in nearby Wiltshire.

The distant toil of farm machinery glistening in the sun, weaving across fields on the far side of the valley a constant companion while studying yellowing newspaper clippings from the local paper containing Salisbury's Southern League fixtures for seasons now long gone.

The cool, empty clubhouse felt like so many other non-league bars up and down the country.

The walls lovingly decorated in team photographs that drifted from colour into faded black and white images dating back to before the First World War, pinned notices on cork notice boards fluttered gently on the warm breeze drifting in through the open door; pre-season training session dates and club socials trying to attract attention.

On the far wall, near the door to the toilets, hung a framed shirt that, on closer inspection had nothing to do with Sherborne Town or Yeovil, but was in fact the shirt of the Pohnpei National team, a tiny island in the Pacific that was a part of the Federated States of Micronesia. A laminated sheet beneath the shirt explained that the Pohnpei National Team was being coached by a man from Bristol, charged with creating a football league for the Island's players, as well as a national team to represent them – all with the ultimate goal of gaining FIFA recognition.

Paul Watson, brother of the comedian Mark Watson, sent requests to as many clubs as he could think of asking for any unwanted old shirts, in order to kit out these new teams in this new far-flung Micronesian league. From that original request, only three clubs responded with kit: Norwich City, Yeovil Town, and Western League Sherborne Town, which is why, above the text, sat a photograph of the Pohnpei Premier League side SDA FC lined up proudly wearing the black and white stripes of Sherborne Town.

It is a worthy tribute to the soul of football that exists beneath the bright lights at the very top of the game. It is this happiness to reach out to far flung friends through football that makes the game so special. It is also a fitting venue, beneath the Pohnpei National Team shirt, and among 100 plus years of photographic Western League history, to meet one of the games true unsung heroes; an inspirational character and a role model for the true spirit of football.

To be Sarah Wiltshire takes dedication, passion, determination, and a love for the game that reaches deep into every fibre of your being. Because being a WSL 2 player is not easy, and there are many sacrifices that you need to make. As we sit down to talk that becomes very apparent.

Off the pitch, Sarah appeared nothing like the tenacious player she transformed into on it.

Quietly spoken, she cuts a slight figure in her Yeovil Town training gear, and this seemed completely at odds with the player I had seen taking on some of the games physical and metaphorical giants out on the pitch. But as with all things beyond the bright lights of the game's elite; size counts for nothing.

Sarah began her senior career with hometown club Watford, before moving to Yeovil when WSL 2 was formed in 2014. And despite being the second tier of the Women's game, it is a hand to mouth existence for Sarah, and for many of the league's players.

'I am on a part-time contract here. You only ever really get one year contracts in WSL 2, that run from February to October, so sometimes it can be hard,' she says. 'I also work part-time at a primary school where I do some coaching during the afternoons, which helps. My fiancée works full time in banking, so between the two of us we make ends meet.

'Some of the girls in the team have to work full-time to supplement their income, fitting in training and games around it, which is tough. You have to sacrifice an awful lot to make it work. Spare time is a luxury! At least a lot of the girls live a little nearer to Yeovil than I do, which makes things a bit easier in getting from work to training. I drive up to training on a Thursday from home, which can be a long and lonely journey every week. Sometimes I stay over with one of the girls that lives locally, otherwise it is a very long and tiring day where you don't get home until very late.

'We don't earn very much from playing.' She continues, 'It is passion and a love of the game that fuels you, not money, because we do have to give up a lot of our time in order to play for Yeovil in WSL 2.'

Unlike many of the semi-professional leagues in the Men's game that are dissected into regional competitions, WSL 2 is a national league that stretches from Yeovil in Somerset all the way to Durham in Northumberland, which necessitates overnight stays for the further flung fixtures, and a juggling of working schedules for many.

'We have to stay over for the matches against Everton, Sheffield, and Durham. We came back from Durham only last week. I met up with the coach in the midlands, so as I didn't need to drive all the way to Yeovil first. But even then, it was a good five hours on the coach. I dread to think how long it took from Yeovil!'

Sarah's sparkling performances for Wales and Yeovil in 2014 resulted in interest from the big WSL 1 clubs for the following season, and at the start of 2015 she signed for Manchester City.

'It was a dream come true, to become a full-time professional football player. But things didn't work out. It was a long way from home and I got homesick. I missed my fiancée. I was lonely,

Most of the girls lived locally,' she went on, 'so they would come in to training, then head on home. I found myself on my own by 1pm every day, and there were only so many times you could walk around the shops, or go out for a coffee.

'I think by not being happy and being homesick, affected my performances. I wasn't getting picked and I wasn't playing, which only made things worse.

'Yes, it was full-time, and my fiancée did offer to come up with me,' She said. 'He could have managed a transfer through his work. But the contract I had was only for a year. I missed home, I had to weigh everything up, and the decision I made was that it wasn't worth it; to be a full-time professional that wasn't playing. All I have ever wanted to do was to play football. And our careers are short, I didn't want to waste any time.

'What made matters worse was that I knew what I had left behind at Yeovil: a lovely team with great characters, great coaching staff and people behind the scenes. It was,' she said 'and is a progressive, family club; we are a family in the dressing room, and out in the stands, and I was very happy when I was given the opportunity to move back here. This is my third year here now, and I am very happy, we are doing well in WSL 2.'

Returning to Yeovil has brought the best out of Sarah once more, and, as we sat chatting and looking at photographs of her injured ankle that ruled her out of that day's cup match against Notts County, her season's statistics of nine goals from 11 matches spoke volumes about her wellbeing. In fact one week later and those statistics rose to 11 goals in 12 matches!

When I mentioned being a Southampton fan, and that Matt Le Tissier had stayed put where he was happy, and had achieved great things in his career despite it, the analogy between two similarly creative players felt apt. With Yeovil three points clear at the top of the table at half way, I suggested that Sarah could yet find herself right at the top of the game without compromising on her happiness.

She smiled, daring to dream for only a second before the pragmatic nature in all football players sprang into action, knowing that a job half done was nothing.

'If we go up it will be great. To get to play right at the top of the game, like I hoped I would with Man City, would be amazing. It would be a massive challenge for a small club like Yeovil in WSL 1, playing against proven international players every week.' She said, 'But it's what we want, all the players. We want that challenge.

'And if we did it with Yeovil, with a team of great people, where I feel happy and comfortable, where everyone is so friendly, that would make it even more special. It is a small, family club, where you genuinely feel a part of it, whether a player or a fan. It is a club that cares about you, wants to look after you.'

WSL 1 is not the end of her ambitions either.

'I really would love to get back playing for Wales again.'

That first match that I saw her play against England in 2014 turned out to be one of her last for the national team. Shortly after the World Cup campaign had been completed the coach was replaced by another who clearly didn't rate Sarah, and stopped selecting her. At the same time as I had been spellbound by her performance that night, spellbound enough to want to write about her, her future Wales National Team coach had been a pundit for the BBC, and had been far from complimentary about Sarah's contribution to the game.

'She just doesn't rate me,' Sarah said with a shrug when she saw the confusion on my face.

'Football is a game of opinions.'

When I mentioned that surely her goals to games ratio this season couldn't be ignored, that in a Wales squad made up equally of WSL 1 and 2 players, her performances at the top of the league couldn't be overlooked she shook her head, paused.

'I really do miss it. Playing that night at the Cardiff City Stadium is one of the highlights of my career so far. It is one of the best grounds I have ever played at.'

When I press her for other highlights, it is clear that Sarah really does appreciate and cherish everything that football has given her, and everything she has achieved through it.

'One of the best moments ever was playing at the under-17 World Cup in New Zealand when I was 16. I was playing for England back then. We played in an amazing ground over there. I can't remember the name, but it was an amazing experience. It is the best ground I have ever played at. It was enormous. Empty, but enormous!' She said and smiled in her typically humble, self-depreciating way.

Her humility came into sharp focus after a little research, where it became apparent that the stadium she was talking about was Auckland's North Harbour Stadium, and one of the two matches she played there was a third-place play-off match against a German side that included some of the best players currently playing in the Women's game in Alexandra Popp and Dzsenifer Marozsan.

Neither did she mention that she had played in a World Cup semi-final against North Korea with some of England's current senior side in Lucy Bronze, Jordan Nobbs, Danielle Carter, and Isobel Christiansen.

That semi-final match at the QE II stadium, Christchurch, in the winter of 2008 would be one of the last major matches played there before it was completely destroyed by the devastating earthquake of 2011 that claimed 185 lives.

That she didn't mention these achievements serves to underline her humble attitude, but it also hints at her passion for the sport, where her focus is always on the next game, and her next opportunity to express herself out on the pitch; the time for reflection on past experiences left for another time a long way down the line.

It is the attitude you would maybe expect of someone who plays with such flair and imagination, I offered, who has never lost that fundamental joy of expression first discovered running about as a young child in the local park; who keeps it in her game even now, much to the pleasure of those that watch her (Welsh National Team coach apart).

She smiled, laughed, then shrugged her shoulders.

'People do say that I play like that, like a kid. I'm never sure if it is meant as a compliment or not!'

I tell her it is a compliment. It is great to see; that basic elemental expression that a ball at your feet can offer.

'I do think that sometimes players can get that childlike joy coached out of them. Which is a shame. It is only passion after all.'

It is clear that passion is one thing that Sarah will never lack.

'I just love football. I love playing it, I love watching it. I am just as happy watching Tottenham in the Premier League as I am watching kids in the park. My fiancée does some coaching with Cambridge United's Women's team, and sometimes we go over there to see the men's side play in League Two. I love the atmosphere of the lower leagues. We always stand near all the noisy fans. It's great.'

She is equally passionate about the Women's Super League, and can only see great things for it.

'The standard is getting better and better all the time. Attendances are rising across the board, teams are turning professional. If things keep going like this then before long the entire league will be full-time, probably after I've retired though!' But at only 25, Sarah has a long time left in the game, and the highest levels of it at that, I suggest.

'I just want to play as much as I can, achieve as much as I can. I want to enjoy it all. There are only 20 or so matches in a WSL season, so I don't want to waste any time. That's why I came back from Man City – I just want to play, I want that more than I want to be a full-time professional.

'In the WSL off season I go on loan to a team in the Women's Premier League. Below the WSL all the Women's leagues are winter leagues, which is a bit strange really as promoted teams to the WSL, like Brighton who won the league in May, then have to wait until the following March for the next WSL season to begin. It is a long time to wait, and a lot of momentum can be lost.'

Ironically only a week or two after our chat the WSL announced that it would be moving to a winter league from 2017, to move in line with the other Women's leagues in Europe. Another positive step in the evolution of the Women's game, a step that should offer even more opportunities to the next generation of players; opportunities that Sarah is forever thankful to have experienced herself.

'Football has given me so much, so many wonderful opportunities. I have travelled to the other side of the world, I have played in big stadiums, against some of the World's best players. I have played international football, and I play in the WSL in front of passionate supporters and for a great club'.

As she speaks Steve Allinson, Chairman of Yeovil Town Ladies stops by to say hello to her, to see how the injury is coming along. Steve had been on the board of Yeovil's men's team for many years, but had become a little disillusioned with it all. Thankfully for him a trip to see the Women's team rejuvenated him, and inspired him to get involved once more.

'I am really proud of this club, of the girls in what they have achieved in WSL. We are a part-time outfit having to try and compete against some sides that are full-time and on far greater budgets than ours. To be top of the league at the half way stage is a great accomplishment.'

It was clear that Steve was excited about the prospect of promotion to WSL 1, but also more than a little nervous.

'The girls deserve, for all their hard work and dedication, to get the chance to compete against the very best. However,' He continues, 'It would be a massive challenge. We are a small club, and we would be up against sides like Chelsea and Manchester City whose playing budgets are massive by comparison. A lot of clubs in WSL 1 can't compete with them,' He went on 'let alone the promoted sides from WSL 2 who are really struggling this year. I don't think last year's WSL 2 runners-up; Doncaster Belles have even won a game yet this year in the higher league.

'I have a model in place in case we go up, to give us the best chance, if it happens,' he said, 'But this club will always be a family club. That is the most important thing. It is for the fans, and for the girls that play for the club. I really don't care what league we play in as long as both are happy.

'After a couple of seasons here at Sherborne, we now play our home games at Huish Park,' he said 'which means more of the town can come and see the girls play. And with us getting crowds around the 700 mark now, we are the best supported club in WSL 2, which bodes well if we did go up'.

'Playing at Huish is great', Sarah added 'the pitch is immense, and we all love playing in front of the bigger crowds. They really get behind us.'

But for now, while the Huish Park pitch is being re-laid, it is a welcome return to Sherborne, seven miles east of Yeovil. As Sarah has to head off to see the physio, and Steve continued on his rounds saying hello to all and sundry, there is enough time before kick-off to enjoy a walk around the sun-drenched Jones Stadium.

Beyond the small stand that sits atop a grassy slope, rising up sharply just beyond the edge of the pitch, sits an old park bench made up of fading green metal slats. Sitting just off the hard standing and among a sea of wild grasses left well alone during the off season, it looks as idyllic a spot to take in the sun and some football; looking out as it does on the pitch and the rolling hills of Somerset beyond.

The setting may be quaint, but the football on offer once both sets of players had finished their warm-ups was anything but.

One of the biggest misconceptions about the women's game is that it lacks the intensity and ability of the men's game. In truth, the only thing it lacks is the histrionics and play acting that can blight top flight matches in the men's league.

Notts County's WSL 1 side contains England internationals that shone on the biggest stage during the 2015 World Cup. Captain Laura Bassett, whose last gasp own goal during the World Cup semi-final was swiftly forgotten with a heroic display of courage against Germany in the third-place play-off, once again ran the show for County. Her composure on the ball setting up attack after attack that a young and injury hit Yeovil side struggled to contain.

Up front Ellen White, another England regular looked a different class in her hold up play and her movement, while Jess Clarke dominated possession and the wings with scintillating runs and defence splitting passes.

It was no surprise when Ellen White converted twice in the early stages of the first half, the second a sublime header that any centre forward would cherish.

With Sarah on the side-lines, along with influential skipper Ellie Curson and a couple of other first team regulars, Notts County's dominance didn't really offer a true reflection of the gap between Yeovil and WSL 1.

However, it did show the levels of skill, fitness, experience, and tactical know-how that would need to be bridged if cup match became league fixture the following season. With the unwavering support from Yeovil's young fans in the stands, at least their enthusiasm could be guaranteed to be first class, regardless of the league their team found itself in.

As the game wound down after a lengthy injury delay to Yeovil's Ellis Hillman, and a routine 3–1 win for the visitors was confirmed, there was much to feel positive about. For County, they were one step closer to the cup that eluded them in the final the year before. For Yeovil, some of their younger players had been given a taste of playing against the very best. And for the spectators they had been treated to some impressive performances from some of England's Lionesses; a sight that would hopefully become common occurrence the following season.

If Yeovil do make it, WSL 1 will be enhanced by having a player of Sarah Wiltshire's calibre in it, and a club that sees its true purpose with such refreshing clarity and perspective.

Either way, the future is bright for both.

The slogans used by the Women's game to underline its importance, such as 'We Can Play', 'She Who Dares', and most tellingly 'A League of Our Own', speak volumes of the institutionalised prejudice that generations of Women in football have had to endure. These mantras are displayed in programmes, across websites, on pitch-side hoardings, to help steel and educate the young players of the future; emboldening them to reach out and dream even further than this current generation of players.

In some respect the decades' long closed-door policy to women in the boardroom, management offices, and coaching positions by the professional men's game has led to this current and exciting set-up of the Women's Super League.

Untold years of unsung work, building the Women's game in an environment of disinterest and apathy by football's ruling elites, has resulted in the creation of a league with strong principles of fair play and inclusiveness, that espouses many of the values now seemingly lost at the pinnacle of the Men's game.

Respect isn't just a slogan in the WSL, it is a simple fact. Respect between players on opposing sides means there is no gamesmanship, no attempts to get players sent off or booked, no play acting. Respect on the terraces means there is no segregation, and fans of competing sides can cheer their teams on next to one another.

The WSL is a league that supporters of Premier League clubs, old enough to remember a time before it, will recognise, or current supporters of lower league and non-league clubs will empathise with. It is a league of vibrant play, skill, and endeavour out on the pitch, where player and fan mingle as one before and after the 90 minutes. It is a league of clubs by a community, for that community; where all are valued, all are welcome to contribute. It is a thing to be very proud of, and deserves more media coverage, more respect.

It may well still be at the fringes of football, in the UK at least, but what the women's game has done, in creating this league of their own, is to offer an environment for a brand of football that every fan of the game can relate to.

For what it brings to the game, women's football deserves so much more credit than it currently receives. In nurturing and enabling players like Sarah Wiltshire in an environment of fair-play and respect, some might say that it is leaving the men's game at the elite levels way, way behind.

'A League of Our Own' is fast becoming a slogan not simply for girls and women that love the sport and follow WSL, but a slogan for all those that love the true spirit, the true soul of football. In the WSL, like the lower and non-leagues in the men's game, that timeless soul, that eternal heartbeat of what makes football so special to so many is alive and kicking.

Long may it continue to do so.

Postscript:

Three weeks later

Sarah looked emotional as, after 63 minutes of the WSL 2 fixture at Huish Park against Durham, she saw her manager beckon for her to come off, her replacement Nadia Lawrence stretching out, jumping up and down on the touchline in preparation for her introduction.

It seemed a routine swap after a yet another sparkling display by Sarah; during which she had scored after five minutes with an exquisite lob of the keeper from the edge of the box, then a mazy run caused a desperate defender to bring her down, with the equally impressive Helen Bleazard converting the free-kick. A missed penalty that she had created from another scintillating run, an audacious turn and shot from the edge of the box that had the keeper scrambling to tip over the bar, followed by a venomous strike that stung the gloves of the over worked Helen Alderson in the Durham goal, all looked to be the result of a typical Sarah Wiltshire performance.

However, just after the hour mark, and having been brought down with an industrial tackle from another desperate Durham defender, she landed heavily, and stayed down for a moment or two, before getting back to her feet. She looked up to see her manager, Jamie Sherwood, immediately calling for her substitution.

She was in tears before she reached the touchline, and as the game continued after the 700 plus crowd had applauded her off and a long hug from Jamie before she sat down in the dugout suggested only that he was consoling a disappointed player at being taken off. It wasn't until the final whistle and an exhilarating 4-0 win against a decent Durham team that the announcement was made, that this would-be Sarah's last game for Yeovil. Sarah was pregnant.

In a league in which virtually every player has to make great sacrifices to play the game that they love; juggling a full-time job with their part time football responsibilities that leaves no room for a social life, spare time or rest days, Sarah is putting this passion, that she has dedicated her entire life to, on hold in order to create something else that she has dreamt of: a family with soon to be husband, Steve.

Though her tearful speech on the pitch after the match won't be the last that football will see of Sarah. After a typically self-depreciating dig at her performance when I congratulated her on her news and her goal:

'Yeah but I should have scored a few more!' Sarah confirmed that this isn't the end of her love affair with the beautiful game: 'I will definitely be back. I love football so much, and if Yeovil offer me a contract I will sign for next season.'

With statistics after her final match of the season standing at 12 goals in 14 games, you can imagine that Yeovil would be more than happy with that. And if the team can keep up the momentum, she could even return as a WSL 1 player.

No matter what league Yeovil are in in 2017, football needs Sarah Wiltshire. Her performances lift you out of your seat, they are the essence of everything that makes the sport so special. And like a good number of the players at the very top of the women's game, motherhood needn't mean you can no longer live your dreams out on the pitch. The sacrifice and dedication of the players of the WSL means that everything is possible – you just have to want it.

And with Sarah, that is never in doubt.

CHAPTER 12

Displaced, Refugee, Unrecognised: Three National Teams in Search of a Nation

IT IS A simple municipal pitch in Remscheid, near Dusseldorf, Germany. There are no stands, or terracing, or supporters. There is, however, floodlights, that are needed to illuminate a match played out in the cold, fading light of an early spring evening in March.

Two teams give their all, like the thousands upon thousands of other amateur matches played out across countless anonymous local council pitches, the length and breadth of Europe every week.

The only thing separating this fixture from the myriad of others is meaning.

Because unlike the vast swathe of park football matches, whose results quickly become lost, the league tables those results affect slipping into obscurity in recycling bins along with the local papers that printed them, this match in Remscheid is of national importance. It may not be of a national importance in the traditional sense, in as much as the game's victors, Tamil Eelam, no longer have a nation to call their own.

But to the exiled and displaced Tamil community that once called the northern and eastern coastal regions of Sri Lanka home, this national team for a displaced nation, playing under the banner of a lost home, representing the rich culture, history, tradition, and language they struggle to maintain; for them, this anonymous looking match in the failing light of a cold German night means so much.

Their 4-1 victory over the Roma National team, a traditionally dispersed ethnic group spread across Europe, is a rare opportunity to play and to represent a forgotten people, albeit it on the most obscure of international football stages.

Post-match celebrations, where both teams came together for a group picture, were heightened beyond the joy of this rare opportunity to wear the orange and yellow striped shirts of their homeland. Because victory in this Remscheid Challenger Tournament qualified the Tamil Eelam National Team for the CONIFA World Cup 2018 edition.

No matter that it was over three years away, and is a tournament that most football loving people the world over have never heard of; the opportunity to play, to represent your nation, even in exile, and in relative obscurity is something worth celebrating. In a world where so much has been taken from you, where you are far from home, unrecognised by the international community, cut adrift from international law, the promise of identity through football, no matter how distant, how low-key, is no small thing.

Post-match, talking to the exiled Tamil community, head coach Ragesh Nambiar exclaimed his delight at winning the match, and qualifying for the tournament. Jonathan Chandran, captain of the team, went on to explain the importance of the Tamil Eelam football team in giving some voice to the exiled and home-based Tamil community:

'We want to thank all the supporters and fans that motivated us to achieve this victory. We need also at the same time remember that we are playing in the Tamil Eelam football team to represent our identity and our nation in the international sport arena. We want also to express our support to the Tamil political prisoners that are fighting for freedom in our homeland.'

For some, like Jonathan Chandran and his team-mates, the luxury of World sports governing bodies mantra that 'sport and politics don't mix' is one they cannot afford, and a reality they do not recognise; a post-match football interview being a rare opportunity to put a voice to a largely voiceless people. Thankfully for Ragesh and Jonathan the fundamentally flawed notion that sport and politics must be kept separate (after all UEFA and FIFA ensure that politically sensitive or explosive matches between hostile nations are avoided where possible) isn't accepted by CONIFA, or the Confederation of Independent Football Associations.

CONIFA is the football association for associations that fall outside the remit of FIFA, who only accept National Football Teams from nations recognised by the United Nations. CONIFA describes itself as being:

A global acting non-profit organization that supports representatives of international football teams from nations, de-facto nations, regions, minority peoples and sports isolated territories.

With high ethical standards and dedicated members CONIFA is the world leading organization for people, nations and sportingly isolated regions whom share the joy of playing international football. CONIFA contributes to the enhancement of global relations and international understanding.

We aim to build bridges between people, nations, minorities and isolated regions all over the world through friendship, culture, and the joy of playing football. We work for the development of affiliated members and are committed to fair play and eradication of racism.

This statement of building bridges is one that nearly every world sporting body mimics, however it is CONIFA that actually carries through with it, ignoring the politics that prevents certain states or regions from competing at the Olympics, or attempting to qualify for the FIFA World Cup.

In the mainstream global sporting community, sport and politics *do* mix, on almost every level, and in almost every decision made, always to the detriment of those that don't comfortably fit into the self-prescribed notion of nationhood. CONIFA recognise those that have been forgotten by the international communities governing bodies, that history, politics, diplomacy have forsaken, places like Tamil Eelam.

Tamil Eelam is the name of the proposed independent state that Tamils both within Sri Lanka, and among the exiled diaspora aspire to. Stretching along the northern and eastern coastline of Sri Lanka, it is a region that traditionally has always spoken Tamil, rather than Sinhalese that is spoken by the rest of the country.

The Tamil community's roots in Sri Lanka stretch back to ancient times, and though it isn't known when ethnic Tamils first came to the island, by the 11th century there was a significant population in the northern regions. The Tamils of the 20th and 21st centuries came from a rich and long history, a distinct culture, with traditions and language separate from the rest of the island.

However long perceived injustices, a lack of equal opportunity and rights for the Tamil community in the majority Sinhalese Sri Lanka, led to political movements in the '50s and '60s calling for greater autonomy and self-determination. A lack of progress caused disillusionment among the Tamil community, who became ever more isolated economically until the

'70s, when the newly elected United Front government implemented discriminatory laws against the Tamil community, cementing what had been a perception of being second class citizens into a harsh reality: The intake for Tamil students into universities was regulated, and Tamil pupils had to attain higher grades than their Sinhalese counterparts to study on the same course. Employment in the public sector was also capped at just 10 per cent for the Tamil community.

In the face of such discrimination a movement for an autonomous Tamil state grew in stature during the late '70s, resulting in the Tamil United Liberation Front political party winning a landslide victory in an election to determine the creation of a self-governed Tamil region. In retaliation, the Sri Lankan Government demanded all elected members of Parliament, including the TULF to take an oath of allegiance to a unitary state of Sri Lanka, forbidding the advocacy of a separate state, even by the peaceful and democratic means that the TULF had used. Upon refusing to take the oath, TULF were expelled and a civil war between the Tamil north and the Sinhalese majority broke out.

The Liberation Tigers of Tamil Eelam, or Tamil Tigers as they were known internationally, protected the Tamil communities and their traditional homeland. From behind this people's army a government ran the de-facto state of Tamil Eelam from 1983 to 2009, when the Sri Lankan army finally broke its resistance, and crushed all opposition. Channel 4's chilling documentary *Sri Lanka's Killing Fields* captured the terrible loss of civilian life during the final push to eradicate the Tamil Tigers. One UN report estimated around 40,000 civilians lost their lives during the Sri Lankan government's last decisive assaults; assaults that included bombing what had been prescribed safe zones for civilians to flee the fighting. Other Human Rights groups that had been working on the ground at the time estimated up to 100,000 fatalities would be a more accurate reflection of the horrors faced by the Tamil people.

As a result of more than a quarter of a century of civil war, and in the aftermath of such a catastrophic loss of self-determination in 2009, countless Tamil's fled Sri Lanka in search of a safer future. From that diaspora, the Tamil Eelam National Football Team was formed in 2012; a small symbol of identity, of defiance in the face of such cultural devastation and isolation.

In the west, a saturated football calendar results in many journalists, supporters, and officials bemoaning what is often referred to as 'meaningless international friendlies', played out in apathetic half empty stadiums in-between qualifying campaigns and major international tournaments. For the players of Tamil Eelam, and the other teams that fall under CONIFA's umbrella, meaning is everything, even for friendly matches with nothing riding on them. They are opportunities to wear the shirt of your homeland beneath the flag of your forefathers, to sing the national anthem of a nation lost among the fog of war and politics; no matter the size of the crowd, or stature of the ground, the significance of it is fathomless.

To those that have lost everything, or are clinging on to fragments of a rich and vibrant culture, there is no such thing as a meaningless friendly; the ghosts of past horrors, of injustice and abuse, as well as all that has been lost see to that.

The mainstream football hinterland of CONIFA and the list of its member nations reads like a concise history of 20th and 21st century political failings. Tamil Eelam's first foray into the world of international football for nations that don't exist was held in Erbil, Iraqi Kurdistan, in June 2012, a region as beset with tragedy and suffering as the lost home of the Tamils.

Just 220 miles from Baghdad, Erbil, the capital of Iraqi Kurdistan, had endured a bloody history for more than 60 years. Having been granted autonomy in 1970 after heavy fighting with the Iraqi government, Kurdistan was again plunged into conflict when the treaty was never honoured.

During Saddam Hussein's reign the Kurdish people were subjected to an onslaught of traditional and chemical warfare that devastated whole towns. In the vacuum left by the dictator's fall, Kurdistan's Peshmerga fighters have had to defend its people from the unspeakable atrocities meted out by the terror group ISIS, and resist its advances from the south and the west.

The host's 2-1 victory over North Cyprus (a country only recognised by Turkey as an official state) in the final was witnessed by a crowd of 22,000, and represented a rare opportunity to celebrate the identity and culture that they are forced to defend in a seemingly never ending cycle of war.

Making up the lower placings with Tamil Eelam in Erbil were Western Sahara, a disputed territory in Northern Africa whom Morocco claim sovereignty over, and Darfur, a region in western Sudan that is blighted by genocide and mass-displacement. Heavy defeats against more established sides in Erbil were met with a sporting magnanimity, suggesting they had experienced far worse in their short lives. Indeed they had.

When war broke out in Sudan in 2003, a programme of ethnic cleansing began against Darfur's non-Arab population. Carried out by the Janjaweed militia, the military and police, hundreds of thousands of Darfuris were killed, and many more were displaced into vast refugee camps in Chad and the Central African Republic. More than 13 years on the refugee camps remain, as does Sudan's president Omar Bashir, despite the International Criminal Court issuing arrest warrants against him for crimes against humanity and genocide. The Sudanese Government have refused to give him up, and since the warrants were issued violence has increased within the country and aid agencies have been expelled. United Nations resolutions remain vetoed by China and Russia, leaving the international community impotent. Still haunted by the lack of action in Rwanda a decade earlier, the UN have declared the situation in Darfur 'one of the worst humanitarian disasters in the world'; a small comfort to the 400,000-strong refugee community still living in an overcrowded, degenerating state of perennial limbo.

It is from these camps that the players from the Darfur United team were picked for their CONIFA adventure in Erbil. One such individual is Mahamat 'Iggy' Enigy, a refugee from Eastern Chad, for whom the team has given hope where there appeared none.

'Darfur United makes a lot of difference and changes our lives and the lives of all our people,' he wrote from Toulum refugee camp, near the Sudanese border in eastern Chad. His written English, though slightly erratic, was impressive given that Arabic is the prominent language in Sudan, and education within the camps being far from comprehensive 'We stayed 12 years as Sudanese refugees in eastern Chad on the border in very bad conditions and in isolated camps. The international community – I mean the United Nations – forgot us and our problems.

'When the war began,' he went on 'there's genocide, killing without mercy, rapes, fires from the sky by government planes, and from the ground by the Janjaweed militia, and even words are not enough...' It is clear that the horrors he witnessed have left an indelible mark on Iggy, but so too the positive effect of Darfur United, which he is happy to share when asked.'

'First of all, before Darfur United, we stayed in our camps without any programmes,' he wrote, 'We didn't know anything outside our camps: no media and with nothing to do. I don't even think the world knew about us.

'Darfur United is a team selected from 12 camps from different tribes. Darfur United helped us to know about the life outside our camps and also helped other to know about us. We play as brothers, as one body, like one family.' To add a little context, Iggy explained that he had come from a small village called Kornoi, which had been part of the Zagawa tribe. 'I said my tribe is Zagawa. Never mind, we are all united. Zagawa, Fur, Masalit, Dago... we are united!

'It was our first time travelling by plane (to Erbil),' he wrote. 'We stayed in a five-star hotel in Erbil. It was unbelievable that one day we were representing our people. We played with real teams and on real fields, and we really enjoyed the experiences we had.

'In spite of difficulties and obstacles, we participated in a very important and amazing event,' Iggy continued 'It was unbelievable and unforgettable. When we came back to our camps our families, friends and people were so happy. Their behaviour towards us changed. They respected us and saw us as leaders.'

'We love football so very much,' Iggy wrote, his enthusiasm bursting from the page. 'We played with passion, hope, joy, and fun, and we enjoyed every second of the tournament. Though we lost the games by a big number, we enjoyed ourselves, our heads are still up and we are still strong with passion and hope.

'We had a lot of unforgettable experiences and brought the world awareness of how we Darfuri refugees have suffered in our lives. We also improved our skills and played with very strong teams in a real stadium; it was amazing.'

A 15-0 defeat by eventual finalists Northern Cyprus; a team made up of semi-professional players from Cyprus and Turkey, was followed by an 18-0 loss to Provence in the group stages.

However, in the match to determine who would finish ninth out of nine, a small piece of history was made when Moubarak Abdallah Ahmat scored Darfur United's first, and to date, only international goal in a five one defeat to Western Sahara.

Two years on, the 2014 CONIFA world cup would see them lose by 20, 19, 12, and ten goals without reply against the likes of South Ossetia and Nagorno-Karabakh; two disputed states from the Caucasus region of the former Soviet Union: South Ossetia in dispute with Georgia over autonomy,

Nagorno-Karabakh being in the centre of a bitter stand-off between Armenia and Azerbaijan.

The final 10-0 defeat came at the hands of Jonathan Chandran and his Tamil Eelam team-mates.

To the players of these teams from the forgotten conflicts and diplomatic vacuums of Africa, the Caucasus region of the former Soviet Union, the Indian Ocean, and the volatile Middle East – the meaning in being able to celebrate your people, your identity, to proudly wear the football shirt of your nation, your home, even in a tournament devoid of the world's media, is enormous. In finding solidarity with others, and empathy where there hadn't been any before, the CONIFA tournaments these teams populate must be some of the most important the world over; if not for their size, then their significance in helping people find a voice, find themselves.

As Iggy, an otherwise forgotten face and voice from the refugee camps of Eastern Chad describes, far more comes from these tournaments than the simple act of being able to play football.

'I am happy and lucky enough to be from the Darfur United team. I am very proud. Darfur United is not just a soccer team; the team represents amazing millions of people from Darfur who are suffering from genocide and displacement from home.

'Darfur United is a movement to bring hope, joy and inspiration to the displaced people of Darfur. We love football, and we are a voice for Darfur. We are the voice of people who have spent 12 years isolated in camps and bad conditions. Twelve years means 12 generations, so this team can bring leaders and freedom. I believe that soccer can bring peace. Soccer has strong power to bring peace and inspiration and joy. It's great.'

It is this joy that Iggy describes, this potential that a place at the CONIFA World Cup can offer that Jonathan Chandran and his players expressed at the final whistle that cold day in March 2015. No matter that that opportunity is still some three years away – it is something where, almost exclusively, there is nothing for these forgotten football communities of the world. And as the players of Tamil Eelam began their long wait for 2018, they could at least follow the 2016 edition from afar, and begin to dream.

Abkhazia lies on the eastern coast of the Black Sea, another state from the Caucasus region of the former Soviet Union still struggling in the vacuum left by the fall of one of the world's former super powers. Sandwiched between the sea to the west, Russia to the north, and Georgia to the south and east, Abkhazia declared sovereignty from Georgia in 1990 to form its own independent state that is only officially recognised by Russia, Venezuela and Nicaragua in the international community. In the eyes of Georgia and the United Nations, Abkhazia is still a region of Georgia, though an uneasy militarised stalemate has existed since the 13-month long Abkhazian – Georgian war that spanned 1992 and 1993. Backed by Russia, who themselves see Georgia as rightfully theirs, the small republic of Abkhazia survives as an independent entity within this fractious atmosphere.

To help underline Abkhazia as an independent state, the Abkhazian Football federation was formed in 2007, though initial 'international' fixtures were limited to playing fellow Caucasian rogue states South Ossetia (again in dispute with Georgia) and Nagorno-Karabakh. Abkhazia's position firmly in the hinterland of international officialdom saw it as an ideal location for the 2016 edition of the Confederation of Independent Football Associations World Cup. Despite numerous diplomatic warnings declaring that travel to Abkhazia was dangerous and not recommended, 11 teams joined their hosts in the capital Sukhum in late May 2016 for what would be another successful edition of the international tournament for countries that don't exist. Among them were Somaliland – a disputed autonomous region of Somalia, North Cyprus, Iraqi Kurdistan, Panjab – representing the Panjabi people across India, Pakistan and beyond, United Koreans in Japan – made up from the largely discriminated against population of Koreans living in Japan, and the Szekely Land and Sapmi teams representing traditional ethnic minorities living in Hungary and Finland respectively.

To the packed crowds in the national stadium, the Abkhazian team worked wonders on the pitch to overcome the tournaments stronger nations of North Cyprus and Punjab, both of whom contained semi-professional players, to win this alternative world cup. An unprecedented success on the pitch, the tournament also did much to bring together both the host nation, who could rise above the uneasy peace of their everyday lives and celebrate their country, their identity, that had survived through hardship and struggle; but just as previous editions of the CONIFA World Cup had done, also celebrate the identities of the 11 other teams taking part.

Through shared struggles, through a mutual connection in being the unknown, the unrecognised, the disregarded, the forgotten; cultures were explored and enjoyed, and fortified through the raising of flags, the singing of national anthems. For a precious few days in late May and early June, even if it was away from the majority of the mainstream media, who chose to focus on preparations for the European Championships and the Copa America, these 12 teams, 12 cultures, had their moment in the sun.

Even those who thought they had no interest in football found themselves caught up in such an uplifting spectacle. Twenty-two-year-old Lana Tarnava, resident of Sukhum, wasn't born until after the Abkhazia – Georgia war had ended. However, her life, like the lives of every Abkhazian, is dictated to by the hardships of living within a nation that doesn't exist. Even for her, someone with no apparent interest in the sport, having the CONIFA World Cup in her country, her home town was a life-changing experience.

'For my country, being a part of this kind of championship is one of the most important events, like the day when Russia recognised us as an independent country. Because of Georgian propaganda, Abkhazia has an image of a dangerous country, but we showed the world the real situation: a beautiful nature, hospitality and a high level of organisation. It's so important for us', she went on 'that everyone can hear our national anthem and see Abkhazian flags waving under a peaceful sky.

'I think our guests were so proud to for this opportunity to represent their countries as independent states.' She said 'Sport is the good way for people to come together. I never was a football fan before, but CONIFA has changed me a lot. The atmosphere in Sukhum was amazing! I never expected how cool the Abkhazian team was! It is difficult to describe all of the emotions during the week of the CONIFA tournament. My biggest dream is to see my country recognised by all of the countries.'

For Lana and for her country success on the pitch helped to fortify the pride of its people and strengthen resolve in the face of a continued uneasy future. However, simply taking part in such an affirming environment, even among the lower placings of the tournament's final reckoning, can have an equally powerful effect.

Far from the medals in Sukhum, far even from the knockout stages, The Chagos Islands came to Abkhazia for its first taste of a CONIFA tournament with altogether different expectations.

For them, like Darfur United in the 2014 edition, representing their forgotten people at this tournament would always rank higher than any sporting success out on the pitch.

Until the story of The Chagos Islands, the tales of human rights abuses that pepper the histories of some of CONIFA's more troubled members have come from far flung, distant lands.

But with the inhabitants of The Chagos Islands, their hardship and suffering is a truly British affair, and a shameful one at that.

The Chagos Archipelago comprises more than 60 islands in the Indian Ocean that forms a part of the British Indian Ocean Territory, and lies 300 miles south of The Maldives. Its strategic position, being equidistant from the Middle East and Asia, interested the government of the United States of America, who in the 1960s was looking for a military base to monitor the region from.

The British Government agreed to lease the largest of the islands, Diego Garcia, to the Americans, and in the early '70s proceeded to evict the Chagossian community from its home, citing a self-penned report that suggested the Chagos community were simply migratory fishermen who had no physical ties to the islands.

That a history of more than 150 years could be charted of the islanders and their island held little truck, and a programme of deprivation and deception began to clear the population. Members of the community were asked to sign papers written in English, a language that they didn't understand, thinking that they were documents for home ownership. In fact they had been deceived into agreeing to leave Diego Garcia for Mauritius. Medical aid was withdrawn, and when people needing a doctor travelled to Mauritius to seek help, they were denied passage back to their home. Indeed, any Chagossian travelling to Mauritius for whatever reason found themselves denied a return journey.

The remainder of this peaceful community of subsistence fishermen found themselves rounded up and transported to the tin shack slums of Port Louis, Mauritius' capital, and left to fend for themselves. Many could not adapt to a life as far removed from what they had known. Suicide rates among the Chagossian community rocketed, as did reports of elderly members 'dying of broken hearts'.

Unable to cope with an impoverished life in Mauritius among a refugee shanty town with no opportunities, many Chagossians eventually fought their way to the UK, where after years living in temporary accommodation they were finally resettled in Crawley, Sussex. There, among a fractured community torn from their homeland, elders struggled to keep the memory and culture of Diego Garcia alive, by any means available to them.

As MarieSabrina Jean, chairwoman of the Chagos Islands Football Association, explains, one of those means is football:

'Our small community was united not just by our shared history of adversity, but also by our shared love of football. This led to the birth of the Chagos Football Association which consists of second and third generation exiles representing the country of their ancestors.'

With little or no equipment or funding, the Chagos Islands National Football Team offers a vital outlet of identity and connection for young Chagossian exiles to connect with their roots, and the history that was taken from them. Even in the obscurity that a lack of status, money, and respect affords them, the exile community of the Chagos Islands resists the passing of their sad story into the annuls of forgotten history. Every training match, every opportunity to represent the nation that the British Government wants us to forget, is a small victory in maintaining a vibrant and proud culture.

No matter that money meant only a threadbare Chagos squad could travel to Abkhazia; the CONIFA World Cup enabled another people with no voice on the world stage to shine a light on the injustices meted out to them, and to play the game they loved so much.

Heavy defeats against the hosts and then Western Armenia (an ethnic population from the Armenian highlands, that geographically now finds itself a part of eastern Turkey), was followed by a narrow three two defeat to Somaliland in the first placement round, and a penalty shoot-out loss to Raetia (a former province of the Roman Empire that once spanned parts of Switzerland, Bavaria, and the Tirol, and whose unique language still persists among the small pockets of its descendants) after a three all draw.

For a team devoid of resources, finances, or support, other than what can be provided by their small exile community, a five-goal haul over four games, the opportunity to compete beneath the flag of The Chagos Islands, and the opportunity to represent their people is a success far greater than any victory or trophy win. That during an opening 9-0 defeat to Abkhazia, a packed Sukhum stadium chanted the name of The Chagos Islands in support of their endeavour out on the pitch, and the players, supporters, and media at the tournament finally knew about them and their people, their struggle, must surely be more precious than any gold medal.

Not long after their return from Abkhazia, representatives of the Chagos community were in the high courts after petitioning for their return to the islands. The 50 year lease the Americans and British signed for Diego Garcia was up for renewal; and high profile figures like naturalist Ben Fogle and investigative journalist John Pilger supported a report detailing how the Chagossians could safely return to the islands even if the military base remained. The lease was renewed and the report dismissed. For MarieSabrina, the Chagossian elders, and their grandchildren doing the community proud out on the football pitch, the wait for justice goes on.

But after all these years, and because what they are fighting for is so precious, there is no doubt that their attempts to return home will continue, for as long as it takes.

In the two years between each CONIFA World Cup, football among the forgotten nations and peoples of the world can grind to a complete standstill. To refugee communities like The Chagos Islands, Darfur United, and Tamil Eelam – communities devoid of any official status as a recognised entity – there are no lucrative sponsorship packages or government subsidies. Funding for football, or anything for that matter, has to come from within. Which is easier said than done.

Fundraising coupled with investing what savings they had, and borrowing what they could, enabled only the bare minimum of Chagossian players to travel to Abkhazia. Though it proved to be a life-changing experience, it would also be one that some will be paying off for quite some time. Finding even more money to maintain what had been built during the CONIFA tournament is often a step too far for the players and supporters of many unrecognised national teams; momentum and continuity a luxury out of their reach.

For Darfur United, living in refugee camps in Chad means that gainful employment is virtually impossible. Having fled a genocide with what little they could carry, the resources to travel in the name of football lies firmly in the hands of charitable donations and aid agency assistance.

Attempts to compete in a small competition against The Chagos Islands and Tamil Eelam in England in August 2016, which would count as a qualifying tournament for the 2018 CONIFA World Cup, saw Darfur United have to withdraw at the last minute.

With fundraising for the players travel expenses coming up short, followed by the hammer blow that the teams travel visas had been denied by the British Government (having refugee status in the modern political climate closes far more doors than it opens) meant that for Iggy and his teammates the wait to return to the football pitch continues. No one knows when they will be able to continue the vitally important and life affirming work that they had started, work that was helping not only them, but also their fellow Darfuri refugees. Their last appearance, that 10-0 defeat to Tamil Eelam in June 2014, could stand for quite some time, though hopefully not as long as fellow CONIFA member Tibet's last venture into the world of football for the forgotten.

The last appearance by this team of exiled refugees based in Dharamsala, northern India, dates back to another 10-0 defeat, this time against North Cyprus in 2006. The global financial crisis of 2007–08 saw a dramatic fall in charitable donations to the Tibetan National Football Association; donations that were their only source of income. An entire generation of refugee Tibetan men (but not necessarily women, as detailed in chapter six) have been denied the honour of pulling on their national shirt and representing a homeland lost to the invader/occupiers China in 1950. A life among the unrecognised and forsaken footballing nations is an unspeakably tough one forged out of patience and persistence. But because of what it means to represent a community bound together by injustice, players keep on training, hoping, just in case.

Who knows when Darfur United, or Tibet will play again.

With a mainstream media that remains focused solely on the money at the top end of the game, who appreciates the physical, financial, and emotional hardships that saw The Chagos Islands team struggle to find the funding for a mini bus to take them the 26 miles from Crawley to Sutton, to play in the tournament that money and politics denied Darfur a place?

For most, wearing the shirt of your national football team, be it out on the pitch as a player, or in the stands as a supporter, is a given. The meaning and pride in wearing the badge of your nation and representing a culture, your culture and identity, is a relatively routine honour. It is the source of great pride and passion; a focus for hope, a beacon of unity and belonging. A national team badge has the power to bring people together, even in the face of seemingly impossible division.

After the 1994 genocide, Rwanda re-integrated Hutu and Tutsi people through its national football team. Where one tribe, incited by the Hutu majority government's call to arms, killed one million of their Tutsi neighbours in little over 100 days, the nation was re-forged through truth and reconciliation hearings, and its fully integrated football team.

Identity, culture and the past, present and future of an entire people can be carried in the fabric of a national team's football shirt. And when that nation, and the people it represents are shunned by world politics, the injustices befallen them forgotten and shunted to the very fringes of existence, that meaning can be amplified to levels those of us lucky enough to live under the umbrella of recognised statehood can only imagine.

The singing of the national anthem, beneath a national flag, the playing of a match for your people; to the unrecognised of the world this honour, this celebration of identity that most take for granted, it must feel priceless, overwhelming, near-indescribable. For those of us who take our basic freedoms for granted, we can't possibly know. Sadly, there are people who do. One can only hope that, for the footballers of Darfur, The Chagos Islands, Tamil Eelam, and the many other lost and unrecognised people of the world, that life-affirming honour soon befalls them once more.

CHAPTER 13

Southampton A and B – Discovering Football's Forgotten Teams

A FOOTBALL CLUB, no matter how big or small, is almost always at the very heart of its community, a focal point for so many. As a child, you dream of making it as a player for your team, and as an adult you enable those that did to live out your hopes and aspirations out on the pitch. To the fan, their club can mean everything, a physical manifestation of a large part of their identity, the club crest their badge of honour, the club's home ground a kind of Mecca, their team running out onto the pitch a spine-tingling euphoria. A football club, no matter how big or small, can mean all this and more. It can mean everything.

But for every one of those lucky few who get to live the dream of pulling on the shirt of their beloved team, and playing on the hallowed turf of their home town club just as they'd imagined and played it out over and over again in local parks and their back garden as a child, there are infinitely more that never do. In an era of elite academies, under-21 development squads, and a global scouting networks searching for the best talent, it must seem doubly daunting for the children of today as they play out their aspirations in the streets and on any scrap of grass they can find.

However, it wasn't always as seemingly impossible to play for the team you loved. There have been those that managed just that, though it is quite likely that only a precious few have ever heard of them, and whose feats have seemingly faded, unrecorded into history – not possible, you might think, in this world of statistics, facts, the internet, where the history of each team has been lovingly collated by its passionate fans as a further act of devotion. Definitely not possible in the case of Southampton, where a group of dedicated supporters have published numerous forensically detailed books on the club; painstakingly compiling a list of every player to have ever played a first team game during its entire history. Another book includes every reserve team line up since the end of the Second World War. As club histories go Southampton's must be pretty much sewn up. Or is it?

Hidden among the archives of Southampton central library, seemingly lost to time, is another part of Southampton's history that so few know anything about. Between 1932–1939 and 1947–1985, playing beneath the first and reserve sides in the Hampshire League were Southampton 'A', and between 1950–1955 and 1964–1968 playing beneath the 'A' team in the lower divisions of the Hampshire League were Southampton 'B'.

Used as nursery teams for up and coming local players, and in the case of the 'A' team, a place where, on occasion, reserve team players recovering from injury could get their match fitness, Southampton A and B helped knit the club into the fabric of the town, where a player that could say they played for Southampton could quite literally be found on any street, any neighbourhood, even if it was in Hampshire League Division Three West. Southampton were far from unique with their A and B teams; these junior sides were the norm at professional clubs the length and breadth of the country for decades.

That the professionals of the first and reserve teams above these junior sides were on a wage similar to those who stood on the Milton Road terrace watching them during the '50s and '60s, also tells a story of just how connected the club, like all the other clubs around the UK must have felt back then to the town; and how it and its players, regardless of ability, truly were a part of the community the club served. They lived side by side with the fan on the terrace, from the first team right down to the B team; a far cry from the numerous open jawed supporters milling past the player's car park at St Mary's on any given match day now, marvelling at some of the cars that cost more than they would earn in a year or two.

There is no way of finding out any information quickly and easily on the Southampton A and B teams, no quick point of reference. If you want to learn about these teams, and get a taste of the players that played in them, Southampton Library and the old micro films of *The Daily Echo* newspaper are your only option, where many a long hour will be spent peering into the corners of the sports pages trying to find a line up or a result. But if you do, a world of Southampton players you never knew existed will open up to you.

In the years between 1950–1955, where Southampton ran both A and B teams, names will begin to filter out of the flickering microfilm machine.

There are names never mentioned before, but they are names of Saints players, players who lived the dream of putting on the red and white stripes.

On 10 November 1950, the *Echo* revealed that 'the Persian, N Makhzani' had signed professional forms for the Saints. Based on the information that could be found among the microfilm, Makhzani had made his debut for the Southampton A side in a 4-2 defeat away at Andover in Hampshire League Division One on 9 September, and his high-water mark for the Saints would be a solitary reserve team game against Aldershot at The Dell three weeks later. After signing professional forms, Makhzani made fleeting appearances for the A and B team, scoring one goal for the A side in a 2-1 loss to Ryde, and two for the B team, one of which coming on his B debut at home to Brockenhurst. By March 1951 Makhzani's Southampton career was over with one final appearance in a Hampshire League Division Three West fixture against Fordinbridge Turks. He had made seven A team appearances and four for the B team to add to his reserve team match at The Dell.

It was an unremarkable Southampton career spanning only 12 games, but what Saints fan wouldn't offer up their right arm for Makhzani's season, living out the dream of playing for the team they love, playing at The Dell beneath stands and terraces they knew in forensic detail, having dutifully spent so many hours sat in and stood on them. What wouldn't they give to score a goal for the team they, their parents and their grandparents supported?

As befitting the Southampton A and B teams' lowly status, information about their matches are incomplete within the archived pages of the *Echo*; a team line up in Friday's edition, a score-line on Monday's is about the most you can hope for. However, through these scraps you can, just like 'The Persian, N Makhzani', start to piece together the careers of Southampton players you never knew.

From 1951–1955 the defender Spacagna (no initial could be found throughout that time) played the majority of his football career for Southampton with the B team in Hampshire League Division Three. Based on the information available he played 81 B team games over those four seasons that included a 13-2 victory over Fordingbridge Turks, a goal (his only for the Saints) in a 5-2 defeat away at Wellworthy's, and two appearances at The Dell (versus West Wight in a Hampshire Intermediate Cup fourth round replay that ended in a seven two victory in February 1952, and against

Blackfield and Langley on Valentine's Day 1953, result not known). He also stepped up to the A team in Hampshire League Division One on 13 occasions in his four known seasons with the Saints, though that was as good as it got for him. The book, *In That Number* by Hagiology Publishing, does not list him as ever having played for the reserves. Spacagna may not have a first name, or even got to play for the reserves, but like N Makhzani, what I wouldn't give for his 94 Saints games, his one Saints goal, and his two appearances at The Dell.

Through the old reels of micro film, acts of amazing Saints endeavour that had been long forgotten, if ever known, came back to life: A W Turley scoring four goals for the B team against Lymington in January '51, a P Brown bagging five against Fordingbridge in that 13-2 win in September of the same year. J Flood and Mason scoring on the opening day of the 1951–52 season in a 2-0 away win for the A team in front of 'nearly 2,000 spectators' at 'a thrilling and entertaining curtain raiser to the soccer season at the Walled Meadow', Andover. All of these players got to live a dream so many of us never did, even if their stories have become lost to time.

How many more Southampton A and B stories are there that weren't chronicled in tiny snippets in *The Daily Echo* among the other names discovered from the scraps found at the library? Whatever happened to R Sievewright, Bodger, Chitty, Griggs, Mignot and T Nekrews?

As the '50s wore on, information about the A and B teams grew more scarce within the sports pages of *The Daily Echo*, and by the mid-60s results and scorers had all but disappeared, and it wasn't until the '70s and '80s when results, tables and match reports on the A team began to appear in the first team match programme that more information about Southampton's Hampshire League exploits became available.

In the summer of 1985 it was decided that Southampton's 89-year association with the Hampshire League (a reserve side first appeared in the League in 1896) would end; the A team becoming a youth team and joining the South-East Counties League, featuring youth teams from other professional clubs.

Like the B team's nine seasons in the Hampshire League, the A team's exploits during the spell researched in the '50s didn't produce a single player that went on to play in the first team, and it was felt that a player's development would be better served in a more professional setting, rather than in an A team playing amateur sides. A fair assumption and undoubtedly true, but what the players gained from this new set up came at a price; and what did the club and the fans lose?

Having an A and B team, having sides that players of varying abilities could aspire to, must have brought the club closer to the community. Its existence at all levels of the game, where anyone could potentially become a part of the Southampton family must have helped the feeling that the club was for everyone, and was everyone's.

And for those players that couldn't make it at Southampton, they had the opportunity to play against these sides, and on rare occasions play at The Dell, which undoubtedly must have been a highpoint of their amateur careers, if not particularly news worthy to the local paper.

Based on the reverence The Dell held, and St Mary's now holds with fans young and old, suggests that statements on 'the day I played for Southampton/against Southampton/at The Dell' would remain proudly at the fore-front of these player's minds; the day they got to live their dream.

Time move on, we cannot stand still. But the absence of that connection that professional football clubs across the land once had with the amateur player and fan (Portsmouth, Bournemouth, Aldershot and Reading also had A and B teams in the Hampshire League at the same time) seems to be every-one's loss.

When working fans are being priced out of the top levels of the game it feels apt, and more than a little poignant to reflect on a time when the local football club really was ingrained in the fabric of its community, when it truly was open to all, or at least seemed that way.

Having spent months in a gloomy corner of a library, you can't help but wonder, with more than a little envy, what it must have been like to play for Southampton A and B, playing in a rich and vibrant league as the Hamp-shire League was back then, being able to say 'I played for Southampton'.

The team that beat Fordingbridge 13-2 in 1951, that played with the Persian N Makhzani and Spacagna, the man with no first name, they would all be very old today, probably in their late 80s, maybe even early 90s. It is very possible that more than a few great stories of life in The Hampshire League, of proudly pulling on those red and white stripes with Southampton A and B, of fulfilling a boyhood dream have been lost forever to the passage of time; all that is left are a few dusty records in the basement of Southamp-ton City Library, maybe the odd football programme tucked away in a box in a loft somewhere.

But at least these snippets exist, snippets that once meant something to someone, and, with a little searching can come back to life through the illuminated screen of a microfilm machine; the incomplete stories of men that once played, albeit virtually anonymously, for their local team.

And that, despite being so fragmented, is at least something.

It is a cold, sharp morning in a cul-de-sac not far from Southampton General Hospital, the frost thick set and not budging from the pavements despite a pale sun rising in the sky. Mick Ellard answers his door awkwardly, his smile trying to mask the discomfort in his hip that is soon to be replaced, and ushers me in, sitting on his sofa with a scrap book resting by his side.

'I'm not sure what use I can be for you, it was all such a long time ago,' he says before standing up and heading in to the kitchen to make us both a cup of tea.

Nine years after the Southampton B team had been mothballed in 1955, they re-joined the Hampshire League Division Three for the start of the 1964–65 season. Among Southampton's new recruits was a young lad just turned 15, who had previously played for both Southampton and Hampshire Boys teams with distinction. Having left school in the summer at the tender age of 14, Mick Ellard signed apprentice forms for Southampton not long after his birthday, beginning a five-year playing career with the club; him and his wife still watch play more than 50 years later.

He set the mugs of tea down and scanned the sheet made up from incomplete Library records of the players' names from that first season of the B team's second spell in the Hampshire League, pausing on the odd one:

'He just lives over there, I play golf with him, and him, Russell, he came all the way down from Scotland to be an apprentice with the Saints. That name I don't remember at all, but look at how many times I played with him... Eddie Stone,' he said tapping another name, 'It would be good to get back in touch with him.'

Mick played two years as an apprentice, the first in the B team, the second with the A.

'The B team used to play up at Victory Transport in Rownhams, it was one of the first grounds to get floodlights. The A team were over at BTC ground in Stoneham. I remember we would meet up at The Dell and get in a mini bus that would take us off to wherever we were playing,' he said 'Pat Parker who ran the A and B teams would hand out little brown envelopes with travel expenses inside to the amateur players who were neither apprentices or on professional contracts.

'I don't remember too much about the matches. I remember that we used to get around 40 or so watching the B team matches, between 100 to 200 watching the A side.' He went on 'I remember playing at Swaythling before they changed their name to Eastleigh. Back then there was just one shed like building alongside the pitch – A far cry from now!' (The day we meet, Eastleigh, sitting in the play-off spots in the National League and pushing for promotion into the Football League are travelling to Bolton Wanderers for an FA Cup Third Round Replay). 'The Hampshire League was a good standard, I remember Fareham Town were the team to beat back then.'

When I mentioned growing up down on the Waterside and watching Blackfield & Langley in The Hampshire League, Mick scrolled down the list of fixtures and tapped one name.

'I remember playing Esso down in your neck of the woods. Do they still play behind that cinema down there?' I nodded. 'They had lovely pitches down there. Ford Sports, I remember playing them too, down on Wide Lane near the airport.'

He picked up the scrapbook that his mum had lovingly compiled for him and flicked to a picture of that young team, or at least the first-year apprentices of '64, pointing at himself. They all looked so young, all around the same age of 15, they seemed much too frail to be playing up against large, burley men's works team like Esso and Fords, and helped to explain their relatively lowly position in that season's final league table.

'Only a couple of the B team made it to the first team, many didn't even get to the play in the reserves.' In his second season as an apprentice Mick graduated into the A team in Hampshire League Division One, where there were better crowds and a better standard of team. At the back of the scrapbook is a team sheet from an A team match against Newport over on the Isle of Wight. 'I don't remember anything about that game, but I recall another trip to the Isle of Wight to play Cowes Sports, that was a lovely ground.'

When I mentioned that I had been there to see a match the season before last, and that the place looked like it hadn't changed in the decades in between the two matches he seemed quietly pleased, maybe relieved in an era where much of what he knew as a player had changed.

With the Dell gone, teams like Swaythling transformed into something barely recognisable to him today, there was at least one spot where time had stood still a little, where memories of matches long since finished still have a home.

Across the pages of the scrapbook were faded articles and photographs of Mick's boys' team all being signed as apprentices, all moving up into the B and A teams together. There was one action shot of Mick playing for Southampton boys away against Rotherham boys in front of a crowd of 5,000, another a team photo of the entire Southampton squad congregated on the pristine Dell pitch during pre-season, the youngsters all looking a little in awe of being alongside internationals and personal heroes.

That he was still friends with a number of his fellow apprentices now, still played golf together suggested the close-knit group those boys were, all playing for their boyhood team, all living out what they had dreamt and hoped for since before they could remember. At the end of his second season Mick played in the final reserve team fixture away at Leicester City, and was then offered his first professional contract. He put his hand down the side of the sofa and carefully pulled out an envelope with that first contract stowed inside and opened it out.

'I was on £12 a week, and I would get an extra £2 for every reserve team appearance. There were all sorts of bonuses: £10 for playing in the first team, £100 for winning the FA Cup!'

Mick played for Southampton as a professional for three years, moving between the A and reserve teams, and he would go on to make a further 43 reserve appearances, playing at The Dell and other famous grounds. Among the scrapbook were a few reserve team programmes, one had him lining up against a Leicester team with a young Peter Shilton in goal.

'I found another one the other day in the garage from when I had to mark Harry Redknapp when he was at West Ham. I remember I also had to mark Terry Paine in first team versus reserve team practice matches! Now he was some player.'

A newspaper clipping from December 1967 entitled 'Reserves unlucky at Birmingham' explained that despite losing 'Martin White and Mike Ellard were outstanding in defence'. Another told of Mick holding Chelsea reserves at bay at Stamford Bridge.

Mick loved playing for the reserves, playing at The Dell and other famous grounds. 'We would get a couple of thousand watching our reserve team games back in those days.'

You get the impression that it was a relatively anonymous life playing for the reserves, A and B teams, however Mick gave a warm, self-depreciating smile when I suggested what a big deal it was to have played for your hometown team.

'A lot of people would probably give their right arm to be able to say "I played for the Saints. I played at The Dell, Stamford Bridge, Craven Cottage, and Highbury for Southampton. Let alone all those matches in the Hampshire League!' I suggested.

Memories seemed to fog his eyes for a moment before he told how his contract wasn't renewed at Southampton in the summer of '69, at the age of 19. Bristol Rovers of Division Three came in for him just before his 20th birthday and gave him a signing on fee of £1,000. 'Which was a lot of money back then. You could do a lot with that sort of money.'

But it wasn't the same. He had grown up playing with the same bunch of mates, for *his* team. The facilities were nowhere near as good; the training pitches were awful, and it just wasn't Southampton.

'I stayed for just the one season, I played in the first team a couple of times, but I was mostly with the reserves. I was sharing a house with Robin Stubbs who had come up from Torquay. His girlfriend at the time was Anthea Redfern, who went on to marry Bruce Forsyth!' Checking Anthea on the internet revealed that she was at the time of Mick and Robin's house share a model, Playboy Bunny, and by the season's end had been crowned 'Miss London'! A far cry from a life of mini bus journeys to Hampshire League matches.

'At the end of that season I packed it in and came home. I got a job at Bowyers, who sold sausages and Pork pies and the like, and stayed there for 35 years,' he said. 'I still played football, for Swaythling, then I became player manager at Totton' – both teams back in the Hampshire League where it all began.

No doubt he would have come up against Southampton A, and a new generation of hopefuls just starting out on their own personal adventure, though with Mick you sense that there wouldn't have been any regrets, just as there aren't any now. He played at a good standard in the Hampshire League, and he enjoyed his football. He played in front of some good crowds and he played for Southampton, at The Dell and elsewhere.

Mick Ellard may not have scaled the heights as some of his contemporaries like Mick Channon, and his career may be unknown to all but his old team-mates and family, but it is a career that those who didn't get to play for the team they loved would be proud to have. And as he waves me off from his front step, shivering in the cold, I hope Mick is proud, along with the countless other A and B team players that have become forgotten over the course of time.

Just one appearance playing for Southampton at The Dell would be a priceless achievement to me, to any fan, and Mick played there many times, in front of a good number of people, joining Spacagna, N Makhzani and the rest in the now, hopefully not quite so unwritten firmament of Southampton's forgotten history. It is just one story among a great many A and B team stories. But like them all, even though sadly some have already been lost to time, they are stories that deserve to be told, revealing as they do a precious time when the roots that cement a football club into its community were buried down that little bit deeper.

CHAPTER 14

Life in the Shadows – Macclesfield Town

A LITTLE OVER 20 miles south of Manchester, the sprawling city that is home to two of football's largest global icons in Manchester United and City, lies the small former mill town of Macclesfield.

Nestled in the foothills of the idyllic Peak District, Macclesfield was once the hub of the silk industry; it's 71 silk mills producing roll upon roll of the sought-after material during the 1800s – transporting it far and wide through the canal system that links the towns that were at the forefront of the great Industrial revolution.

Since then, like so many other small towns in the north of England, Macclesfield was forced to reinvent itself upon the decline of the nation's manufacturing backbone. The few great decaying mills that still remain today, with vast upper floors boarded up or littered with broken windows, now house small workshops that help to complement its modern image as a small market town. It is picturesque, a destination for tourists before heading deeper into the lush greenery of the Peak District. It is not, however, renowned for being a football hotspot.

Living in the shadow of its more illustrious city neighbours, is Macclesfield Town, of the Conference National League, the top division in the non-league pyramid and the last stop before promotion into the football league. It's quaint, 6,000 capacity Moss Rose ground is a world away from Old Trafford, the Etihad Stadium, and The Premier League and Champions League that is often played at both.

For a club like Macclesfield Town, existing in the shadow of such vast institutions, the closest they come to the wealth of the Premier League generated by crowds in excess of 70,000 for every home game, shirt sales to what seems to be every country in the world, and enormous income from television deals, are the homes of some of United and City's players that populate the prettier villages and small towns nearby. To a club in the non-league

with an average attendance of 1,500, having to survive in such close proximity to the very top of the sport, is a daunting, and seemingly impossible
task. How can you compete with the lure of the very best, with their trophy
laden seasons and matches against Europe's elite and the best players in the
world?

However, survive and compete they do.

Football isn't just about trophies and league championships. In fact,
for many, it is an enjoyable sideshow to something much more important
and fundamental that has enabled teams with such seemingly impossible
odds stacked against them to survive, and in their own way, thrive. Identity,
belonging, and meaning founded clubs in the latter half of the 19th century,
and it is those three fundamentals that keep them going, keep them vibrant,
have kept them relevant for more than 130 years, no matter their status.

A club, without the support of its community, would be nothing. It
couldn't survive. The town and its people without their club would be half a
town, bereft, so deeply ingrained one has become with the other over more
than a century of co-existence, regardless of the size of either. Generation
upon generation of families have stood on the same spot on the same terrace, or sat in certain seats, in a certain row, of a certain stand. Young boys
have turned into grown men, then old men, selling programmes from the
same corner outside the ground; and others have gravitated toward them,
decade on decade, to buy a copy from them, because it's what they do, it's
what they have always done.

Unwittingly, football clubs have become a living time capsule, a living
history of the community they sprang from – no matter how big or small,
or how close to a global giant they are. The fortune and misfortune of the
community is the fate of the club, and vice versa. Wars have been fought,
player and supporter alike have gone off to fight side by side. Recession and
boom have shaped and re-shaped the landscape.

It is this shared history that has melded club and community into one
over time. And it is this necessity and reliance on a football club to help hold
its community together that helps to keep clubs going, even in the face of
extreme financial hardship. By hook or by crook, no matter what, just about
enough money is found to keep a club afloat, because for the community
that it serves, no matter how small, the result of it failing, disappearing,
would be catastrophic to those that had invested so much of their heart and
soul, their identity, into it.

Keeping a club the size of Macclesfield Town afloat, running it on a day to day basis, given its fundamental importance to the community, and its location so close to a number of greater propositions (indeed there are many more clubs in and around Macclesfield, either in the leagues above or below, that further restrict the possible fan catchment area) is both a daunting task and a role that comes with a tremendous responsibility.

The fate of the club in your hands is the fate of the people that love their team, who have invested their lives into it, whose joy and pain is interwoven with the success or failure of the club.

Running a club in the present is to undertake preserving the past, all the memories of those that have gone before that are held so dear, and have soaked into the steps of the terraces and rows of old seats.

Who on earth would want to take on such responsibility, to endeavour to keep such a small, but vitally important institution afloat, facing down the harsh financial realities of a life down the leagues and in the shadow of much bigger fish? People like Rob Heys, the General Manager of Macclesfield Town.

It isn't just a life of struggle, being a Macclesfield Town fan, there have been great sporting highs along the way. Promotion into the football league in 1997 was quickly followed by a second promotion into the third tier of English football where, remarkably, given where they are now, Macclesfield found themselves in the same division as Manchester City. But while their neighbours won promotion through the play-offs, Macclesfield were relegated back into the fourth tier, where they stayed until relegation back into the non-league in 2012.

Driving through the beautiful country roads of rural Cheshire on a hot August afternoon, the sun dappling the water of the Macclesfield canal through a canopy of lush trees, lovingly painted narrow boats moored alongside towpaths populated only by clouds of flitting mosquitoes, the floodlights of The Moss Rose, home of Macclesfield Town finally came into view. From the road, the old main stand, a fading homage to a mostly lost golden age of football architecture, and freshly painted terracing behind one goal that came into view after one final bend hinted at a ground full of character. What the Manchester City of today would make of having to play here is anyone's guess.

That there is little chance of that happening, barring a freak cup draw, is City's loss, as the Moss Rose is a wonderful setting for a football ground.

'I know I've only been here a few months, but I don't think you could ever get tired of that view,' Rob Heys, General Manager at Macclesfield Town says, looking out from the large bank of windows running along the open plan office above the relatively modern Moss Lane stand. As he waits for the kettle to boil, the rolling hills of the Peak District bask in the summer sun beyond, while the immaculate pitch below, fresh from an off season of recovery and repair, glistens an emerald green as sprinklers water it in preparation for the second match of the new season later that night.

'Being General Manager means that I do a bit of everything, whenever it needs doing,' He says as we settle down in a couple of seats in the stand not far from the half way line. 'We all chip in to get things done. That is the only way clubs like Macclesfield keep going.'

Macclesfield Town, much like Accrington Stanley, Rob's hometown club and where he worked in a similar capacity for many years before coming to The Moss Rose, is the true definition of a community club. It simply couldn't survive without the support of the town.

'As you can see we have an office staff of about five or six people, but most are volunteers. They don't draw a wage. They just do it because they love the club' he said. 'Without the community coming in through the turnstiles on a match day, or volunteering through the week, or sponsoring players' kit, without local businesses advertising around the ground, or hiring our hospitality suite, a club the size of Macclesfield just couldn't survive.' As he talks we watch a point in hand, as two volunteers on the far side of the ground sort through the puzzle of new advertising boards, getting them in the right order before nailing them into place.

'Macclesfield is very similar to Accrington in many ways. It is a small club from a small town, but both have real ambition' he went on. 'The aim this year is promotion back into the Football League, despite the fact that there are a good 14 or 15 teams in the National League with bigger playing budgets than ours. We have a small squad, but it has some real quality in it.

'We signed Mitch Hancox from Championship side Birmingham City in the summer when he was released' he said. 'You can just tell he has played at a higher level. He always seems to find that little bit of extra time on the ball. We are very happy he decided to sign for us! I think he will be surprised at the quality of football in the National League. It is non-league, but many of the sides are full-time professionals, and could hold their own quite comfortably in League Two, possibly even in League One. It is a good standard of football. So far this season it has been great to watch. Long may that continue.'

As we begin to wander around the ground we watch the Groundsman Gary Lewis tending to the pitch, painstakingly dragging sprinklers and their hoses from spot to spot to make sure the whole playing surface gets an even soaking, pausing in the heat to wipe at his brow.

'We are hoping to get an under-pitch sprinkler system for next season, so as he won't have to keep doing this all the time. If we can get the money,' he said. 'I remember when we got it at Accrington. We bought it second hand from Morecambe when they moved to their new ground. We had to hire a van, drive up and dig the system out of the pitch. We hired a plumber to install it, but he had never done anything like it before, and of course there were no instructions being second hand, so we put it together through trial and error!' he smiled as he thought back. 'There were a few false starts when we tested it with some of the sprinklers having the wrong water pressure, and they went off like a rocket! But we got there! When you are down the leagues, and money is very hard to come by, sometimes you have to make do and mend.' As we walk, Gary pauses to watch the sprinklers at work, wiping the sweat from his hands on his vest, before wandering to the next sprinkler.

'Gary has been here since 7am.' Rob continues, 'He probably won't leave till after tonight's match has finished. Just so as he can give the pitch the once over. It is a real labour of love: Gary and his job. He isn't doing it for the money that is for sure, as the pay isn't great,' he said. 'I believe the average wage for a groundsman in the Football League is around £32,000. We can just about afford to pay half that. It is pretty much minimum wage. But he loves his job. You can see that every day.'

After moving another set of hose, Gary spots Rob, waves, and wanders over. Rob introduced me as having written about Accrington Stanley in a book. Gary smiled, then chuckled.

'And are you here to write about Macclesfield as well!' He seemed shocked, bewildered a little when I nodded, confirmed that that was the plan. He had clearly not expected that response.

Gary's assumption was a small slice of the self-depreciating humility that is a mainstay of the supporter in the lower leagues; their passion and love for their team tempered only by the knowledge that, in relative terms, so precious few others care as much as them; though a life of supposed obscurity could never dilute the importance of a club to its supporter, no matter the size.

'Really?' He asks, 'Well. That's great. It is a smashing club, this. I hope you enjoy your time with us,' and with that he headed back out on to his field of dreams to continue working on his pride and joy.

Walking along the still terraces, the financial realities of running a club the size of Macclesfield become stark as Rob explains that gate receipts, sponsorship, advertising, takings from the little club shop, supporters bar, and kiosks selling tea and pies on a match day, along with hospitality packages are the only revenue streams that they can rely on. And in the National League all can add up to a very modest amount.

'We do get a small sum from the league because of the BT Sport television deal that screens some National League games live, but in the scheme of things it isn't very much. Every club in the lower leagues and non-league wishes that more of the fortunes generated by the Premier League television deals would be handed down the football pyramid, to help maintain the grassroots. If we did get a little bit more it would probably go to paying the players a little better. I doubt it would mean we could have a bigger squad, it would just mean we would have a slightly better paid small squad like we have now.

'We are a sensibly run club. We only have one or two players on £400 a week, the rest are on less, and we have some on non-contract terms, so they don't earn a wage at all. Like most clubs in the National League we can't afford to sign big players,' he explained. 'We get players that have been let go by larger teams up the food chain, for whatever reason, and are desperate to prove themselves and to make the most of what they see as potentially a last chance to make a career in professional football.

'As a result we play some nice football, on the floor, the manager making the most of the talent that they have, that those larger teams saw in them in the first place.' With the sun on his back, Rob looked out at the pitch, the quiet main stand beyond as we walked. 'You can come up against some big, bruising teams in the National League, full of seasoned non-league players. We're hopeful that skill and effort will always come out on top.'

It is the glass half full attitude that someone involved in running a club in the lower reaches of the professional game seems to always have, I suggest; knowing that anything less in such a challenging financial environment, with extremely limited resources at hand is just not an option if you want to survive, let alone prosper.

Rob shrugs.

'You just have to get on with it. For the sake of the supporters, the club. You could always do with more money, but you just make the best with what you have.'

Even such a positive attitude must have been tested to the full during Rob's last season with Accrington, where terrible weather meant that five home games were postponed in a row, stretching over a two-month period. As clubs in the lower leagues are so reliant on their match-day revenue to keep themselves afloat, postponements must be a real strain, and five in a row a borderline disaster. How on earth does a club the size of Accrington Stanley, Macclesfield cope with such a financial hit, I wondered?

'It's not easy, for anyone. After one or two postponements we have to tighten our belts, the financial hit in losing games to the weather can really hurt a club, the whole club. Backroom staff and players have to agree to receive only a part of their wages, until the club can afford to pay the rest' he said. 'We also need to always be in good communication with our creditors, we need to have a close relationship so as we can approach them and explain that we can't afford to pay all of their bills right away.

'We have to show good-will by paying even a small amount of it,' he went on 'and we have to prioritise what bill gets paid first, depending on which businesses that we owe money to is in greatest need. It is their livelihoods that an unpaid bill effects, and we don't want to leave them in trouble.

'Thankfully football clubs are unlike any other business,' he said 'in that there is a real emotional attachment to it, and many of the companies we buy from are local, and they care about the club too. Often, they are supporters, they understand and make allowances where they normally wouldn't, and in fact couldn't. They wait until our income stream is back up and running again.'

Re arranged matches can often bring in far fewer supporters through the turnstile than the original fixture would have done, being crammed into a mid-week slot later in the season that often results in fewer away supporters turning up to boost the gate.

In Rob's final season at Accrington, their lucrative home match against League Two giants Portsmouth was lost to a frozen pitch just before

Christmas. An estimated 1,500 fans had travelled up from the south coast, and would have been a welcome boost to the finances, given that Accrington's attendances, including both home and away support, rarely crept much higher. The re arranged mid-week fixture attracted less than 700 away fans; that potential pre-Christmas income remaining forever lost in the ether.

On such tight finances and limited budgets, I asked, what happens if Macclesfield's star striker gets a bad injury in the first game of the campaign, and is ruled out for the rest of the season?

Rob laughed, joked with that lower league self-depreciation:

'We don't have a star striker! But if a key player did get injured there is no budget for a replacement. If we were fortunate we might be able to get a good loan deal, but more than likely the manager would just have to make do with what he had.

'We want to stretch ourselves a bit, we want to get promoted' he went on. 'But we can't stretch ourselves so much that club isn't being sensibly run. We can't put the club in any kind of financial jeopardy. It's hard enough as it is without any kind of extra financial burden. It's a constant juggling act between ambition and sustainability, and I think the supporters appreciate that.

'Luckily the great thing about Macclesfield Town is that we have great hospitality facilities which can help to raise extra income, and "Butch's Bar", the supporters bar has just been refurbished. It is a really nice place where people can go, meet up before or after the game, it helps to create a nice community feel to the club and the ground.

'It's named "Butch's Bar" after Richard Butcher' he explained, 'who played here for years, but died in his 20s while playing for Kidderminster Harriers. It was a nice touch for the club to name it after him. His name, his memory is a part of the fabric of the ground now and a part of the club's history. I'm trying to learn about it all; the promotions and relegations, cup wins, famous victories, important characters like Richard. Knowing about all that is as important as knowing how to do your job. When you work for a football club you need to understand its past, and the people that love it, because you are working for them, you are helping to keep one of the most important things in their lives afloat.'

As we turn the corner toward the terrace where two volunteers are finishing off attaching new advertising hoardings, Gary the groundsman, looking deep in thought as he studied a patch of sun-drenched pitch, lost track of the nearest sprinklers whereabouts, backing away from it quickly as it threatened to drench him. At a new safe distance, he watched its progress as it carried on along its slow arc.

The old main stand at The Moss Rose is an iconic blast from the architectural hey-day of football stadia, where every ground looked different, and had its own peculiarities of construction. Its roof, like the lid to a fading blue shoe box, stretched over the steep rake of seats beneath. Cracked Perspex panels each end had protected the spectator from the wind for decades, providing a little shelter as generation upon generation climbed the steep steps up into the stand. Small terraced paddocks in front of it had no doubt always housed the more vociferous support, who wanted their thoughts to be known by the countless managers that had sat in the dugouts just in front. In the still of a hushed summers afternoon, hours before that evenings match, the ghosts of past games and seasons lingered heavily in the heat, drifting about the old stand amongst the erratic patterns of gnats and mosquitoes.

From the player's tunnel, this old stand gave up a wonderful warren of corridors that wound beneath it and the terraces, carefully maintained, but unaltered since the day they were built. Rob moved from door to door, opening them up to reveal what lay beyond them.

'It's good that I get to show you around. It gives me a chance to have a wander about parts of the ground I haven't had a look at yet. I have no idea what is behind some of these doors!'

Though there were plenty that he did, like the changing rooms; a little rundown, but cared for and functional. In the referee's room next door, he couldn't help but press the bell that would call the players to the tunnel on a match day.

'This room is pretty nice. The one at Accrington is a quarter of the size and is very cramped on a match day, when the referee, the two assistants, and a fourth official all have to cram into it. New rules mean that you have to have two showers in the referees changing room now,' He said pointing to the two shower cubicles in the corner, 'But at Stanley there just wasn't the room to add a second cubicle. So, what we did was add a second shower head, splicing the water for it from off the hose to the first one, and there we had it: two showers! They were, however, both in the one cubicle, and if ever two people tried to use them at the same time they would be bunched up like sardines. But by the letter of the law we had the right number of showers!'

Doors opened up onto physio rooms, a steward's room, a windowless but welcoming boardroom whose ceiling followed the contours of the raked seating above, storerooms and a kit washing room, the fresh smell of washing powder lingering over the washers and dryers.

Rob laughed when I made a comment that there probably wasn't much call for swapping shirts at the end of a match in the National League.

'No! The players get one shirt for the season. It only gets replaced if it is literally falling off them and is good only for the bin. There just isn't the money for that kind of thing in the National League, or League Two for that matter.

'When Macclesfield got relegated back into the non-league in 2012 money got even tighter again. There is precious little television money that makes its way down to League Two, but there is even less in the non-league. The loss of that, lower gate receipts and everything else means a tightening of the belt even when you thought there were no more notches left.

'Relegation meant the club had to disband its youth sides and its reserve team', he explained. 'It just couldn't afford them. All it could manage was a small first team squad.

'We are starting to try and get the youth of the town back involved in the club, in a greater capacity than simply a potential supporter on a match day. We have kid's community projects through the school holidays', he said, 'where they learn about what it takes to run the club, and they help out with various roles around the ground. One group are outside now doing a charity car wash in the car park.

'We're also starting "Project 21", which is being funded by us and money raised in the name of Richard Butcher. The aim is to provide a football provision for the kids of the town. It's not really a replacement for a youth set-up, but it is engaging the kids to get involved in the club, and give them a place to play football. And through that, you never know, we might unearth some talent that could benefit the club. But it is more a community project, and a really nice legacy for Richard.'

As we step back out into the sunshine and continue to wander, Rob looks out at his new surroundings.

'The Moss Rose is great. It is exactly what we need. It is a ground that can be grown into with a couple of promotions,' He looks across at the far terrace, the newer stand that runs the length of the pitch. 'It holds just over 6,000 now. Some people only see progress in moving to a new stadium. But we can develop here. It is the club's heartbeat, it means so much, it is so full of character and history, and look at that view!' He says, pointing away at the hills of The Peak District. 'It doesn't get much better!'

It is clear that in his short time at Macclesfield he has really understood the club, its meaning, its importance, even in the supposed relative obscurity of the National league. No doubt his years working for Accrington Stanley, and the many before that where he was simply a supporter watching their rise through the non-league, had schooled him in the reality that a life on the fringes of mainstream football doesn't mean a life devoid of meaning, of importance. In fact even, it has taught him the opposite.

'It feels like a proper football club here, just like it did at Accrington', he said wistfully as we watched the sprinklers on the pitch. 'The fans really get behind the team, who give their all out on the pitch, and then afterwards the players and fans mingle, have a drink together in the bar, kids get autographs in their programmes. It is how it should be.

'We're not trying to knock down any walls here', he said. 'The aim is promotion, but there is a bigger aim, maybe a far more important aim, and that is to preserve the club for past, present, and future generations. People are proud of their club, and rightly so. Who cares that they aren't in the Premier League, or on *Match of the Day* on a Saturday night? Macclesfield Town is just as important to them as Manchester City or United are to their fans down the road.'

It's just that precious few outside the towns and communities that these small clubs serve bother to notice the passion that Rob described. Mainstream media pay only a passing interest when a David versus Goliath cup draw pits one against the other; the rest of the time, they are on their own, which must be tough in an uncertain economic climate. Working for a lower league or non-league club must be a precarious one. Rob had already mentioned the loss of the youth set-up and the reserves when Macclesfield dropped out of the Football League, and every season there are stories of relegated clubs having to let go of office workers and backroom staff. Postponed matches and other losses of revenue, relegation and the ever-increasing financial burdens needed to just tread water must make job security a luxury out on the fringes of the professional game.

'You just have to work very hard to make sure the club remains in a healthy position. If you can do that then everyone's jobs are safe.' Looking out at the emerald green pitch on a hot summers day, the lazy drone of the odd car on a road nearby, the expectation of a new season drifting about the empty terraces, it must be the dream job, I suggest, working in football, for something you care so passionately about, despite the precarious position you might sometimes find yourself in?

'It is,' Rob said, 'But it is very, very hard work. You work all hours so as to try and keep everything running smoothly. As I said, we only have a few paid staff. It is a constant battle, juggling resources, finances. It can be very stressful', he went on, 'working to ensure there is job security for everyone, working to maintain a club with such a long history, that people rely on, care for so much.

It can be a real burden. And some days, when everything is going wrong, you wonder what on earth you are doing!

'But then there is that one per cent, that little piece of magic, that little snippet of hope that fuels you, it is what made you fall in love with the game in the first place, as a little kid. It could be a last-minute winner, a promotion push, a cup win and a tie against one of the big boys. It can be that hope that keeps you going.

'Seeing everybody happy on a match day after a win', he said, 'seeing big smiles all about the club keeps you coming back to work on a Monday, only to find a desk piled high with more stress and more problems that need solving!'

Though having worked in the lower leagues and in non-league for a long time must help; having lots of connections must be useful when you have to run a club on a strict budget?

'Yes, it does. You never know when you might be able to call on someone, for something. I was at Stanley for a long time. I got to meet a lot of great people. In fact my girlfriend gets sick of me pointing out people I know when we are watching some football on the television! It was surreal to see the Irish keeper Darren Randolph at the summer's 2016 European Championships. He had had a spell at Stanley on loan, and there he was, on one of the biggest stages in world football!'

Macclesfield's opponents that evening, Southport, had signed striker James Gray from fellow National League side Wrexham in the summer, where he had played with Adriano Moke – a beneficiary of Macclesfield's nurturing environment as he recovered from depression.

Before Wrexham, James had been at Accrington for a number of years. Would Rob get the chance to say hello, I asked, despite the fact that both would be very busy?

'James is a good friend. He stayed with me at my house for a while when he first came to Stanley. He is a lovely bloke, and we'll definitely meet up after the match, even if it is only for a brief chat.'

We had taken a seat back in the main stand after we had completed our walk around Moss Rose, and fell silent for a while, looking out at this quiet, picturesque football ground, floodlight stanchions stark against a backdrop of a brilliant blue sky, their shadows, and the shadows of the old stand on the far side of the pitch creeping and stretching slowly across the bank of terracing that led on toward the far goal.

'Football grounds just look amazing at this time of year,' Rob says to no one in particular. 'The pitch looks great in the sunshine, ready for the season.' Maybe a little bit more of that 1 per cent of magic that Rob had described had bubbled to the surface. 'I could sit here and watch the grass grow all afternoon,' He says with a smile, though with just under four hours until kick-off he knew that was a luxury neither he nor the club could afford. As if to underline the point, the clatter of plates and cutlery echoed from the open doors of the hospitality suite behind us, as the catering staff began to prepare for the evenings proceedings.

'Well, I had better get back to it. It never stops!' He says, as we shake hands. 'Enjoy the game tonight.' However, as his office door closes behind him and he makes his way back to his desk, I can't help thinking that there would no doubt be a lot of work to be done before he could even think about kick-off and a simple game of football. But you also can't help but feel that, despite the stress and everything else that goes with running a club this size, the passion, endeavour and dedication that had poured out of him as we walked around the home of Macclesfield Town meant that there really was, fundamentally, no other place that he would rather be.

The start of a new season always carries with it a heightened excitement and thrill at the potential of what the next nine or ten months may bring. And as the supporters of Macclesfield Town, proudly decked out in the new season's shirt, slowly began to congregate in Butch's Bar, outside the turnstiles on the road, the small club shop, that excitement was palpable. A fixture list stretched out ahead of them that would take them through the balmy summer evenings of August where, like tonight, they could sit in their seat, or stand on their spot on the terrace in shorts and T-shirt, through autumn afternoons with a hint of a chill creeping in on stiff breezes that scuttled fallen leaves across the pitch. Through bitter winter storms beneath ashen skies; howling gales and lashing rain whipping across the floodlights' beam, ice and snowfall with the potential to hit any time from November to March, right the way through to the schizophrenia of April with its chill that lingers in the shadow of the stand, but casting a deceptively hot sun out on the terrace. And with it promotion? The Play-offs? Or another season of mid-table mediocrity?

Through it all these die hard supporters will turn up no matter what, in the hope of a sustained promotion push, or cup win, or simply just an entertaining game of football with a goal or two to cheer. Because, ultimately, it is that over everything else that supporters miss the most through the dormant months of the off-season; not being able to meet up with their friends, or terrace companions, to do the thing they had been doing since before they could remember: watch their team play.

Never mind promotion, cup wins, everything else that the hope of a new fixture list can offer. It is the fundamentals that really matter; the re-emergence from its moth-balled state of the club that offers, has always offered identity, belonging, meaning to those that care for it. A new season is a new opportunity to stand with your friends, have a drink, watch a game of football, like your parents did, and their parents before them; to go on a journey far more important and meaningful than any league table can detail.

Though promotion would be a very nice bonus all the same, the prospect of which had groups of friends discussing over a pint or a cup of tea the new signings that had arrived for the season ahead, and where the team needed strengthening still, who just wasn't up to the job if promotion was the aim. It would be that desire, that wish for a good win that would see them cheer, shout, despair throughout every 90 minutes of football that season. Though often the perspective of that fundamental bigger picture will have returned by the time they had queued and got their post-match pint, and a bad loss met with the gallows humour that is the lot of most supporters.

As the players came out to begin their warm up, Gary the groundsman was still out there, lugging hose and sprinklers from spot to spot, dodging wayward balls as well as the jets of water that pulsed as they span slowly about.

'He'll be doing this all day,' Rob had said more than four hours earlier, 'As the manager likes a slick surface. It helps our players to pass the ball about. Make the most of their technical ability.'

Twelve hours on from when he had first arrived that morning, Gary was living up to his billing as another of the lower league and non-league's unsung, dedicated mainstays.

Finally, as kick-off approached, Gary and a couple of volunteers switched off the sprinklers and trailed the hoses to the side of the pitch, tucking them alongside the advertising hoardings. A crowd of 1,300 had gathered for this match in the fifth tier of English football against Southport. Not bad considering near neighbours Manchester City were on the television in a Champions League qualifying match against Steaua Bucharest.

As the setting sun cast a reddish hue to the ever-darkening pastel blue sky, Macclesfield began to dominate. Three quick goals effectively killed off the game within the first 25 minutes, and helped to give proceedings as relaxed a feeling as The Moss Rose had appeared in the calm of the afternoon. Supporters that normally hunched in agony in their seats, willing their team on, sat back and smiled, chatted to their neighbours, enjoying the spectacle and the heat of the evening. Shirt sleeves billowed on a soft breeze that brought gnats flitting about the floodlights down among the seats; the odd programme batting them away.

It felt more like a scene from an idealised Hollywood vision of a minor league baseball game from any small-town stadium, USA. You could almost hear the faint sounds of cicadas, the crack of ball on bat, the organ music between innings among the singing from the Macclesfield support in the paddocks in front of the old stand.

For Rob's friend and Southport striker, James Gray, it was far from a relaxing time. An under-siege Southport defence had long resorted to hoofing the ball away from danger, leaving him to feed off of high balls that the much taller Macclesfield defenders mostly dealt with comfortably.

A rare opportunity with the ball at his feet led to him laying it off to the lively looking winger Jamie Allen, only for the attack to be halted by a crunching challenge by a Macclesfield defender that sent the ball careening into the stand for a throw in. The speed with which the ball travelled meant that the poor bloke sat with a cup of tea in the front row could do nothing to stop it from smashing into his chest, his tea and polystyrene cup exploding all over his shirt.

With good grace, and in the face of the hysterical laughter which his friends sat either side of him offered as condolence, he stood up, raised his arms to the crowd who had cheered his misfortune, and took a bow, before heading under the stand to the toilets to clean himself up. A few minutes later, holding another cup of tea, he re-emerged, raising it up to the crowd and pronouncing: 'Bring it on!'

In the least malicious way possible, I don't think a single person that had seen the events unfold didn't pray for another wayward ball to wipe him out once more, purely for the twisted irony of it. Sadly, for everyone that had had a little devilment in their hearts, he was able to finish his tea uninterrupted.

As the skies drained of colour with the setting sun, the moon crept above the hills of the Peak District and slowly drifted toward the flood-light stanchion in the far corner of The Moss Rose. Its passage across the skies was as inevitable as Macclesfield's impending victory, which was only blighted by a consolation goal from a Southport team that had rallied in the second half. Among it all, among stands of expectant faces hoping for a fourth goal to finish the night off, among the singing contingent behind the far dug-outs, among the staff that worked the kiosks, the stewards, and countless other volunteers dotted about the ground, Rob Heys wandered, stopping to chat with anyone that wanted to. Even among the dying embers of a match well won, his focus, as it had been throughout, remained on the people in the stands, and the mechanics that ran a club on a match day. Only rarely did he afford himself a few moments to look out at the action on the pitch that shimmered beneath the floodlights' glare, pausing in the balmy heat of a summer's night to view the spectacle that all his hard work had been in aid of.

What he saw no doubt fell under that 1 per cent, that sliver of magic that made all the effort worthwhile; because beneath the lights the strong home win that was being played out set the club up nicely for the season ahead.

All the expectation that came with a new fixture list had been consolidated, for one glorious summer's night at least; the supporters draining away at the final whistle into the dark streets beyond, happy that their club was back from its off-season doldrums, and heading in the right direction.

They all, no doubt, as I did, couldn't help but look back over their shoulders one last time to look at their spiritual home lit up in the darkness, glowing against the shrouded backdrop of the Peak District. How many times they would do that this season, maybe muttering under their breath after a bad defeat, or chatting excitedly after a good performance; huddling beneath a collar from the wind and rain, or checking their step among snow and ice.

Memories of the time they walked home in shorts and T-shirt after the South-port game long since consigned to their own personal histories of their club.

It would be a match that would be to most only a small footnote in the columns of newsprint and league tables produced for the following day, dwarfed by headlines of Manchester City's thumping 5-0 Champions League victory. That wouldn't matter a jot to those Macclesfield Town supporters, who knew the true worth of their club, just as those that first took them did, and those that took them way back in the day.

It is a worth Rob Heys understands through instinct, through his love of his home town team Accrington Stanley, and his knowledge of life far from the riches of the elite levels of the sport. Though it is clear that instinct was being fast replaced with a genuine passion for his new employers; the burden of maintaining such an institution sitting proudly on his shoulders. Whether he got to see his new home lit up as he left after another long day at work is extremely doubtful; that luxury for the supporters only. No doubt he would have been one of the last ones out after all the lights had been extinguished on another small chapter of the Macclesfield Town story. A small price to pay for working an exhausting, stressful, infuriating, impossible, intoxicating, exhilarating, life-affirming job in the lower reaches of the professional game. And despite it all, maybe indeed because of it, you can't help but feel that ultimately, he really wouldn't want it any other way.

CHAPTER 15

Full Circle – More European Dreaming

DAYS BEFORE THE official end of one season, another had already begun. The week before Cristiano Ronaldo lifted the European Championship trophy for Portugal, heralding the end of the 2015–16 campaign, the minnows of European club football had already embarked on what would be for most a short and anonymous campaign in the 2016–17 editions of the Champions and Europa Leagues. While the continent's heavyweight nations battled it out in front of a global television audience for the big prize, the last days of June also featured 48 first qualifying round ties in the Europa League and four in the Champions League.

Among them, Alashkert of Armenia defeated Santa Coloma of Andorra 3-0 at the Vazgen Sargysan Anvan Hanrapetakan Marzadasht stadium in Yerevan in the Champions League. Also going through to the next round were Lincoln Red Imps of Gibraltar, whose 2-0 win against Flora Tallinn of Estonia set them up for a dream second qualifying round match against Scottish giants Celtic. The high-water mark in this competition for the semi-professional players from Gibraltar would come a full 11 months before the final, with an improbable 1-0 victory over their illustrious visitors, before a brave 3-0 defeat at Parkhead, Glasgow.

Elsewhere, in the Europa League, matches were being played out between the gloriously obscure Zimbru Chisinau of Moldova and Chickhura Sachkere of Georgia, Rudar Pljevjla of Montenegro and Kukes of Albania, Ordabasy of Kazakhstan and Cukaricki of Serbia. 'Small-time' matches were being played out in 'small-time' stadiums from the northern regions of Scandinavia all the way down to the competitions southernmost fixture at Israel's Hapoel Beer Sheva, whose Turner Stadium stands some 50 miles from the Egyptian border. From the extreme west in Reykjavik, Iceland to the towns of Shymkent, Almaty, and Astana in Kazakhstan in the east, matches with little or no significance beyond the supporters, players, and officials of the clubs involved were met with a predictably deafening indifference. But not here. Not me.

With memories of that World Cup '82 sticker album and the fascination my ten-year-old self felt in peering into rows of obscure El Salvadorian, Cameroonian, and Kuwaiti players faces; wondering at the far-flung stadiums they were pictured in, and the exotic sounding teams they played for – for me, the high point of the Europa and Champions Leagues start and finish at the first qualifying round stage.

Just as that old England–Luxembourg programme sent to me by my grandfather, and the brown parcels of obscure programmes from Steve Earle, that World Cup '82 sticker book exposed a world of football that ran far deeper than just the very elite; a world of football typified by these 52 virtually anonymous first qualifying round fixtures. The sticker book back then showed me that football was about far more than just winning the World Cup; it was a game that had permeated every corner of the planet, and had crept into the most distant and remote, and to a ten-year-old boy the most mysterious and exciting of places. Football programmes, World Cup sticker books were my *National Geographic;* opening up a world of the unknown, the unexplored.

The sense of adventure, fascination, wonder at the possibilities of the world outside my door, as well as my love for football made me hold the information attributed to El Salvadorian striker Mauricio Quintanilla in that sticker book in as high regard as that of Kevin Keegan. It made me wonder what the stadium looked like beyond the limited frame of the Kuwaiti team photograph, and what the ground of Al-Qadesseyah, Kuwait striker Jasem Yaqoub's club looked like. It made me realise that there was so much more to football, and so many more stories than those from the top flight. There was a rich, vibrant diversity that, no matter being largely unknown to the wider world, was so important to the very fabric of the sport.

It was what made football magic; that such a simple sport could seemingly unite every tiny village, average town, and sprawling city metropolis across the planet. Transcending language barriers, football truly is as universal a language as mathematics. The same sense of meaning, identity and belonging that both the village team and the Premier League team's supporters feel the foundation blocks that enabled it to become the global necessity it is today. And more than 35 years on from that first taste of football at its remotest fringes, those same feelings of excitement and adventure at the strange sounding names of teams never heard of before, of stadiums yet to be explored; of first time nations appearing in new World Cup sticker books as Angola did in 2006, well, they haven't diminished any.

The stories, history, legend waiting to be discovered, like in 1982 El Salvador's 'El Meurte' Joaquin Alonso Ventura's chaotic route to the CONCACAF Champions Cup final, or Ernest Lottin Ebongue's only international goal for Cameroon – though relatively obscure, and seemingly destined to remain so, for me it felt as a young boy, and still does today, far more vital than any Premier League statistics on passes completed or fouls committed.

These histories of unknown players and obscure teams from little known nations and leagues, they mean something, they are the true heartbeat of football, and they mean everything to those whose lives are enriched by them. No matter how few or how far away they may be. Football is the same sport wherever it is played; attacking flair a thing of poetry at the Nou Camp, Forfar Athletics' Station Road, or the Stade Ahmadou Ahidjo – home to Ernest lottin Ebongue's Yaounde Tonnerre in Cameroon.

And as the 52 fixtures were published for the first qualifying rounds of Europe's two club competitions, complete with stadium names and club badges of those taking part, the magic that had been felt pouring over the obscure details of the players of El Salvador, Honduras, Kuwait at World Cup '82, the names and clubs of the Luxembourg team from that programme that Grandad sent me in December later that same year came flooding back. Just as I had wondered at the names and club badges of Differdange, Dudelange, and Niedercorn back in 1982, so to the wonder grew at the hidden histories behind the beautifully colourful and strange (some from the further reaches of Europe featuring indecipherable Cyrillic script), mostly never seen before badges of 2016's early European hopefuls.

Internet searches (the 21st century version of brown envelopes stuffed full of programmes from a mail order service from Suffolk) began to offer up sometimes grainy pictures of stadiums and kit, along with a sense of their geographical location. And from these strange names and club badges stories began to surface; some funny, some tragic, some simply interesting, all detailing their meaning and importance, the origins of identity, even if only for a small number.

Zagledie Lubin of Poland was formed in 1945, when the town of Lubin was technically still a part of the greater war-time German Reich that had absorbed Poland through invasion and occupation.

With Lubin returned to Poland after the war, Zagledie Lubin Football Club was founded by ethnic Poles who had been forced to abandon their homes and lives in former eastern Poland when it was annexed into the Soviet Union as part of the post war Yalta agreement. Zagledie became a symbol and focal point for remembering an old life, while helping to forge a new one in a new town for those who had spent the war in the shadow of one dictator in Hitler, and had no interest in a life after it under another in Stalin. Seventy-one years on from its formation, Zagledie beat Slavia Sofia and Partizan Belgrade before losing to the Danes of Sonderjyske in the third qualifying round.

B36 Torshavn were formed in 1936 simply because there were too many players wanting to play for HB Torshavn, their now capital rivals on the Faroe Islands. Their Champions League campaign ended in the first qualifying round with an away goals defeat to Valletta of Malta.

Teuta of Albania began life as the ominous sounding 'Uranium Sports Club' before changing their name in reference to the queen of Teuta of Illyria in 231–227 BC. Their Europa League dreams were ended in Almaty, Kazakhstan in the first round.

Odd Grenland, Norway's oldest team still in existence went one round better than Teuta, beating IFK Mariehamn of Finland before losing to PAS Giannina of Greece. Odd were formed in 1885 and named after a character in Viktor Rydberg's 1882 novel *Segerssvardet*, called Orvar Odd. Maybe the only football team ever to be inspired by 'Sweden's last Romantic'!

Among the vast swathe of clubs populating the early rounds of European qualification, among the incomprehensively obscure and the not quite so, was one familiar name: F91 Dudelange. Having put the disappointment of defeat to UCD in the first round of the Europa League last time out, F91 went on to win the Luxembourg league for the 12th time, earning them a place in the Champions League second qualifying stage.

Looking at their badge among the sea of logos of other European hopefuls, a colourful mural of the F91 part of their name, it was easy to remember back a year to the sights and sounds of Dudelange preparing for its part in the opening round of European competition. Old-timers had tended to the pitch at the Stade Jos Nosbaum in the hush of an expectant afternoon, while others swept between the banks of exposed, sun drenched seats that looked out over the town, the water tower turned art gallery that dominated the skyline, the deep swathes of forest beyond. Through a cloud of cigarette smoke, others prepared sausages and kegs of Bofferding beer in the pitch side bar near the corner flag, while a woman lovingly displayed badges, pennants and scarves around her tiny club shop kiosk counter in anticipation of some brisk business that evening.

The excitement among the club's staff while setting up, and the 1,200-strong crowd in anticipation of seeing their team play in European competition spoke volumes. No matter that it was the first qualifying round, and few beyond the supporters of the teams taking part would even learn of the result; to them it meant everything, because it was their team taking part.

Just as it was easy to remember back to the very start of my adventures and an obscure European night in Luxembourg, so to it was easy to imagine the similar scenes as those same volunteers prepared for their second qualifying round second leg in the Champions League one year later.

With the sun shining once more, and the Bofferding ready to go, even the reality that a 2-0 defeat in the first leg had all but sealed their fate for another year would have done nothing to dampen their pride that it was their club, F91, representing their country in Europe again. For small teams like F91 Dudelange, it is their opportunity to celebrate who they are, and where they are from; two legs in European football being a thing to be rightly proud of. And though they cannot hope to win the competition, there is always the dream of making the next round, then maybe the next. Small victories in the scheme of things, but try telling that to the F91 faithful, a microcosm of all that is great at the fringes of football.

Identity, meaning, belonging: three words that validate every single team and supporter that have featured on this book long journey from Luxembourg to Macclesfield were present that idyllic summer's night in Dudelange, and would have been at every qualifying match across Europe a year later.

No matter the size of the team or nation in status, the people that care about them, they matter, their stories matter, even out here among football's forgotten hinterlands. And if there was ever one story that deserved the last word on life at the fringes of world football, that defined the power of identity, meaning, and belonging that exists among these little-known teams, then the story of F91 Dudelange's opponents in their second qualifying round of the Champions League would be a very strong contender.

Qarabag Agdam FK's 2-0 victory against F91 at the national stadium in Baku, Azerbaijan in the first leg seems an appropriately obscure and forgettable qualifying round fixture. However, how Qarabag came to be playing in Baku is not. Qarabag Agdam were formed in 1950 in the then Soviet region of Nagorno-Karabakh, an area between what is now Armenia and Azerbaijan in the troubled Caucasus region, and was home to a mix of ethnic Armenian and Azerbaijani. Qarabag, based in the small town of Agdam, one-time home to a population of 40,000 mostly ethnic Azerbaijani played in the lower leagues of Soviet football, and would play friendly matches against their neighbours FK Karabakh Stepanakert from the predominantly ethnic Armenian town 25 miles away.

However, with the fall of the Soviet Union, and the formation of the independent states of Azerbaijan and Armenia, war broke out between Azerbaijan and the Armenian backed Nagorno-Karabakh in February 1988. Azerbaijan claimed that this mountainous region had always been a part of Azerbaijan under Soviet rule, and is to this day recognised internationally as a part of the country by the UN, while Nagorno-Karabakh demanded recognition as an independent state in its own right, allied to Armenia.

The politics of a fracturing region meant that the peaceful world in which FK Qarabag and FK Karabakh Stepanakert played friendlies was shattered forever; and as war broke out between the two sides Stepanakert disbanded to join the ranks of the Nagorno army, while Qarabag played on among an increasingly dangerous and volatile time.

During the six-year war that ended with a fragile ceasefire in 1994, and loosely remains in place today, thousands were killed in a brutal battle played out along ethnic lines. Matches continued to be played at Qarabag's Imaret Stadium in Agdam, though some were abandoned when the shelling by Nagorno and Armenian troops came too close.

Finally, with the war right on their doorstep, the team were forced to move to Baku, and only five days after they claimed their first ever Azerbaijan league title, the town of Agdam finally fell to the advancing Armenian army following a six-week siege that claimed 6,000 Azerbaijani casualties.

Agdam had been completely destroyed, and remains to this day a decaying ghost town of shelled out buildings. Upon hearing that the town had fallen, Qarabag's players headed back to the border to try and find friends and family among the 200,000 ethnic Azerbaijani refugees that had fled Nagorno-Karabakh. Though some moved to Baku and other towns in

Azerbaijan, many refugees preferred to stay nearer the border and their fallen home. Temporary tented refugee camps developed into towns of more permanent brick buildings where lack of opportunity, unemployment, boredom and poverty have become the norm, and roughly 30 people, civilians included, are killed by sniper fire every year.

One in eight of the population of Azerbaijan today came to the country as a result of the Nagorno Karabakh-Azerbaijan war.

In order to maintain some kind of morale, and preserve the identity of the lost town of Agdam and its displaced people, FK Qarabag, finding itself permanently exiled in Azerbaijan's capital began to lay on coaches to Baku for their refugee supporters, so as they could continue to cheer on their team now based more than 100 miles away. An arduous journey across Azerbaijan's interior, it remains their supporters only way to connect with their lost home, and is an exercise still taking place more than 20 years on. Though how many made it all the way from the uneasy peace of these refugee towns to Stade Jos Nosbaum, Dudelange will forever remain an unknown.

While Qarabag have at least continued, albeit far from their homeland, to play football, and have achieved success within the Azerbaijan league that has enabled them to regularly play in Europe, the same cannot be said for their pre-war friendly opposition FK Stepanakert Karabakh. Despite the war freeing Nagorno-Karabakh from any kind of control by Azerbaijan, it also isolated them on the world stage. With the United Nations recognising them formally as a region of Azerbaijan, the players of Stepanakert Karabakh that returned from the frontline found themselves a part of a nation that didn't exist. While their colleagues from Agdam continued to play under the umbrella of FIFA and UEFA, the footballers of Nagorno-Karabakh found themselves shut out of the game in their newly formed rogue state. Those who made up a part of the 350,000 ethnic Armenians that fled the fighting by moving to Yerevan and Armenia's other towns, the possibility of playing within the Armenian leagues presented itself. For those left behind, football played out a sporadic existence for a decade before the first Nagorno-Karabakh National League was attempted.

A few years later, and inspired by other 'nations that didn't exist' in the region in forming a 'national' team, a Nagorno-Karabakh side was created, though coming nearly 18 years after the end of the war, this national team arrived too late for the players of FK Stepanakert Karabakh that put down a ball and took up arms back in 1988.

However, after all the conflict and suffering, being able to witness a debut victory on home soil, and in Stepanakert no less, of the Nagorno-Karabakh National team, must have overwhelming; no matter that it was experienced among the stands rather than out on the pitch. A 3-1 victory against Lana Turnava's Abkhazia had been preceded by a one all draw in Sukhum, and was quickly followed by membership of CONIFA, where they came up against, among others, Iggy's Darfur United in the 2014 CONIFA Cup, running out 12-nil winners.

Since 2014, and among escalating tensions that spilled over in April 2016 into renewed military activity, resulting in 30 fatalities of soldiers from both sides, the national team have become inactive; another victim of the paucity of opportunity afforded national football teams that 'don't exist'.

Where football has been able to build bridges, as witnessed with Rwanda's post genocide truth and reconciliation national team that contains both Hutu and Tutsi, in some instances, as it is here, football remains helpless. With all communication broken down, and the horror of war still fresh and raw, the names of Armenia and Azerbaijan are kept apart in draws for World Cup and European qualifying campaigns; as are the names of club sides in these first qualifying rounds of the Champions and Europa leagues.

It is not football's only failing in keeping sport and politics separate. The young women of Cassie Childers' Tibetan Women's Soccer programme are still unrecognised by FIFA, and indeed the exiled Tibetan National Football Association, and are therefore denied many opportunities afforded to others. Despite their passion for the game, it is politics rather than sporting ability that holds them back.

The people and footballers of Gaza, Palestine are still denied a freedom of movement, along with many other freedoms. The small concession by the Israeli authorities and football association to allow the annual Palestine Cup, between the champions of the West Bank and Gaza remains fraught. Like the 2015 edition, the first Palestine Cup fixture of the 21st Century, there were huge delays in allowing players to cross from one to the other. Indeed, the 2016 matches between Gaza's Khan Younis and Ahli Al-Khaleel of the West Bank, though completed successfully after long delays and interrogations at the border, resulted in two players who hailed from Gaza, but who had forged careers for themselves playing in the West Bank for Ahli, being denied entry back into their adopted homeland after the first leg at Gaza City's Al Yarmouk Stadium. Mahmoud Wadhi, Ahli's leading goal scorer, remains stranded in Gaza still, his future far from certain as the Israeli authorities give concessions with one hand, but take away more with the other.

Despite all the hardships, the impossible hurdles, football endures; the power, the freedom, the hope it inspires in anyone with a ball at their feet means that the young Women of Tibet, the footballers of Gaza, the forgotten teams of the Chagos Islands, Darfur, Tamil Eelam, Nagorno-Karabakh, the perennially overlooked at Port Talbot, Accrington Stanley, Berwick Rangers, no matter what, they will forge on.

In the face of seemingly impossible odds, be it financially, geographically, politically, or status, they will continue to celebrate the game they love and help it to thrive, whether anyone notices or not. The people that make these clubs and teams what they are will carry on doing what they do, as did the generations that went before them, and those before them. People like the exiled supporters of an obscure Azerbaijani team from a war-ravaged ghost town, the few that had been able to make the long trip to Luxembourg from Baku, or the refugee towns near the Nagorno-Karabakh mountains for their Champions League match no doubt enjoying what they were seeing.

A one all draw in Dudelange secured a relatively comfortable three one aggregate victory, meaning that any Bofferding consumed among the sun-drenched seats of the main tribune went down smoothly and untroubled.

While F91 went back to preparing for their domestic season, and dreams of qualifying for Europe once more, Qarabag's narrow defeat on the away goals rule to Viktoria Plzen of the Czech Republic in the third qualifying round earned them a spot in the play-offs for the Europa league group stages.

Victory against IFK Gothenburg guaranteed at least another six matches in group J against Fiorentina of Italy, PAOK of Greece, and Slovan Liberec of the Czech Republic.

Six more opportunities to celebrate and maintain the identity of this team from a lost town on the fringes of football; and three more long bus rides across Azerbaijan for the refugee supporters of Qarabag Agdam FK.

Where in 1982 there was wonder at the hidden worlds of the El Salvadorian team, the Luxembourg squad, the strange sounding teams at the foot of the classifieds; spawning footnotes about abandoned CONCACAF semi-finals, a single international goal in front of 35,000 people in Dakar, and the one club career of Jasem Yaqoub of Kuwait – these adventures more than 35 years on have revealed even more stories to join them in the annals of minnow football.

From the journeyman career of William Dominguez da Silva, the Brazilian winger playing on a remote volcanic peninsula in Iceland, to the dedication of Alec following Clyde across Scotland and into the European wilds of Berwick for more than 70 years. From young Tibetan, Sonam Dolma playing football in the face of seemingly impossible odds, and the injustices faced by Mahmoud Al Sarsak for simply trying to play the game he loved. To the tragedy of his Palestinian team-mate Mohammed Zash, losing his dream of owning a home and having a family, though realising another in playing for his beloved National team; these stories of hope, determination, passion, and despair from the fringes of football reveal a world of infinite depth and importance.

The fathomless weave of stories beyond the media glare of the world's big leagues and competitions, like a cloud of gnats beneath the shade of a tree on the towpath of the Macclesfield canal, remain seemingly lost in their anonymity. The obscurity of the leagues, countries, or teams that they come from condemning them to a life often devoid of any outside attention.

However, without them football could not be all that it is, all that it can be. Far from the media frenzy around the elite levels of the game, they have the time, the space to tell the story of football, the story of the people who invest their heart and soul into it; and it was there, at Blackfield's roped off pitch, and the quaint Victoria Park, Salisbury that football first truly captivated me.

These clubs, the others in the preceding pages, and the fathomless numbers yet to be discovered, they have the time to reflect on what the game can mean to the people at its very core; what it can offer, and what people offer it. Through their clubs, the story of a place, an ideal, a nation, a people is played out; a living history of the past, and a focus for the present and future.

The fringes of football may be a place rarely visited by mainstream media, but it is by no means an irrelevance. In fact, it is vital in keeping the spirit of the game pure, in maintaining that fundamental magic which captivates generation upon generation of people the world over.

It is a place where part-time footballers can dream of playing in European competition or the FA Cup, and supporters can dream of following them, maintaining that simple joy of expression, of hope eternal that fuels the game. It is a place where those forsaken by the world can pull on the football shirt of their people, and represent something more precious than money. It is a fascinating place, with a seemingly infinite number of uplifting, inspirational, and sometimes heartbreaking stories waiting to be discovered; and an untold number of adventures to be explored among the sea of humanity that calls the fringes of football home.

Indeed, how many more stories got to be played out and expressed, whether anyone was taking notice or not, across the 52 first qualifying round matches that preceded Qarabag's trip to Luxembourg? How many stories that we may never get to learn about?

Whether Víkingur Olafsvik, from a remote fishing village of 1,000 people, maintain their place in Iceland's top flight (injuries to an already tiny squad decimated any hope of staying near the top of the league, leaving them in a relegation battle that they won on the final day of the season; Herman Heriardsson's Fylkir dropping out of the Pepsi Deildin instead), whether Sarah Wiltshire's Yeovil Town Ladies will make it to the Women's Super League One (they do, gaining promotion with one game to spare).

Whether Iggy and his exiled and refugee Darfur United will break free from their situation to play out more life changing experiences on a football pitch any time soon are questions rooted in the present.

However, win, lose, or even failing to make it to the pitch are fleeting.

For Anton in Olafsvik, Sarah at Yeovil, Iggy in a refugee camp in Chad, and everyone else on the fringes of football, their innate love for the game, for what it means, what it will always mean, ensures that they will keep on keeping on, regardless of any obstacle or indifference. Because of it the true soul of football and the stories played out among it remain safe, preserved sometimes in just a fragile oral history echoing about old and ramshackle stands the world over.

And if things don't quite work out for Anton, Sarah, Iggy, and everyone else this season, then there is always the next, or the one after that.

Whether anyone notices or not is immaterial.

Because when it comes to your club, your team, and what it means to you, then all of that really doesn't matter.

Also published by **LUATH** PRESS:

Another Bloody Saturday
Mat Guy
ISBN: 9781910745724 PBK £11.99

Why do people head out on windswept Saturday
afternoons and wet Wednesday evenings watch lower
and non-league teams play when they could watch
Premier League football from the comfort of their
living rooms?

Does an international match between two countries
that technically don't exist have any meaning?

Why do some people go to so much trouble
volunteering to support clubs which run on a
shoestring budget and are lucky to get even a glimpse
of the limelight?

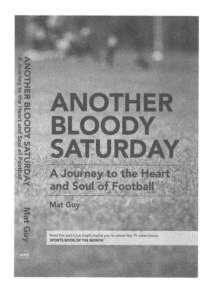

Over the course of a season, Mat Guy set out to
explore the less glamorous side of the beautiful
game, travelling the backwaters of football across the
length and breadth of the country – and beyond. He
watched Bangor as they were cheerfully thrashed by
Reykjavik's UMF Stjarnan, was absolutely won over by
the women's game, and found a new team to love in
Accrington Stanley.

From Glasgow to Northern Cyprus, Bhutan to the
Faroe Islands, Mat discovered the same hope, sense
of community, and love of the game that first led him
to a life in the stands at Salisbury FC's Victoria Park,
where his own passion for football was formed.

Details of this and other books published by Luath Press can be found at:
www.luathpress.co.uk

Luath Press Limited

committed to publishing well written books worth reading

LUATH PRESS takes its name from Robert Burns, whose little collie Luath (*Gael.*, swift or nimble) tripped up Jean Armour at a wedding and gave him the chance to speak to the woman who was to be his wife and the abiding love of his life. Burns called one of the 'Twa Dogs' Luath after Cuchullin's hunting dog in Ossian's *Fingal*.
Luath Press was established in 1981 in the heart of Burns country, and is now based a few steps up the road from Burns' first lodgings on Edinburgh's Royal Mile. Luath offers you distinctive writing with a hint of unexpected pleasures.
Most bookshops in the UK, the US, Canada, Australia, New Zealand and parts of Europe, either carry our books in stock or can order them for you. To order direct from us, please send a £sterling cheque, postal order, international money order or your credit card details (number, address of cardholder and expiry date) to us at the address below. Please add post and packing as follows: UK – £1.00 per delivery address; overseas surface mail – £2.50 per delivery address; overseas airmail – £3.50 for the first book to each delivery address, plus £1.00 for each additional book by airmail to the same address. If your order is a gift, we will happily enclose your card or message at no extra charge.

Luath Press Limited
543/2 Castlehill
The Royal Mile
Edinburgh EH1 2ND
Scotland
Telephone: +44 (0)131 225 4326 (24 hours)
email: sales@luath. co.uk
Website: www. luath.co.uk